Rural Livelihoods and
in Developing Co

WA 119684

D0351700

Rural Livelihoods *and* Diversity *in* Developing Countries

— FRANK ELLIS —

OXFORD
UNIVERSITY PRESS

OXFORD

UNIVERSITY PRESS

Great Clarendon Street, Oxford OX2 6DP

Oxford University Press is a department of the University of Oxford.
It furthers the University's objective of excellence in research, scholarship,
and education by publishing worldwide in

Oxford New York

Athens Auckland Bangkok Bogotá Buenos Aires Calcutta
Cape Town Chennai Dar es Salaam Delhi Florence Hong Kong Istanbul
Karachi Kuala Lumpur Madrid Melbourne Mexico City Mumbai
Nairobi Paris São Paulo Singapore Taipei Tokyo Toronto Warsaw

and associated companies in Berlin Ibadan

Oxford is a registered trade mark of Oxford University Press
in the UK and in certain other countries

Published in the United States
by Oxford University Press Inc., New York

British Library Cataloguing in Publication Data

Data available

Library of Congress Cataloging in Publication Data

Ellis, Frank, 1947–
Rural livelihoods and diversity in developing countries / Frank Ellis.
Includes bibliographical references.
1. Rural development—Developing countries 2. Rural poor—Developing countries.
3. Agriculture—Economic aspects—Developing countries. I. Title.
HN981.C6 E45 2000   307.1'412'091724—dc21   00–035692

ISBN 0–19–829695–9
ISBN 0–19–829696–7 (Pbk)

1 3 5 7 9 10 8 6 4 2

Typeset by Hope Services (Abingdon) Ltd.
Printed in Great Britain
on acid-free paper by
Biddles Ltd.,
Guildford & King's Lynn

Contents

— Part I. Concepts, Definitions and Framework —

— Part II. Dimensions of Diverse Rural Livelihoods —

— Part IV. Looking Ahead —

To Jane, Clare and Josie
one more time

Preface

Both livelihoods and diversification have become popular topics in development studies. Livelihood seems to offer a more complete picture of the complexities of survival in low-income countries than terms formerly considered adequate like 'subsistence', 'incomes' and 'employment'. Diversification recognises that people survive by doing many different things, rather than just one thing or a few things. Interest in livelihood diversity in developing countries also coincides with labour market changes in the industrial countries. More flexible labour markets mean more switching of occupations during the lifetime of an individual, and, for low wage and low skill work, they also often mean a necessity to engage in multiple part-time occupations in order to earn a minimally acceptable level of income.

In rural areas of developing countries, livelihoods and diversification have always, of course, been there. Their relatively recent 'discovery' by the development profession should not be confused with the advent of something startlingly new in the experience of achieving rural survival under difficult circumstances. In a profession that is notoriously prone to fads, it is a mistake to confuse increased awareness of a phenomenon with changes in its nature, incidence or importance.

This point is made because this book utilises a framework for livelihood analysis that, at the time of writing, is gaining ground rapidly as a 'new' approach to rural poverty reduction in low-income countries. Perhaps increased awareness of livelihoods and diversity can lead to better formulated rural poverty reduction policies than those based conventionally on sectors and sub-sectors; however, this conclusion should not be taken as axiomatic. It makes sense to start out with a moderately sceptical view of the claims of the livelihoods approach to represent a leap forward in rural development policy, and to become enthusiastic when demonstrably beneficial outcomes become apparent.

Having got this note of caution out of the way, this book does, however, swim with the tide. It espouses the livelihoods perspective on rural household strategies, and it sets out to investigate seriously the complex ramifications of diversification as a fundamental characteristic of such strategies. It advances a policy framework that is livelihood based and that enables diversification to be explored as a central feature. It concludes that under a wide variety of circumstances in the poorest developing countries the capability of individuals and households to diversify their livelihoods should be facilitated rather than inhibited or discouraged by policy. This is so for a number of reasons, but the main one is that diversity enhances the resilience of hazard-prone livelihoods by spreading risk and increasing the options for substitution between diverse livelihood components.

Some readers may note that the term 'sustainable' is utilised infrequently in the book, and is really only addressed in any serious way in a chapter that considers environmental aspects of diverse rural livelihoods. This reflects a personal feeling that 'sustainable' has become one of the most over-used and degraded words in development studies, rendered practically meaningless by the multiple aspirations it seeks to placate. However, it is recognised that others find the term useful for various purposes, and that the livelihoods framework utilised here is often referred to elsewhere as the sustainable livelihoods framework.

Chapter 1 sets the scene. It provides definitions for the concepts that surround livelihoods and diversity, and it discusses the ambiguities of the household as the social arena around which much livelihood analysis inevitably takes place. It describes the different mainstream narratives that have provided the intellectual foundations of rural development policies in the past, and locates the livelihoods approach and diversification in relation to these and to more recent approaches.

Chapter 2 sets out the livelihoods framework that guides much of the subsequent material of the book. This framework is a version of the 'assets-mediating processes-activities' approach to livelihoods that is encountered in a lot of recent literature on poverty, vulnerability, coping and adaptation. The framework places emphasis on the asset status of households, and the productive uses to which those assets can be put, as well as on substitutability within and between assets and activities as a fundamental source of strength in achieving livelihoods that are viable in the long term.

The second part of the book explores a number of different policy dimensions of diverse rural livelihoods. Chapter 3 considers the factors causing rural households to diversify their income sources. The primary distinction is made between diversifying out of necessity and diversifying by choice. The chapter considers seasonality, risk, coping, labour markets, credit markets, and asset strategies as reasons for diversification. It also draws attention to the special features of migration and remittances in livelihood strategies.

The next four chapters apply the livelihoods framework, and examine the arguments and evidence surrounding the implications of diversification strategies in the four main areas of poverty, agriculture, environment and gender. Chapter 4 does this for poverty and income distribution, introducing key concepts and debates concerning the character and measurement of poverty, and utilising empirical studies to explore poverty-diversity and income distribution-diversity interrelationships. Chapter 5 conducts a similar exercise with respect to agriculture and farm performance; first, setting out the growth linkage model that puts agriculture in the driving seat of rural change; second, considering opposing explanations of the outcome of agriculture-diversity relations; and, third, discussing on-farm diversification as an option within diversification strategies overall.

Chapter 6 explores interactions between diversification and environmental change. It does this by linking diversity as a theme to arguments about poverty-environment relationships, and to the concept of sustainability. This provides an opportunity to deconstruct the concept of sustainability, and to consider caveats about its use to describe desirable long-term attributes of rural livelihoods. The chapter also considers land tenure and common property issues that arise in the context of rural livelihoods. Chapter 7 takes a slightly different approach. It begins by strengthening the gender dimensions of the topics of the preceding three chapters, namely, poverty, agriculture and the environment. It then proceeds to look at labour markets, migration, and assets from a gender perspective, highlighting the difference between the experience of women and men with respect to these aspects of rural livelihood strategies.

Chapter 8 examines macro policies and reform from a livelihoods and diversification perspective. Macro policies determine the large-scale economic context within which rural citizens make livelihood decisions. The chapter examines the chief features of stabilization and adjustment processes and the pathways by which these are expected to influence livelihood options and the choices made by rural households. It also shows that this is a two-way process, with diversified livelihoods modifying in unexpected ways the distributional impact across sectors of macro policies. The chapter ends by suggesting that macro policy reforms may have encouraged diversification and created more livelihood alternatives in economies previously stifled by over-extended states.

The third part of the book is about research methods for policy work on livelihoods. The livelihoods approach requires timely and cost-effective means of capturing the livelihood strategies of the poor as a prerequisite to good policy or project design. Chapter 9 compares and contrasts formal sample survey and Participatory Rural Appraisal (PRA) methods for investigating rural poverty and its attributes, and suggests that selected elements from both types of methodology are required in order to undertake livelihoods policy work effectively. Chapter 10 illustrates this discussion of methods by reference to fieldwork undertaken in three villages in Tanzania, aimed at discovering differences in the livelihood strategies of the poor from the non-poor. The chapter focuses on the advantages and limitations of the particular combination of methods that were chosen, and the conclusions reached for good practice in this area.

The final chapter of the book, Chapter 11, begins by summarising key points and issues that emerge from the preceding chapters. It sets out some criteria that would seem central to the practical implementation of the livelihood approach, and to the recognition of diversity as a central feature of rural survival strategies. The chapter also seeks to identify promising future directions for poverty reduction policies, utilising the livelihoods approach. This leads to a consideration of access failures that result from an inhibiting rather than enabling governance context, in local settings, as having a debilitating impact on the achievement of viable livelihoods by the rural poor.

This book is written from an economic perspective, but the non-economist may rest assured that it contains very little technical economics. Economics has a tendency to explain almost all decision-making as a matter of freely-made choices, albeit subject to economic constraints (resources, assets, skills, incomes etc.). However, this book takes for granted that social and familial constraints also apply, and that not only what people do, but their capability to change what they do, is influenced by their social and institutional context. The expression 'socially-embedded' conveys this idea of the non-economic constraints on individual economic action.

Overall, the book hopes to stimulate discussion, debate, and new ways forward for poverty reduction policies in rural areas of low income countries. In the past it has often been assumed that farm output growth would not only secure rising incomes for farmers, but would also create plentiful non-farm income earning opportunities in the rural economy via linkage effects. This assumption is no longer tenable, even if it was arguably valid under some circumstances in the past. For the majority of poor rural families, farming is no longer able to provide a sufficient means of survival on its own, and the yield gains of new technology are levelling off, particularly in those regions where they were most dramatic in the past. The livelihoods approach offers a more holistic view of the survival strategies of the rural poor, and emphasises diversity and adaptability as positive attributes in the construction of rural livelihoods that exhibit resilience in the short term and viability in the long term.

Acknowledgements

A large number of people have contributed directly or indirectly to the development of the ideas contained in this book. In terms of insights into the topic, discussions on different themes, comments on draft work, help with contacts, and all-round encouragement to proceed, I would like to thank Neil Adger, Piers Blaikie, David Booth, Kate Brown, Debbie Bryceson, Diana Carney, Stefan Dercon, Charlotte Elton, David Gibbon, Martin Greeley, Barbara Harriss-White, Gillian Hart, Judith Heyer, Diana Hunt, Karim Hussein, Cecile Jackson, Andrew Lawson, Catherine Locke, John McDonagh, Adam Pain, Richard Palmer-Jones, Carole Rakodi, Tom Reardon, Ben Rogaly, Jim Sumberg, Jeremy Swift, Steve Tabor, and Martin Upton

Short visits to four countries were made to collect secondary data, test ideas on local researchers, NGO personnel, and government officers, and visit a selection of livelihood oriented projects in a variety of rural locations. In Tanzania, special mention should be made of Brian Cooksey of the Tanzania Development Research Group (TADREG), Bernard Kasimila of the Development Studies Institute at Sokoine University, David Kwimbere of the Central Bank of Tanzania, Joseph Semboja of Research on Poverty Alleviation (REPOA), and Wilbard Maro of the Economic Research Bureau, University of Dar es Salaam, for facilitating the work there. Particular thanks are due to Ntengua Mdoe of the Department of Agricultural Economics, Sokoine University, for carrying out, very professionally and effectively, the small-scale sample survey on diversification described in Chapter 10 of the book.

In Kenya, Jim Harvey and Sheila Chatting of the British Development Division in Nairobi were excellent and helpful hosts. I would also like to extend special thanks to Lucy Emerton of the Policy Research Group for research and administrative support, Elizabeth Kiruki for providing research assistance; and Benno Ndulu of the African Economic Research Consortium, Peter Ngau of UNCRD, and Edward Okeyo of the Central Bureau of Statistics for their advice, support and help with statistical data.

In Sri Lanka, thanks are due to Piyadasa Senanayake for being a very helpful colleague and research collaborator, and to Professor W. D. Lakshman, Vice-Chancellor of the University of Colombo, Terrence Abeysekera of the Colombo office of the World Bank, David Dunham of the Institute of Policy Studies, G. A. C. de Silva of the Department of Agriculture, and Wijaya Jayatilaka, Dean of the Faculty of Agriculture at Peradeniya for their help and support in various ways.

In Ghana, Tei Quartey of the Ministry of Finance guided me through the intricacies of gaining access to available secondary data from a wide variety of sources in Accra, and also accompanied me on several field trips outside the capital. I am indebted to Wilbert Tengey, head of the African Centre for Human Development, and to the team of the Sankofa Programme in Kadjebi District of Volta Region for an enlightening field visit to a large number of village projects based on the group credit approach. Thanks also to Professor Forsuu, head of the Department of Agricultural Economics, University of Ghana at Legon for bringing together a lively audience for a seminar presentation of the research.

Research assistance in the preparation of the book was provided, in different phases, by Lisa Tang, Robert Lancaster, Angela Milligan and John Mims. The entire manuscript was read and commented on by Catherine Locke, Richard Pearce and an anonymous referee, and I am truly indebted to them for helping to turn the draft manuscript into, I hope, a reasonably coherent and readable final piece of work. Needless to say, neither they, nor anyone else mentioned here bear any responsibility for the quality or lack of it of the final outcome.

The research represented by the book was made possible by a grant from the Economic and Social Committee for Research (ESCOR) of the UK Department for International Development (DFID). I am very grateful for this research funding, and would like to thank Charles Clift, the then chief adviser to ESCOR, for his support and encouragement throughout. The ideas and views expressed in the book are solely my own responsibility and are not those of DFID.

Frank Ellis

Norwich, July 1999

Tables

Illustrations

Boxes

PART I

Concepts, definitions and framework

— CHAPTER 1 —

Livelihoods, Diversification and Agrarian Change

rural families increasingly come to resemble miniature highly
diversified conglomerates

(Cain and McNicoll, 1988: 105)

This book is about livelihoods, diversification, and the survival strategies of rural households in developing countries. Its key point of departure is that for many such households farming on its own does not provide a sufficient means of survival in rural areas. For this reason most rural households are found to depend on a diverse portfolio of activities and income sources amongst which crop and livestock production feature alongside many other contributions to family well-being. Engagement in a diverse portfolio of activities also means nurturing the social networks of kin and community that enable such diversity to be secured and sustained. Thus livelihood diversity has both economic and social dimensions and must be approached in an interdisciplinary way.

The book has five broad objectives. The first objective is to bring awareness of livelihood diversification more centrally into thinking about rural development than has hitherto been the case. The second objective is to put forward, and utilise, a framework for the policy analysis of rural livelihoods. The third objective is to examine livelihoods and diversification in relation to rural poverty, agricultural productivity, natural resource management, and gender relations in rural areas. The fourth objective is to advance the policy understanding of diverse rural livelihoods, including local level approaches to reducing rural poverty and links to macro level structural adjustment policies. The fifth objective is to contribute to the search for low cost and effective methodologies for investigating diverse rural livelihoods for policy purposes.

Household level diversity often seems to pose problems for economic and social analysis, and these problems then spill over into policy prescriptions concerning income levels or farm productivity. Conventionally, both official statistics and social scientific analyses prefer to identify people's place in the economy according to their main occupation and profession, and then to develop a body of theory and policy around that activity. Hence in developing countries a huge amount of attention over many years has been paid to the small farm household; its efficiency as an agricultural enterprise, its responsiveness to new technology, the removal of barriers to raising farm output and incomes, and, latterly, concerns with its environment and gender characteristics.

When diversification is discussed in the rural development context, it is usually posed in terms either of the need for on-farm changes in the mix of agricultural activities or of the desirability of developing rural-based non-farm industries. The former sets out to correct the dangers of undue reliance on a single main farm output when it faces unstable or declining prospects in national or international markets; while the latter seeks to provide alternative full-time employment for rural dwellers in locations other than cities. In both cases, diversification is thought of as changing the nature of full-time occupations rather than enabling a single individual or household to engage in multiple occupations.

Yet, as has been demonstrated by several comparative studies (Haggblade *et al.*, 1989; von Braun and Pandya-Lorch, 1991; Sahn, 1994; Reardon, 1997), it is the maintenance and continuous adaptation of a highly diverse portfolio of activities that is a distinguishing feature of rural survival strategies in contemporary poor countries. This household level diversification has implications for rural poverty reduction policies since it means that conventional approaches aimed at increasing employment, incomes and productivity in single occupations, like farming, may be missing their targets. One reason for this is that when both rural and urban households pursue multiple livelihood strategies that cross the sectoral divide, it becomes unclear who, spatially, are the gainers and losers of economic policy changes that act on costs and prices (Jamal, 1995).

Some clearing of the ground is in order. First, participation in multiple activities by farm families is, of course, not new, nor only confined to the rural sectors of developing countries. In the industrial country agricultural economics literature, it has been referred to as 'pluriactivity' (Shucksmith *et al.*, 1989; Evans and Ilberry, 1993), and there is recognition of the likelihood of its increasing prevalence as agricultural income supports are gradually removed (Benjamin, 1994; Kelly and Ilberry, 1995; Hearn *et al.*, 1996). It also as much characterises the livelihoods of the urban poor as those of the rural poor in developing countries (de Haan, 1997; Moser, 1998).

Second, what is distinctive about diversification in many of the poorer developing countries, amongst which virtually all sub-Saharan African countries are counted, is its pervasive and enduring character. It is pervasive in the sense that it is not just an isolated or scattered phenomenon corresponding to a few farm families in particular locations. Livelihood diversification is widespread and is found in all locations, as well as across farm sizes and ranges of income and wealth. It is enduring in the sense that it is not merely a transient feature in the otherwise smooth transition from agriculture to industry, which would be the orthodox interpretation of its occurrence (e.g. Saith, 1992; Bryceson, 1999b).

Third, livelihood diversification in poor countries is not farming combined with occasional short periods of wage work on a neighbour's farm, or in a nearby rural town centre. Nor is it part-time or hobby farming associated with permanent wage or salary earning in full-time, non-farm occupations. Most rural families have truly multiple income sources. This may indeed include off-farm wage work in agriculture, but it is also likely to involve wage work in non-farm activities, rural non-farm self-employment (e.g. trading), and remittances from urban areas and from abroad. Studies show that between 30 and 50 per cent of rural household income in sub-Saharan Africa is derived from non-farm sources (Reardon, 1997). In some regions, e.g. southern Africa, this can reach 80–90 per cent (May, 1996; Baber, 1996); and in others, e.g. Pakistan, Bangladesh, Sri Lanka, around 15 per cent of rural household incomes are accounted for by remittances from family members working in the Persian gulf (von Braun and Pandya-Lorch, 1991).

Fourth, diversification does not necessarily conflict with the conventional notion that specialisation and division of labour are essential ingredients for the transformation of national economies (Johnston and Kilby, 1975; Tomich et al., 1995). While an individual person diversifying his or her livelihood sacrifices specialisation in order to operate concurrently in several different labour markets, the household or any larger social grouping can diversify by placing different individuals in single occupations, thus allowing for specialisation and skill development by each member of the group. A frequent finding of livelihoods research is that individual level diversity tends to characterise the diversification strategy of poorer households, while household level diversity combined with occupational specialisation tends to characterise the diversification strategy of better off households. Since this finding has implications for poverty reduction policies, it is explored in more depth later in the book (see Chapters 4 and 11).

Livelihood diversification cuts across a number of typically self-bounded arenas of policy discussion in rural development, including household coping strategies (Davies, 1996), household risk strategies (Carter, 1997), intrahousehold relations (Hart, 1995), rural growth linkages (Hazell and Haggblade, 1993), rural non-farm activity (Fisher et al., 1997), rural-urban migration (Stark, 1991), and rural poverty (Jazairy et al., 1992). While overlaps occur between these arenas, they each tend to bring rather partial insights to bear on the causes, opportunities, effects and policy implications of diversification.

The fragmentation of insights into diversification means that the literature abounds with conflicting propositions about its causes and consequences. Diversification may occur both as a deliberate household strategy (Stark, 1991) or as an involuntary response to crisis (Davies, 1996). It is found both to diminish (Adams, 1994) and to accentuate (Evans and Ngau, 1991) rural inequality. It can act both as a safety valve for the rural poor (Zoomers and Kleinpenning, 1996) and as a means of accumulation for the rural rich (Hart, 1994). It can benefit farm investment and productivity (Carter, 1997) or impoverish agriculture by withdrawing critical resources (Bryceson, 1999a).

It is not the intention of this book to suggest that these conflicting interpretations can be resolved. The causes and consequences of diversification are differentiated in practice by location, assets, income level, opportunity, institutions and social relations; and it is not therefore surprising that these manifest themselves in different ways under differing circumstances. Nevertheless, a useful purpose is served by disentangling the different strands in the arguments and evidence concerning diversification, especially in so far as this can assist rural poverty reduction policies to achieve better their goals. With the dismantling of sectoral level policies in many countries, something of a vacuum has appeared in the understanding of the links between local-level development initiatives and macro policies emanating from structural adjustment programmes. In this respect, livelihood strategies forge essential connections between micro circumstances and macro contexts (Berry, 1986; Lipton and Ravallion, 1995).

There are several considerations that inform the approach and coverage of this book, and that are elaborated, where appropriate, elsewhere in this chapter or later in the book. These are set out as follows:

1. recognition of livelihood diversity requires an extended concept of the rural household, beyond the resident social unit to include spatially dispersed contributors to household welfare (Bruce and Lloyd, 1997);
2. rural-urban links are pervasive in the livelihoods of both rural and urban dwellers in poor countries; transfers of money, goods, and individuals are commonplace between the rural and urban branches of extended families (Hoddinott, 1994; Jamal, 1995);
3. household level livelihood diversity is not necessarily synonymous with sectoral diversity (i.e. agriculture, manufacturing, services etc.) within the rural economy, since a high degree of household level diversity may exist even in the context of a relatively undiversified rural economy in sectoral terms (Bryceson, 1996);
4. rural communities are not homogeneous social entities in which all families can be supposed to share similar adversities and prospects—households and individuals are differentiated by their assets (especially land and education), income and social status in their local communities (Bernstein *et al.*, 1992; Leach *et al.* 1997);
5. individual and household livelihoods are shaped by local and distant institutions (e.g. local customs regarding access to common property resources, local and national land tenure rules), and by social relations (gender, caste, kinship and so on), as well as by economic opportunities.

The present chapter provides some foundations and discusses key contextual considerations that inform the rest of the book. The next section is concerned with concepts and definitions related to ideas of livelihood and diversification. This is followed by a discussion of the extended household as the social unit appropriate for the analysis of diversified rural livelihoods. Finally, the chapter considers the evolution of ideas and theories about agrarian change and rural development, and examines the place of livelihood diversification in relation to those ideas.

Concepts and definitions

Livelihood

The concept of a livelihood is widely used in contemporary writings on poverty and rural development, but its meaning can often appear elusive, either due to vagueness or to different definitions being encountered in different sources. Its dictionary definition is a 'means to a living', which straightaway makes it more than merely synonymous with income because it directs attention to the *way* in which a living is obtained, not just the net results in terms of income received or consumption attained. A popular definition is that provided by Chambers and Conway (1992: 7) wherein a livelihood 'comprises the capabilities, assets (stores, resources, claims and access) and activities required for a means of living'. This definition, with minor modifications, has been utilised by several researchers adopting a rural livelihoods approach (Carswell, 1997; Hussein and Nelson, 1998; Scoones, 1998).

The important feature of this livelihood definition is to direct attention to the links between assets and the options people possess in practice to pursue alternative activities that can generate the income level required for survival. For example, lack of education means low human capital, one of several types of asset, and this excludes the individual from activities that require a particular level of educational or skill attainment for participation in them.

The term 'capabilities' in the foregoing definition is derived from Sen (1993; 1997) and refers to the ability of individuals to realise their potential as human beings, in the sense both of being (i.e. to be adequately nourished, free of illness and so on) and doing (i.e. to exercise choices, develop skills and experience, participate socially and so on). Strictly, capabilities refer to the set of alternative beings and doings that a person can achieve with his or her economic, social, and personal characteristics (Dreze and Sen, 1989: n.18). As such the use of capabilities as a component of a livelihood definition is potentially confusing since its meaning overlaps assets and activities. The problem is one of confusing process and outcomes. Capabilities as states at points in time both influence and are influenced by personal and household livelihood strategies as they evolve over time.

Assets in the Chambers and Conway livelihood definition contain a number of components, some of which belong to recognised economic categories of different types of capital, and some of which do not, namely, claims and access. There is no difficulty in accepting assets as an essential component of any definition of livelihoods, however, there remains scope for disagreement as to what types of capital or stocks can legitimately be included under the overarching description of assets. Followers of the Chambers and Conway line of thinking about livelihoods (e.g. Scoones, 1998) have tended to identify five main categories of capital as contributing to assets in the livelihood definition, and these are natural capital, physical capital, human capital, financial capital, and social capital.

In brief, natural capital refers to the natural resource base (land, water, trees) that yields products utilised by human populations for their survival. Physical capital refers to assets brought into existence by economic production processes, for example, tools, machines, and land improvements like terraces or irrigation canals. Human capital refers to the education level and health status of individuals and populations. Financial capital refers to stocks of cash that can be accessed in order to purchase either production or consumption goods, and access to credit might be included in this category. Social capital refers to the social networks and associations in which people participate, and from which they can derive support that contributes to their livelihoods.

Amongst these categories, physical capital and human capital obey the orthodox economic definition of capital, whereby an investment is made in order to achieve a future flow of returns, and a conventional rate of return to investment can be calculated. In the case of human capital, this investment is often public in character (education and health services are supplied by the state), although the benefits have both private and public dimensions, permitting individuals to command higher incomes as a result of their improved health or greater skills, as well as raising the productivity of labour more generally. The natural resource base, or environment, has relatively recently come to be thought of as a capital stock in this pure economic sense, although difficulties then arise concerning its valuation as an asset when little is known about the stream of benefits it yields, and the time horizon involved stretches far beyond the 'economic life' of conventional investments.

The term financial capital is somewhat ambiguously designated an asset in the livelihood context, because financial stocks (e.g. savings) may be used for either consumption or investment; moreover, loans obtained through credit contracts can be used for a variety of purposes of which investment designed to raise future productive capacity is only one. Nevertheless, the access status of an individual or household with respect to savings, loans or other forms of finance or credit clearly makes a big difference to the livelihood choices that are open to them, and therefore financial capital is recognisably an important component of individual or family assets.

The relatively recent concept of social capital (Coleman, 1990; Putnam *et al.*, 1993) departs even further from narrow economic definitions of productive assets. Social capital is the subject of continuing debate concerning its definition, its coverage of personalised networks compared to more formal manifestations of community organisation such as co-operatives, farmer associations, village committees and so on, and its efficacy as a vehicle for describing political, social or economic change (J. Harriss, 1997). However, rural households in developing countries are observed to devote a lot of attention to personalised networks, setting up complex, but informal, systems of rights and obligations designed to improve future livelihood security (Berry, 1989; 1993). Whether or not this accords with particular definitions of social capital, it is certainly regarded by individuals and households themselves as an asset requiring investment with a view to securing potential future returns.

Notwithstanding the definitional and conceptual difficulties that surround some of these types of capital, all five types are adopted in this book as analytically useful components of the assets that underpin individual and household livelihood strategies. They are therefore included as part of the definition of a livelihood under consideration here, and their significance for a livelihood approach to rural poverty policies is elaborated in Chapter 2 below.

An important attribute of livelihoods that is subsumed under assets in the Chambers and Conway definition is the access that individuals or households have to different types of capital, opportunities and services. Access is defined by the rules and social norms that determine the differential ability of people in rural areas to own, control, otherwise 'claim', or make use of resources such as land and common property (e.g. Scoones, 1998: 8). It is also defined by the impact of social relations, for example gender or class, on this ability. Access in addition refers to the ability to participate in, and derive benefits from, social and public services provided by the state such as education, health services, roads, water supplies and so on. An oft-stated finding of poverty research is the tendency for public service provision to be biased towards the better-off and more accessible locations, communities, and social groups, thus exacerbating the material deprivation and poor future prospects already experienced by the poor as a result of inadequate levels of assets and income (World Bank, 1990b; Lipton and van der Gaag, 1993; Blackwood and Lynch, 1994).

The definition of a livelihood adopted in this book makes a modification to the Chambers and Conway definition in order to bring out the notion of access rather more strongly. In particular, it is considered important that the impact of social relations and institutions that mediate an individual or family's capacity to achieve its consumption requirements is recognised in the definition. In this context, social relations are taken to be those of gender, family, kin, class, caste, ethnicity, belief systems and so on. Social and kinship networks are essential for facilitating and sustaining diverse income portfolios (Berry, 1989; 1993: Ch.7; Hart, 1995; Bryceson, 1996). At the same time social proscriptions on, for example, permissible courses of action by women can make big differences to the livelihood options available for women compared to men (Dwyer and Bruce, 1988; Davies and Hossain, 1997).

Institutions have been described as 'regularised patterns of behaviour structured by rules that have widespread use in society' (Carswell, 1997; Leach *et al.*,

1997). Alternatively, following North (1990: 3), they are the 'rules of the game in society or, more formally, are the humanly devised constraints that shape human interaction'. Institutions determine, for example, the way markets work in practice, including the degree of trust (or lack of it) in markets, and the mechanisms adopted to overcome lack of trust; the local rules governing access to community resources such as grazing and forest; the customs and rules regarding access to land, land tenure and security of tenure. Local level institutions may work differently from those operating over a larger territory, with overlaps and conflicts between them, for example, customary land tenure may conflict with land ownership regulations passed in capital cities.

In the light of this discussion, the following definition of livelihood is proposed as describing the meaning of the term as it is utilised throughout this book:

Definition

A livelihood comprises the assets (natural, physical, human, financial and social capital), the activities, and the access to these (mediated by institutions and social relations) that together determine the living gained by the individual or household.

A risk that attaches to any definition of this kind is that it fails to convey change over time and adaptation to evolving circumstances. A fundamental characteristic of rural livelihoods in contemporary developing countries is the ability to adapt in order to survive. The construction of a livelihood therefore has to be seen as an ongoing process, in which it cannot be assumed that the elements remain the same from one season, or from one year to the next. Assets can be built up, eroded, or instantaneously destroyed (as, for example, in a flood). Available activities fluctuate seasonally, and across years, especially in relation to larger economic trends in the national economy and beyond. Access to resources and opportunities may change for individual households due to shifting norms and events in the social and institutional context surrounding their livelihoods.

Activities and income

While it is clear from the foregoing discussion that the terms livelihood and income are not synonymous, they are nevertheless inextricably related because the composition and level of individual or household income at a given point in time is the most direct and measurable outcome of the livelihood process. Income comprises both cash and in-kind contributions to the material welfare of the individual or household deriving from the set of livelihood activities in which household members are engaged. The cash earnings component of income include items like crop or livestock sales, wages, rents, and remittances. The in-kind component of income refers to consumption of own-farm produce, payments in kind (e.g. in food), and transfers or exchanges of consumption items that occur between households within rural communities, or between urban and rural households.

Non-economists may not be familiar with the economic definition of income that treats non-monetary contributions to household consumption as income in addition to the cash earnings of the household. The most helpful way of grasping this is to consider that a bag of maize produced on the farm may be either consumed directly by the family or sold for cash. In both cases its net contribution to the material standard of living of the household is its value at market prices, less the cash outgoings (fertiliser, wage labour etc.) incurred by the household in its production. Economists adopt this approach to income, that is, valuing all items at the market prices they could have fetched if sold, less the cash costs of their production, in order to sum together unlike items such as rice and pineapples, wages and firewood.

Total household income is usefully disaggregated into different categories and sub-categories of income sources or activities, these reflecting different features of the resources required to generate them, their seasonality, accessibility to them depending on assets and skills, and their location nearby or remote. Within rural communities different individuals possess differing potential access to alternative activities, and, therefore different income sources convey varying impacts on poverty and income distribution. A basic classification is to distinguish farm from off-farm and non-farm income sources (e.g. Saith, 1992; Leones and Feldman, 1998):

Definitions

Farm income. This refers to income generated from own-account farming, whether on owner-occupied land, or on land accessed through cash or share tenancy. Farm income, broadly defined, includes livestock as well as crop income, and comprises both consumption-in-kind of own-farm output as well as the cash income obtained from output sold. In all cases, reference is to income net of the costs of production. The cost items included in this calculation vary according to the measure of farm income sought. Typically, outlays in cash or in kind on land rent, variable inputs (fertiliser etc.) and hired labour are deducted from gross income in order to obtain the desired net income figures. Family labour inputs are not deducted in this way when the objective is to describe the net contribution of farming to household income.

Off-farm income. Off-farm income typically refers to wage or exchange labour on other farms (i.e. within agriculture). It includes labour payments in kind, such as the harvest share systems and other non-wage labour contracts that remain prevalent in many parts of the developing world. It may also include, although classifications sometimes differ in this respect, income obtained from local environmental resources such as firewood, charcoal, house building materials, wild plants, and so on, where these can be measured and a value attached to them.

Non-farm income. Non-farm income refers to non-agricultural income sources. Several secondary categories of non-farm income are commonly identified. These are: (1) non-farm rural wage or salary employment; (2) non-farm rural self-employment, sometimes called business income; (3) rental income obtained from leasing land or property; (4) urban-to-rural remittances arising from within national boundaries; (5) other urban transfers to rural households, for example, pension payments to retirees; (6) international remittances arising from cross-border and overseas migration.

In the main, this book conforms to this system of classification. Off-farm income is taken as a shorthand to mean incomes generated within agriculture or from environmental resources other than from own-account farming. Non-farm income is usually deployed to mean incomes arising from outside agriculture, although occasionally, in order to avoid the repetition of multiple phrases, non-farm income is used as a shorthand for all non-own-account farming sources of income, therefore taking in off-farm incomes as well. The sense in which non-farm income is being used should always be clear from the text.

There are no hard-and-fast rules governing income classifications however, and not all investigators follow the same conventions. In a detailed study of household incomes in rural Pakistan, for example, Adams and He (1995) utilise the six major income categories of agricultural, non-farm, livestock, rental, domestic remittance and international remittance income (see Box 1.1). In their scheme, wage labour in agriculture is included with own-farm income in the agricultural category; livestock is taken separately from crop income; and non-farm income covers wages, salaries and self-employment outside agriculture, but excludes rents and remittances that are assigned their own categories.

This example illustrates how income classifications are adapted to suit the methods and purposes of analysis. In this instance, livestock income is separated from on-farm income because in rural Pakistan livestock rearing is a major income source for landless rural households in contrast to crop production that is mainly engaged in by landowners. Remittances are divided between two identifiably separate categories because of the widely differing barriers to entry between national and international migration which was one of the factors that the researchers set out to explore. Non-farm income in that study is defined as income derived from non-agricultural activities requiring resource inputs (labour, capital, skills) from the resident household. This meaning of non-farm can also be found in other sources, notably those concerned with rural growth linkages (e.g. Haggblade *et al.*, 1989).

Analytically, the interesting point about different income categories is that they describe different labour markets implying different attributes of security, continuity, gender access, skill requirements, and so on (Reardon, 1997). For example, agricultural wage labour is likely to be intermittent or seasonal, and may follow gender demarcations by different types of agricultural operation (e.g. women weeding and transplanting; men ploughing, ditching).

Box 1.1. Income categories and composition, rural Pakistan

A survey carried out in rural Pakistan over the three year period 1986 to 1989 collected data from households on a range of topics, including the composition of household incomes (Adams and He, 1995). The survey covered 727 households in the three provinces of Punjab, Sind and North-West Frontier. As the data was to be used to analyse income inequality and poverty in selected rural districts, the poorest district in each province was chosen, plus a further district in Punjab province.

In the data analysis, income was distinguished between five main categories:

1. *Non-farm*: unskilled labour, wage employment, and non-farm business profits;
2. *Agricultural*: net income from crop sales, own-consumption, and off-farm labour;
3. *Transfers*: national and international remittances, pensions, and payments to the poor;
4. *Livestock*: net income from sales of cattle and poultry, and own-consumption;
5. *Rental income*: from ownership of assets, including land, machinery and water.

Although typically crop and livestock incomes are combined together under the general agricultural category, in this instance livestock income was divided from crop income because of its different significance for income inequality, related to the unequal distribution of land for crop production. Table 1.1 summarises income data from the survey by source of income and by year.

Table 1.1. Income portfolios in rural Pakistan (mean annual per capita income)

	1986/87		1987/88		1988/89	
	Rps	%	Rps	%	Rps	%
Non-farm	1,007	30.7	1,205	34.6	960	31.2
Agricultural	764	23.2	851	24.5	833	27.1
Transfers	554	16.9	573	16.5	369	12.0
Livestock	535	16.3	444	12.8	435	14.2
Rental	425	12.9	405	1.6	473	15.4
Total	3,285	100.0	3,478	100.0	3,070	100.0

Note: in 1986, 1 Pakistan rupee = US$0.062. All rupees are in constant 1986 terms.

Source: Adams and He (1995: 12).

Despite the dominance of crop agriculture in the Pakistan rural economy, it is striking that crop-related income comprises around only one-third of rural household incomes in all years. Non-farm income, meaning in this instance, self-employment income, is the most important income source, accounting for between 30.7 per cent and 34.6 per cent of household income, compared with between 23.2 per cent and 27.1 per cent for crop agriculture. The importance of non-farm income is supported by the findings of other rural household surveys in Pakistan.

Rural non-farm wage or salary income may involve more continuity of employment, especially if it is in non-agriculture related private sector enterprise or in the local civil service, and access may depend on special skills or high levels of educational attainment. Remittances depend both on the success of family members in gaining access to regular employment in remote locations (including abroad) and on the subsequent reliability and level of income flows back home once employment has been obtained.

In this book, the terms farming and agriculture are used more or less interchangeably. When encountered with a general descriptive intent, they can be taken to encompass not just crop production, but also livestock rearing associated with sedentary agriculture, and pastoralism as an extensive form of livestock management. Of course there will arise instances where these different kinds of natural resource based livelihood activity need to be discussed on their own, in which case the overarching use of agriculture is relaxed in order to explore sub-categories in greater depth.

Diversity and diversification

The terms diversity and diversification in a livelihood context need further clarification. Diversity refers to the existence, at a point in time, of many different income sources, thus also typically requiring diverse social relations to underpin them. Diversification, on the other hand, interprets the creation of diversity as an ongoing social and economic process, reflecting factors of both pressure and opportunity that cause families to adopt increasingly intricate and diverse livelihood strategies.

While both diversity and diversification may be taken overall to mean multiple and multiplying income sources, they are more often invoked in the rural development context to imply diversification away from farming as the predominant or primary means of rural survival. Thus the expression 'highly diversified rural livelihoods' typically conveys the idea of livelihoods in which own account farming has become a relatively small proportion of the overall survival portfolios put together by farm families.

The diversity of agriculture itself, or on-farm diversity, is also a dimension of importance in rural development policy, and this is explored at an appropriate point later in the book (see Chapter 5). Some of the factors that are important in explaining and analysing diversification out of farming are also relevant to farming itself, for example, risk-related reasons for adopting a diverse portfolio of activities. However, on-farm diversity also brings into consideration many factors concerning farm technology, efficiency, sustainability and markets that are specifically agricultural in character.

The preceding discussion enables a definition of rural livelihood diversification to be put forward, and this is as follows:

Definition

Rural livelihood diversification is defined as the process by which rural households construct an increasingly diverse portfolio of activities and assets in order to survive and to improve their standard of living.

An illustration may help to make this discussion of the different concepts involved in livelihood diversification more concrete. Figure 1.1 provides such an illustration in the form of a pie chart in the top half of the diagram, and a summary of the different facets of the livelihood definition in the bottom half of the diagram. The pie chart displays the components of household total income between major categories. This is a livelihood portfolio. While the income proportions in this diagram do not correspond to any particular case-study or location, they broadly correspond to an 'average' livelihood portfolio for a rural household in sub-Saharan Africa, as indicated by the comparative data published, for example, in Reardon (1997).

In terms of the income classifications described earlier, this livelihood is 40 per cent composed of farm activities (own-account agriculture); 18 per cent of off-farm activities (agricultural wage labour and gathering); and 42 per cent composed of non-farm activities. It may be objected that equating the income composition of the household with its livelihood portfolio is to oversimplify the complexity of social and economic dimensions that are involved in a livelihood. However, this is not the intention. As discussed earlier, a particular composition of activities and associated income flows represent the main, visible, outcome of the process by which a livelihood is constructed. Summarising this in income terms merely brings livelihood diversity into sharper focus; it is not meant to suggest that the underlying social processes are made to disappear or are regarded as unimportant for policy purposes.

The bottom half of Figure 1.1 summarises the livelihood definition developed earlier in this section. A livelihood is characterised as comprising assets and activities, access to which is mediated by institutions and social relations.

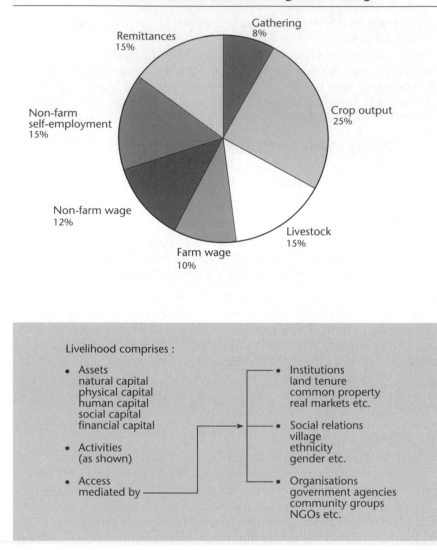

Figure 1.1. A diversified rural livelihood

A digression on entitlements

It is unfortunate that a lot of writing about livelihoods in developing countries mixes terms and concepts borrowed from alternative structures of ideas, without appreciating that the piecemeal deployment of such concepts often serves neither to clarify the new context into which they are inserted nor to remain true to their intent in the body of thought from which they were extracted (Longhurst,

1994). An example of this has already been seen in the insertion of Amartya Sen's concept of 'capability' into the definition of livelihoods advanced by Chambers and Conway (1992), and subsequently modified by others (e.g. Scoones, 1998).

Nowhere is this tendency for borrowing terms more prevalent than with respect to another concept originating from the fertile mind of Amartya Sen, which is that of 'entitlements'. Sen (1981) developed a concept of entitlements within an interlocking structure of ideas aimed to shift radically views about the causes of famine and starvation. The concept was subsequently elaborated by Sen himself and others (e.g. Gasper, 1993; Gore, 1993; Devereux, 1993), and was extended to take into account, for example, the differential food entitlements of men and women within the household (Dreze and Sen, 1989; Kabeer, 1991).

The essence of the entitlement approach is that people do not necessarily, or even mainly, starve due to an insufficient supply of food (food availability decline), they starve because they possess insufficient command over, or access to, food (food entitlement decline). In this food security sense, in a market economy, entitlement refers to the terms of trade under which different income sources such as crop sales, wages and remittances can be exchanged for food. For example, an entitlement decline may occur due to a steep rise in the price of food compared to static or falling income from wages. Direct entitlement is also achieved by own production of food, although this may be compromised early on in a catastrophe such as a drought by the loss of this subsistence basis of survival.

Like the concept of capability, the entitlement approach has some elements that overlap, and others that mean different things, from the set of terms utilised here to describe livelihoods. For example, the notion of endowments in entitlement analysis is quite close to the notion of assets in the livelihood definition. On the other hand, entitlements themselves mean 'the set of alternative bundles of commodities over which a person can establish command given the prevailing legal, political and economic arrangements' (Dreze and Sen, 1989: 9), and this places emphasis on different aspects of survival from the livelihood strategies focus of this book.

Again, a confusion occurs between process and outcomes. Livelihood strategies describe a process unfolding over time, and this process results in evolving outcomes that affect individual or household entitlements in the Sen sense of the term. Moreover, the term entitlement is problematic in a livelihood context not just due to overlapping jargons with different meanings and intents. In ordinary, non-academic English usage it means something over which the individual has a definite right or a claim. While undoubtedly there are some elements of livelihoods that involve rights and claims, for example, rights established by ownership of land or claims on family members based on custom or reciprocity, it is not always the case, overall, that livelihoods can be characterised solely on the basis of rights and claims. Rather, they are constructed, as we have seen, from assets and activities, and differential access to these based on social and institutional considerations.

Social arenas of analysis

For the purposes of this book, the household is regarded as the social unit that is most appropriate for investigating livelihoods and for advancing the understanding of the policy implications of diverse livelihoods. It is understood, of course, that the household is an infinitely variable social arena, difficult to define in many cultural settings, and one that may not even exist with respect to its key attributes in some instances (Crehan, 1992). On the other hand, the household is a site in which particularly intense social and economic interdependencies occur between a group of individuals. This is regarded as a sufficient reason for the household to be a relevant unit of social and economic analysis, since the view is not taken that individual action (i.e. that of women or men on their own) can be interpreted separately from the social and residential space they inhabit.

The household is conventionally conceived as the social group which resides in the same place, shares the same meals, and makes joint or coordinated decisions over resource allocation and income pooling (Meillassoux, 1981; Ellis, 1993: Ch.1). This definition places the emphasis on co-residence as the key attribute of the household. Other attributes may be present or not in varying degrees. In some rural societies co-residence itself needs modifying, due to the different but overlapping spheres of compound and household. The household differs from the family. The household as a co-resident social unit may sometimes have non-family members permanently in residence. The family refers to near and extended kinship relations that may be spread over many households in different locations.

An alternative conception of the household is the idea that it represents a coalition of players committed by choice or custom to act as a unit *vis-à-vis* the rest of the world (Stark, 1991; Preston, 1994). This places less emphasis on co-residence, and allows explicit recognition of the role of non-resident family members in contributing to the wellbeing of the resident group. It has been argued that due to the importance of kinship networks for household survival, the family rather than the household is the appropriate social unit for livelihood research (Bruce and Lloyd, 1997). However, this implies that the extended family could be uniquely defined for this purpose, whereas in practice resident households maintain stronger links with some branches of family than others, and they exercise reciprocal kinship obligations in ways that are impossible to predict for individual cases. Moreover, the social networks that are nurtured by households for livelihood security purposes may often be based on village, ethnicity, and other social ties that are not explicitly familial in content.

Even though it may not be appropriate to invoke the entire extended family in order to describe the livelihood networks of individual households, it is certainly true that a more spatially extended understanding of the household is required than that provided by the conventional definition. Households with members working away in urban centres or abroad are often referred to as 'split families', and their livelihood strategies are described as 'straddling' the rural and urban sectors (Rempel and Lobdell, 1978; Murray, 1981; Stichter, 1982; Heyer, 1996). Migrants to urban centres typically continue to maintain strong rural family connections, even after several generations of urban residence (Lucas and Stark, 1985; Stark and Bloom, 1985; Valentine, 1993; Hoddinott, 1994). Circular migration, in which family members work for periods in the urban economy then return to their family farms, has been observed in several studies (Bigsten, 1988; 1996; Lageman, 1989; Andrae, 1992). Seasonal migration related to cyclical work opportunities in different locations is also prevalent (Agarwal, 1990; Breman, 1996).

A large body of research demonstrates the enormous variation to be found in household arrangements covering access to resources, claims over income, and the relative independence of decision-making between men and women. It is widely accepted that households are sites of conflict and co-operation, and that internal power relations, legitimised by social norms and legal sanctions, have critical effects on the relative welfare of men and women in the household (Folbre, 1986; Guyer and Peters, 1987; Bruce, 1989).

Economic models of the household have evolved over time. For many years, economists found it convenient to treat the household as a single decision making unit, assuming that household behaviour could be adequately described by the single set of preferences of an altruistic household head. Models based on this assumption are termed 'unitary models' of the household. However, recognition of the complex interplay of conflict and co-operation between individuals possessing separate preferences led to alternative approaches termed 'collective models' of the household (Haddad et al., 1997a). These are principally based on bargaining theory in which those with stronger fallback positions in the event that co-operation breaks down are in a better bargaining position with respect to pressing their own preferences than those with weaker fallback positions. Interestingly, the predictive capability of collective models is often indistinguishable from that of unitary models when it comes to explaining household responses to changing labour, resource and output markets (Haddad et al., 1997b).

Even though an advance on unitary models, collective models remain quite limited by the abstract nature of their formulation in economic terms (Hart, 1995). In reality, social norms and rules are not fixed, but adapt and change with the evolving circumstances that confront individuals in a wider social and economic context. This process involves a renegotiation and redefinition of social roles, and it allows women, in particular, a 'voice' in redefining outcomes that is absent when the social relations of the household are treated as an unvarying backdrop to fixed bargaining rules.

In a recent research monograph, Baber (1998) utilises a concept of the household in which four overlapping definitions of social units—homestead units, family groups, co-resident units, and mutual-support units—are mapped against income-generating characteristics described as simple-resident, simple-dispersed, extended-resident and extended-dispersed. These ideas are developed in the context of rural South Africa, where extreme cases of dependence by the resident group on migrant income and other transfers from urban areas are commonplace. However, they take the household as an arena of social analysis in directions that may prove useful in other contexts for capturing the livelihood strategies of sub-groups that experience differing social interdependencies.

The broadest social grouping identified by Baber is the homestead unit. This unit includes all those individuals who 'belong' to a particular rural homestead in the sense that they have the right to be based there and to participate as full members of the grouping. Family groups are sub-units of the homestead held together by bonds between individuals that are stronger than those with other groups within the homestead, for example, nuclear families, single mothers with children. The co-resident unit consists of all those living in the homestead on a daily basis. The mutual support unit consists of the co-resident unit plus migrants who remit on a regular basis. In addition to these four units of co-operation and interdependence, networks of income support can stretch across households, for example, the elderly may transfer income to daughters based in other homesteads.

The apparent complexity of this scheme is simplified when it is considered that in many instances the family group and the co-resident unit may coincide, so that when migrants are added the homestead is complete. On the other hand when homestead composition is truly complex, the subdivision of the larger social group into these sub-groups facilitates livelihood analysis because each sub-group implies different rights and obligations with respect to access to assets and to control over income flows.

The broadest unit, the homestead, captures all those who have a stake in the rural settlement, including non-remitting migrants who can call on the assistance of those living in the homestead. The homestead displays gradations in two main directions that allow the sub-groups already mentioned to be mapped to livelihood sources. One direction distinguishes homesteads with no migrants from those with remitting or non-remitting migrants; while the other distinguishes single from multiple family groups. In this way the kinship composition of the homestead is mapped to the spatial nature of its livelihood sources, yielding four main combinations that are denominated simple-resident (one family group, no migrants), simple-dispersed (one family group, migrants), extended-resident (multiple family groups, no migrants), and extended-dispersed (multiple family groups, migrants).

While not being utilised in an operational way in this book, Baber's approach of taking the rural homestead as the basic unit, and then disaggregating it into analytically tractable sub-groups for livelihood analysis is kept in mind in the arguments about diverse livelihoods found in subsequent chapters. However, the term household continues to be used as the main shorthand for describing the resident social unit, extended where applicable to include migrants and others who make intermittent or regular contributions to household welfare.

Agrarian change and rural development

Diversification does not feature strongly in theories and ideas about agrarian change, and for that reason it has not, until quite recently, emerged as a potential feature of policy significance in the practice of rural development. Theories of agrarian change refer to interpretations of social and economic change in the rural sector in the long run, advanced as possessing broad applicability to the development process across countries and regions. Such 'meta-narratives' do not have as great an impact on the formulation of rural development policies as they did in the past, but they remain important as strands of ideas that are explicitly or implicitly invoked in a great deal of discussion about rural poverty reduction. For this reason it is useful to review briefly what they suggest or imply about the evolution of rural livelihoods. In what follows three main groups of such theories are described, namely, agricultural development; political economy; and population and technology theories.

Agricultural development theories seek to describe the evolving role of the agricultural sector as economic development proceeds. Early models, exemplified by the dual economy approach (Lewis, 1954; Fei and Ranis, 1964), envisaged no prospects for rising productivity in so-called 'traditional' agriculture, which could only therefore passively supply resources to the modern sector of the economy until the latter eventually expanded to take its place. Later models retained the core idea that, as in the history of the industrialised countries, agriculture would decline in its share of GDP as development proceeds. However, the sequence of events came to be seen quite differently, with rising agricultural output and incomes being seen as a prerequisite and stimulant of non-farm growth. In the words of one of the main early enthusiasts for agriculture and small-farm centred paths of economic change 'the faster agriculture grows, the faster its relative size declines' (Mellor, 1966). This is purported to occur because rising agricultural productivity stimulates demand for non-farm input services to agriculture as well as creating an internal consumer market for industrial output.

In the agricultural development tradition, the achievement of rising productivity in small-farm agriculture became the central focus in the 1970s and it remained the orthodoxy well into the 1990s (e.g. Tomich *et al.*, 1995). The overall approach is composed of many interlocking components, some of the principal ones being as follows:

1. small farmers are rational economic agents making efficient farm decisions (Schultz, 1964);
2. small farmers are just as capable as big farmers of taking advantage of high yielding crop varieties because the input combinations (seed, fertiliser, water) required for success at their cultivation are 'neutral to scale' (Lipton and Longhurst, 1989);
3. the substitution of labour for scarce land involved in small-farm HYV cultivation is an 'induced innovation' that accurately reflects relative resource scarcities and factor prices in labour abundant agrarian economies (Hayami and Ruttan, 1985);
4. small farmers are socially more efficient than large farmers because of the intensity of their use of abundant labour in combination with small land holdings and low requirements for scarce capital (Berry and Cline, 1979);
5. these factors lead in the direction of a 'unimodal' agricultural strategy favouring small family farms rather than a 'bimodal' strategy that bets on the strength of a modern farm sector composed of large farms and estates (Johnston and Kilby, 1975: Ch.4);
6. rising agricultural output results in 'rural growth linkages' that spur the growth of labour-intensive non-farm activities in rural areas (Johnston and Kilby, 1975; Mellor, 1976).

Naturally, making a brief list like this greatly understates the complexity of the bodies of thought that gave rise to such propositions, the debates and refinements that occurred around key concepts, and the empirical work undertaken to support or refute key propositions such as the alleged superior economic efficiency of small-farms compared to large farms. However, in the current context, this brevity will have to suffice and the reader is referred elsewhere to sources that provide more complete coverage of the small-farm paradigm of agricultural change and growth (e.g. Ellis, 1993; Tomich *et al.*, 1995).

These ideas had a powerful effect on rural development policy and practice in the three decades from the 1960s to the 1990s. One key attribute is that both growth and equity issues seem to be addressed via an emphasis on small-farm agriculture, since the rural poor are predominantly interpreted as being poor small-farmers. Another attribute is that non-farm rural growth is hypothesised to occur as a consequence of rising farm productivity. As summarised by Singh (1990: xix) 'the growth of the non-farm economy depends on the vitality of the farm economy; without agricultural growth in the rural areas, redressing poverty is an impossible task.'

Livelihood diversity scarcely features in the mainstream agricultural development literature. This could be because writers in this tradition have emphasised specialisation and division of labour as central attributes of rising efficiency and incomes in agriculture: 'The mechanism of economic progress in farming is the same one that operates in every other sector of the economy. The mechanism is *specialisation.'* (Johnston and Kilby, 1975: xx; Tomich *et al.*, 1995: p.36). However, as pointed out early in this chapter, specialisation and diversification are only incompatible at the level of the individual; they can coexist within a household livelihood strategy.

In this same context, it is important not to confuse sector-level diversity with household-level diversity. A lot of rural development literature advocates the encouragement of diverse non-farm enterprises in rural areas (e.g. Mellor, 1976). However, proposals in this direction predominantly envisage individuals and households moving from farm to non-farm occupations, thus enabling the output per person, and incomes, of those left in farming to rise. If this happens, then considerable diversity of rural sector enterprises might be accompanied by specialisation rather than diversity in household livelihood strategies. Conversely, and much closer to reality in contemporary sub-Saharan Africa, highly diverse household livelihood strategies may occur in the context of a relatively undiversified rural sector (Bryceson, 1996; Bryceson and Jamal, 1997).

A second influential body of thought on social and economic change in the rural economy has been the group of ideas and theories that can be broadly described under the label of the political economy of agrarian change (e.g. Ellis, 1993: Ch. 3; Byres, 1996). This has distinct preoccupations from the preceding set of ideas, and, mainly, utilises a different theoretical perspective. Its principle preoccupation is with increasing disparities of income and wealth in the rural economy, and with the viability of peasant agriculture in the long run. Taking its cue from Lenin, writing about peasant agriculture in Russia at the turn of the twentieth century, its view of the latter is pessimistic. It is argued that forces of competition, uneven technical change, and privatisation of land result in increasing differentiation between families in rural society. This eventually leads to the disintegration of peasant communities and the emergence of the two distinct social classes of landless wage labour and labour-hiring capitalist farmers.

Literature within this tradition tends to be critical and sometimes openly hostile to the small-farm strategy of agricultural development. Its emphasis on inequality, power relations, social classes and differentiation in rural areas leads to scepticism about the equity claims of such a strategy. Far from being a scale neutral force contributing to raising the income of poor farmers, new crop technology is interpreted as widening income and wealth disparities. This is due, amongst other things, to the unequal capability of different farm households to finance the new inputs required for successful adoption of new technologies. The critical stance is also, however, political. It reflects quite different priorities and perceptions compared to the agricultural development school concerning economic and political power, the emergence of social classes, the imperatives of industrialisation, the role of wage labour, and the political basis of progressive social policies.

This body of thought concedes various factors that might permit peasants to persist in a competitive capitalist economy. These include their capability to re-treat into subsistence, their adaptability under pressure, and social norms of reciprocity in peasant societies. In its more orthodox formulations, this approach gives little attention to diversification out of agriculture as a peasant survival strategy. However, recent work on 'de-agrarianisation' reverses this dis-regard, explicitly identifying diversification as a response to events and trends that have adverse effects on the viability of agriculture-based livelihoods (Bryceson, 1999a; Bryceson *et al.*, 2000). In sub-Saharan Africa, it is the fall-out from structural adjustment, as manifested, for example, by removal of input subsidies and cost recovery in rural social services, that is held to have acceler-ated diversification in this way.

A third important set of ideas on agrarian change are those inspired by Esther Boserup in her work on population growth and technical change in agriculture (Boserup, 1965; 1981). Boserup's basic proposition is that more intensive farm-ing technologies tend to occur with rising population density. Specifically, rural population growth shortens fallow periods, increases investment in land, switches land preparation from hoe to animal traction, induces manuring in order to maintain soil fertility, reduces the average cost per inhabitant of rural infrastructure, promotes specialisation in production, shifts land tenure from general to specific use rights, and diminishes the per capita availability of com-mon property resources (Boserup, 1965; Rosenzweig *et al.*, 1988).

These ideas have enjoyed a resurgence in the context of debates about rising populations and their effects on agriculture and the environment. The positive relationships between population density and technical progress have been af-firmed by other authors (Simon, 1977; 1981). They have been held to explain the prevalence and success of intensive small-farm agriculture (Netting, 1993). They have also been utilised as the vehicle to demonstrate reversals in environ-mental degradation occurring under high population density (e.g. Tiffen *et al.*, 1994).

Followers of Boserup generally take a positive and optimistic view of the im-pact of population growth on social and economic change, including on the management of environmental resources (e.g. Mortimore, 1998). This places them in contrast to population pessimists who emphasise the difficulty of achieving rises in per capita incomes in the presence of high rates of population growth. Boserup contrasted her ideas with those of the nineteenth-century po-litical economist, Thomas Malthus, who expressed extreme pessimism concern-ing the potential for agricultural output to rise as fast as population growth, such that lack of food itself, and starvation, would in the end become the main check on the rate of population increase. Few people nowadays would argue the extreme Malthus position on population, but debate on agrarian development nevertheless contains every shade of view between these two polar opposites. Supporters of the small-farm model of agrarian change are divided on this issue, for example Netting (1993) adopts an explicit Boserup line, while Tomich *et al.* (1995) regard high rates of population increase as inimical to success in raising rural incomes.

Livelihood diversification does not feature any more strongly in this branch of literature than it does in the preceding two. Here, the central focus is on the positive stimulus to agricultural innovation of rising population density. Another potential implication of such increasing density, that land per farm family might become so subdivided that irrespective of technical improvements it is unable to support the household, does not tend to be pursued by followers of Boserup. Nevertheless, acknowledgement of the diverse income sources of farm families occurs in some of the literature that casts the small family farm in a Boserup-type framework. For example, Netting (1993) interprets income diversification as one amongst several factors enabling intensive small-farm agriculture to persist and to prosper. It does this by increasing the flexibility of the farm family to adapt to difficult circumstances, whether originating in markets (e.g. adverse price trends and fluctuations) or from natural causes (droughts, floods, pests and diseases).

This overview of overarching bodies of thought concerning long-run agrarian change is inevitably somewhat abbreviated. There are of course important overlaps as well as disjunctures between them, and by no means all writers within them would take as strong an agriculture-centred focus as is defined by the main line of argument within each of them. The influence of each of them on agricultural policy and rural development practice differs greatly, with the small-farm strategy school having had by far the greatest influence in this respect. However, for a number of reasons to be described shortly, belief in the veracity and usefulness of overarching theories of agrarian change as a guide to rural development declined markedly in the 1990s. In this context it becomes useful to define more closely the scope of rural development as an arena of policy and practice aimed at poverty reduction in developing countries.

The term rural development first came into widespread usage in the mid-1970s, and is primarily associated with the empirical observation that the vast majority of the poor in developing countries were located in rural areas (World Bank, 1975; 1988; J. Harriss, 1982). Rural development is therefore not a theory of economic or social change as such, nor even an explanation of how spatial patterns of poverty arise. Rather, it is an acknowledgement that the majority of developing-country citizens having incomes below a stated poverty line are resident in rural rather than urban areas, and it is also a call to action to reduce this incidence of poverty. Rural development can therefore be defined as an organising principle for anti-poverty policies in rural areas of low income countries.

Clearly, as so defined, rural development should be about more than just technical change in small-farm agriculture. Nevertheless its overwhelming emphasis for many years was about raising the output and incomes of small, poor, farmers (World Bank, 1988). In this its predominant intellectual influence was the first of the three strands of ideas about agrarian change delineated above. Aside from direct support to this end, in the shape of research, extension, irrigation, credit, inputs and so on, donor and government resources also supported small-farm agriculture indirectly through investment in rural feeder roads, transport, grain stores and other marketing facilities. While other aspects of rural welfare such as education, health services, water supplies and so on were also accorded some weight in government and donor plans and projects, there is no doubt that small-farm output growth was writ large as the dominant strategy for improving rural welfare. Consequently, the livelihood strategies of those of the rural poor for whom own-account farming was unable to provide a sufficient livelihood received scant attention in the rural development mainstream.

This relative neglect of diverse dimensions of rural livelihoods other than success at farming began to be redressed for a number of different reasons from the mid-1980s onwards. One was the powerful disaffection that began to emerge regarding the role of government as the sole or predominant agent for affecting social change and development. The critique of big government was driven largely by agendas of structural adjustment and market liberalisation on the economic side, but this found strange echoes and unlikely allies amongst those seeking to reverse the top-down character of rural development projects, and those impatient with the perceived failure of orthodox approaches to address adequately diverse problems at local levels of action. The advent of 'actor-oriented' approaches to rural policies and projects (Long and Long, 1992), the rise of participatory rural appraisal (Chambers, 1994a; 1997), and the rejection of overarching theories as a useful guide to action (Booth, 1994) all reflect in different ways this major shift in perception regarding the exercise of control by government over development agendas.

The economic dimension of this critique of big government had important implications for rural development. Agricultural policies that had formed the cornerstone of the small-farm strategy such as price, credit and input subsidy policies were found in numerous studies to possess defects that may in many instances have resulted in worse outcomes for rural living standards than the market failures that state action had been designed to overcome. The dismantling of such policies was advocated by the international donor agencies, with the aim of improving the market environment facing agriculture by allowing farm output prices to rise where they had previously been suppressed by government policies, encouraging more efficient and responsive private marketing agencies, and reducing agricultural taxes.

Another important factor in the reassessment of the rural development mainstream was the emergence of the feminist critique of the gender unawareness of rural development policies. This began by placing the internal working of the 'poor rural farm household' under scrutiny in order to identify the different roles, constraints, opportunities and welfare of women compared to men (Guyer, 1980; 1984; Guyer and Peters, 1987). It quickly became apparent that individual livelihood strategies differed between men and women, not only corresponding to gender-defined division of agricultural tasks, but also with respect to domestic roles, cash-earning opportunities, and responsibility for protecting the welfare of children in the face of adverse external events. The placing of gender on the research and policy map made it plain that there was a great deal more to improving rural welfare than just raising the yields of crops in farmers' fields, and, indeed, the latter was sometimes found to erode rather than improve the well-being of rural women.

The outcome of these and complementary changes in the 1990s, for example the rapid rise of non-governmental organisations (NGOs) as the vehicles for implementing rural development projects, amounted to a major shift in the scope and nature of rural development. The shift is from the general to the particular, from seeking single solutions with widespread application to addressing specific problems in a limited context, from implementing solutions from above to permitting solutions to be generated from below.

These changes in perception and practice in rural development facilitate the recognition of livelihood diversity as a potentially important issue for policy and practice. This is the starting but not the end point of this book. Recognising diversity is one thing. Utilising that recognition to advance the objective of reducing rural poverty is quite another. For this objective to be pursued, it is first necessary to elaborate the policy framework that is suggested by the assets-activities-access definition of a livelihood, and that is what the next chapter sets out to accomplish.

Summary

This book is about rural livelihoods and about diversification as a survival strategy of rural households. A livelihood is defined as the assets, the activities and the access that determine the living gained by the individual or household. Diversification is then defined as the process by which rural households construct an increasingly diverse portfolio of activities and assets in order to survive or to improve their standards of living. The livelihood concept is distinguished from ideas of capability and entitlement, which have overlapping meanings but different intentions. An extended definition of the resident household that acknowledges spatially diverse contributions to household welfare is adopted as the basic social unit of livelihood analysis. Broad-scale agricultural development theories are considered from the diverse livelihoods perspective, and it is noted that diversity has featured little in past rural development policy and practice.

— CHAPTER 2 —

A Framework for Livelihoods Analysis

This chapter sets out a policy framework that can be utilised for thinking through diversified rural livelihoods. This is a version of the 'assets-mediating processes-activities' framework that is utilised in various different guises by researchers concerned with poverty reduction, sustainability, and livelihood strategies. It originates from work on vulnerability and famines (e.g. Swift, 1989; Davies, 1996); livelihood systems approaches to gender analysis (Grown and Sebstad, 1989); analysis of poverty-environment interactions (e.g. Reardon and Vosti, 1995); the asset vulnerability approach to urban poverty reduction (Moser, 1998); and research on sustainable rural livelihoods (Scoones, 1998; Bebbington, 1999).

These approaches have in common that they regard the asset status of poor individuals or households as fundamental to understanding the options open to them, the strategies they adopt for survival, and their vulnerability to adverse trends and events. They also therefore concur broadly that poverty policy should be about raising the asset status of the poor, or enabling existing assets that are idle or under-employed to be used productively. Such approaches look positively at what is possible rather than negatively at how desperate things are. As articulated by Moser (1998: 1) they seek 'to identify what the poor have rather than what they do not have' and '[to] strengthen people's own inventive solutions, rather than substitute for, block or undermine them.'

The framework is thought to be particularly useful as a guide to micro policies concerned with poverty reduction in rural areas, although it may also serve a useful purpose for tracing local level impacts of macro policies. In this context the term micro policies refers to interventions that affect livelihood options and strategies at sectoral and local levels. Micro policies may arise from governments, donors, NGOs, or from rural people themselves in participatory interaction with any or several other parties. Micro policies may be economic instruments (e.g. taxes, subsidies, interest rates), advisory or delivery services (e.g. agricultural extension, veterinary services), projects (e.g. microcredit projects based on group lending), facilitation and enabling functions (e.g. formation of groups or associations to achieve specific goals on behalf of their members; reducing bureaucratic barriers to individual or community action), or targeted interventions (e.g. employment guarantee schemes etc.)

While the framework is considered mainly useful as a tool for micro policy analysis, it contains provision for considering macro policy impacts at local levels, and these may, in some circumstances, be highly significant for local-level livelihood strategies. Moreover, the reform end of the spectrum of macro policies (see Chapter 8 below) is just as significant for change at local levels, e.g. simplifying bureaucratic procedures, improving fairness in official decisions, removing barriers to small-scale business activities, as it is at the national level of government operations.

The chapter proceeds as follows. The next section sets out the framework in some detail, considering assets, mediating processes, trends, shocks and activities as components and processes that jointly contribute to rural livelihood strategies. This is followed by a consideration of selected features and applications of the framework in more depth; and by a brief summary of emerging micro policy priorities for sustainable rural livelihoods.

A framework for the analysis of rural livelihoods

The framework is set out in Figure 2.1. The limitations of any such two-dimensional representation of a process as complex as rural livelihood formation are recognised at the outset. The purpose of such a diagram is to organise ideas into manageable categories, identify entry points and critical processes, and assist with prioritising catalysts for change that can improve people's livelihood chances. It is difficult in such a diagram to capture the dynamics of livelihood systems that in practice involve innumerable feedbacks and complex interactions between components. Such dynamic interactions are therefore implied rather than stated in Figure 2.1; however, some key dynamic processes are identified and discussed in the course of describing the framework.

The reference scale of a framework like this depends on the uses to which it is being put (Scoones, 1998). The same diagram can be used to think through the livelihood circumstances of individuals, households, villages, communities, even districts or larger scale geographical zones that share some important features in common, such as their broad agroecological properties (e.g. the cocoa growing forest zone in Ghana). There are important trade-offs with respect to scale. While a large scale perspective may help to identify policies that appear broadly beneficial to all individuals and families sharing certain properties (e.g. cocoa producers), this is offset by their lack of sensitivity to variation within the domain that has been chosen (e.g. the non-cocoa producers; big vs. small landowners within the cocoa zone; the landless etc.).

The recent tendency has been to move away from large domain policies (like cocoa policies, to continue the same example) towards village, household, and individual level policies. However, there is clearly scope to operate simultaneously

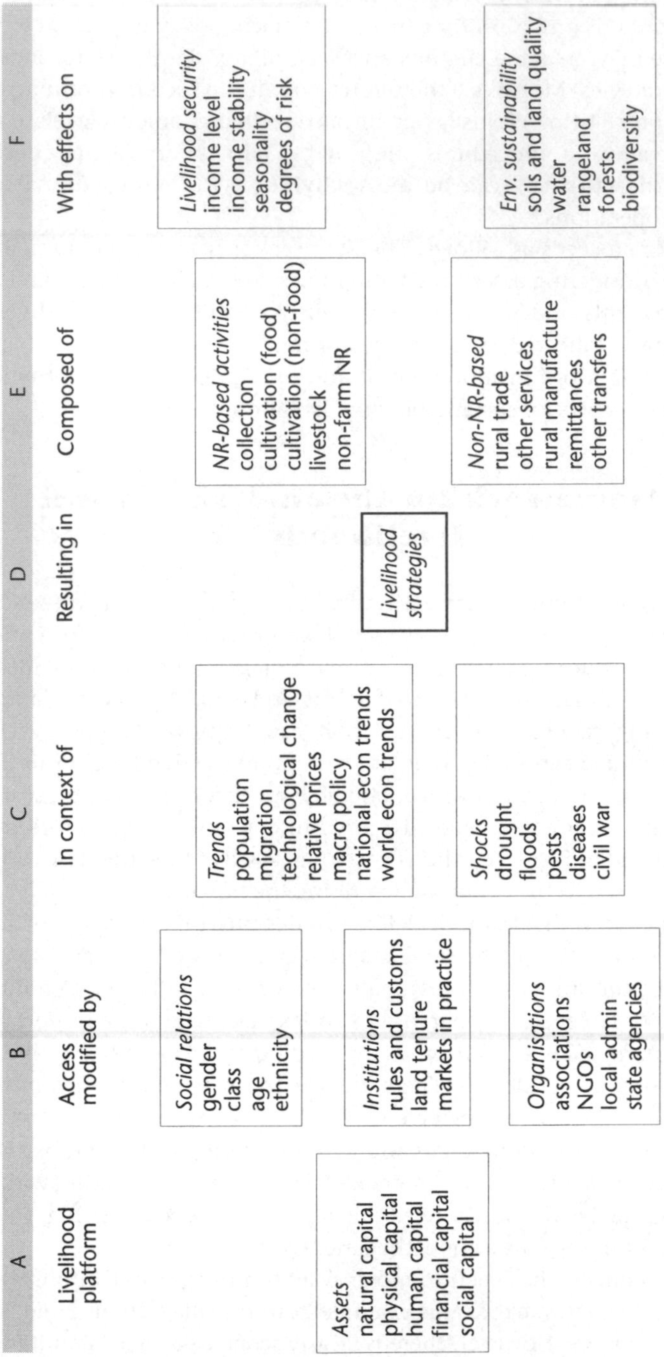

A	B	C	D	E	F
Livelihood platform	Access modified by	In context of	Resulting in	Composed of	With effects on

Assets
natural capital
physical capital
human capital
financial capital
social capital

Social relations
gender
class
age
ethnicity

Institutions
rules and customs
land tenure
markets in practice

Organisations
associations
NGOs
local admin
state agencies

Trends
population
migration
technological change
relative prices
macro policy
national econ trends
world econ trends

Shocks
drought
floods
pests
diseases
civil war

Livelihood strategies

NR-based activities
collection
cultivation (food)
cultivation (non-food)
livestock
non-farm NR

Non-NR-based
rural trade
other services
rural manufacture
remittances
other transfers

Livelihood security
income level
income stability
seasonality
degrees of risk

Env. sustainability
soils and land quality
water
rangeland
forests
biodiversity

Figure 2.1. A framework for micro policy analysis of rural livelihoods

Source: adapted from Scoones (1998: 4) and D. Carney (1998: 5).

at many different scales of policy, provided the limitations of the particular scale chosen are identified and understood. Thus support to cocoa producers, in the form perhaps of disseminating high yielding cocoa hybrids to growers, will improve the livelihoods of a particular set of people in cocoa growing zones differentiated by land ownership, land quality, gender and so on. Such a policy will not improve the livelihood circumstances of everyone in those zones, and other policies are needed to address other constituencies of poor people in the same geographical areas.

In the process of describing the framework shown in Figure 2.1, it is the rural household that is taken as the main social unit to which the framework is applied. This is implied by the use of the term 'livelihood strategy' in which the household as a social unit is observed to alter its mix of activities according to its evolving asset position, and the changing circumstances it confronts. At village or community level, a single livelihood strategy could not apply, since different households will adopt different strategies according to their particular asset and access status. Meanwhile, within the household, the strategies of individuals are likely to be powerfully constrained by, and to overlap, the livelihood strategy of the household or homestead group. The strengths and flaws of the household as a unit of analysis have already been aired in Chapter 1. The household only represents a barrier to understanding interactions between individual and group identities if an unnecessarily narrow, unitary, and static view of the household, its composition, and the roles of its individual members is taken.

Assets

The starting points of the framework are the assets owned, controlled, claimed, or in some other means accessed by the household. These are the basic building blocks upon which households are able to undertake production, engage in labour markets, and participate in reciprocal exchanges with other households. Assets may be described as stocks of capital that can be utilised directly, or indirectly, to generate the means of survival of the household or to sustain its material well-being at differing levels above survival. Some writers refer to assets as resources, while in intention meaning the same thing (e.g. Grown and Sebstadt, 1989). A fundamental feature of assets as stocks of capital is that they either exist as a stock (e.g. land or trees) giving rise to a flow of output, or they are brought into being when a surplus is generated between production and consumption, thus enabling an investment in future productive capacity to be made.

Different researchers have identified different categories of assets as capturing for them strategically important distinctions between different types of capital. For example, Swift (1989) divides assets between the three broad categories of investments, stores, and claims. Here, investments include human, individual and collective assets; stores include food stores, items of value such as gold, and money in the bank; and claims include reciprocal claims on other households, and claims on patrons (chiefs etc.), government, and even on the international community. On the other hand, Maxwell and Smith (1992) in a food security context divide assets between productive capital, non-productive capital, human capital, income and claims. Other variants of the asset list are: natural resource assets, human resource assets, on-farm physical and financial resources, off-farm physical and financial resources (Reardon and Vosti, 1995); and labour, human capital, productive assets, household relations, and social capital (Moser, 1998).

These lists are observed to contain some elements in common, and others that appear unique to each list. Following distinctions first made in Chapter 1, the framework illustrated in Figure 2.1 contains the five asset categories of natural capital, human capital, physical capital, financial capital, and social capital (see also D. Carney, 1998; Scoones, 1998). In amplifying the meaning and scope of these five categories, it becomes apparent that most of the anomalies between the lists of different researchers can be resolved through this classification.

Natural capital. Natural capital comprises the land, water and biological re-sources that are utilised by people to generate means of survival. Sometimes these are referred to as environmental resources, and are thought of jointly as comprising the 'environment'. Natural capital is not static and nor is its utilisa-tion for survival purposes confined to gathering activities, such as collecting wild vegetables or hunting wild animals. Natural capital is enhanced or aug-mented when it is brought under human control that increases its productivity, as has occurred since the beginning of sedentary agriculture with the evolution of farming systems. For some purposes of livelihood analysis, it may be useful to think of natural capital as occurring in a gradient between low and high agroe-cological potential (Swift, 1998; Scoones, 1998). Some locations, for example, hilly and mountainous zones can represent rapid changes of gradient over short distances, allowing for high spatial diversity in livelihood niches; other loca-tions, for example, semi-arid, flat terrains allow for less spatial diversity in the natural resource-based component of human livelihoods.

Within natural capital, an important distinction is made between renewable and non-renewable natural resources. In most rural development contexts, in-terest centres on renewable resources, that is, ones that replenish themselves over time, such as fishery stocks or trees used for firewood or water levels in un-derground aquifers; or that are managed to ensure their renewal, such as soils in farmers' fields or water flows in irrigation canals. However, natural capital also includes non-renewable resources that may be pertinent to rural livelihoods in some locations, or in indirect ways. These are principally extractive resources such as metals, ores and oil, stocks of which in a particular location are perma-nently depleted according to the rate of extraction by human agency.

Physical capital. Physical assets comprise capital that is created by economic production processes. Buildings, irrigation canals, roads, tools, machines, and so on are physical assets. In economic terms, physical capital is defined as a producer good as contrasted to a consumer good. The latter is something that is purchased and consumed for its direct effect on material standards of living; whereas a producer good is purchased in order to create a flow of outputs into the future. Items that are considered to be 'consumer durables' for high income groups, such as refrigerators or sewing machines, are physical capital when they are purchased as a means of generating a future flow of income. Likewise, supposedly unproductive physical assets, such as a house used primarily as a home, becomes a source of livelihood if it is used to generate income flows for its owners, for example, by utilising it for cottage industry or renting out rooms (Moser, 1998). In this way the non-productive capital that enters the asset list of Maxwell and Smith (1992) is included under physical capital here.

It is worth noting that physical or 'man-made' capital can substitute for natural capital in many circumstances. Indeed, the entire long-term process of technological change coupled with industrialisation and urbanisation is one in which physical capital cumulatively substitutes for natural capital over time. This substitution process can potentially help to take the pressure off natural resources that are being depleted in local contexts; for example, water pipes substituting for open channels, with consequent reductions in loss from leakage and evaporation.

An important class of physical assets that facilitate livelihood diversification are infrastructural assets such as roads, power lines, and water supplies. Roads have multiple effects in reducing the spatial cost of transactions in resources and outputs. They also facilitate movement of people between places offering different income-earning opportunities, they create markets that otherwise would not come into existence, and in countries lacking in telecommunication facilities, they play an important role in transfer of information between rural centres and remote settlements (Swift, 1998). The absence of mains electricity inhibits the rural location of manufacturing industries, and constrains small-scale services from arising in rural areas. While this constraint can sometimes be lifted in a fragmented way by the use of technologies such as solar panels, there is no doubt that the availability of an electricity supply has an enormous impact on the diversity of rural activities and on the relative integration of rural areas into the national economy. Finally, in this context, the provision of piped water has multiple beneficial effects on rural livelihoods due to the saving of labour time that it brings, as well as the avoidance of illness and disease if clean drinking water is supplied.

Human capital. It is often said that the chief asset possessed by the poor is their own labour. Human capital refers to the labour available to the household: its education, skills, and health (D. Carney,1998). Human capital is increased by investment in education and training, as well as by the skills acquired through pursuing one or more occupations. Labour as an asset is also made more effective by being free of illness or debilitating health problems. The importance of labour as a resource is emphasised in circumstances where there is little or no labour market, when large household size has advantages since it reduces the risk to livelihood security of illness and permits more diverse occupational strategies to be pursued (Toulmin, 1992). Households as 'groupings' of human capital are not static in composition, either in industrial or low-income societies. The human capital composition of a household changes constantly due to internal demographic reasons (births, deaths, marriage, migration, children growing older), and to deliberate restructuring to meet unexpected events (e.g. divorce) or external pressures (Moser, 1998). As defined here, human capital encompasses at least three of Moser's asset categories listed earlier; namely, those of labour, human capital, and household relations.

Public education and health services are macro policies designed to raise the level of human capital across the country as a whole. Modern theories of economic growth emphasise the significant role of rising human capital in underpinning rapid and sustained growth. A major concern related to structural adjustment since the mid-1980s has been the erosion of state provision in education and health due to budgetary cutbacks (Cornia and Jolly, 1987). However, the evidence about such expenditures fails to confirm the existence of a downward trend in real terms as a general proposition for low income adjusting economies (Sahn *et al.*, 1996). Nevertheless, cost recovery has become more commonplace across developing countries, especially in relation to the dispensing of medicines in rural clinics, and increasingly in relation to parental contributions to schooling costs. It is possible that these trends will result in the future in greater inequality in human capital arising over time in rural areas.

Financial capital and substitutes. Financial capital refers to stocks of money to which the household has access. This is chiefly likely to be savings, and access to credit in the form of loans. Neither money savings nor loans are directly productive forms of capital, they owe their role in the asset portfolio of households to their convertibility into other forms of capital, or, indeed, directly into consumption. Fungibility, meaning ease of switching between uses, is a fundamental characteristic of capital in the form of cash. In many societies, the absence of financial markets or distrust of such financial institutions as do exist, result in savings being held in other forms. In rural sub-Saharan Africa, the keeping of livestock often plays a critical role as a store of wealth and as a buffer against bad times (see Box 2.1). While cattle and goats are considerably less liquid as a form of savings than a cash deposit in a rural financial institution, they possess the same attribute when sold of being convertible into other forms of capital or into consumption. Similar arguments apply also to gold, jewellery, and food stocks as alternative means of holding, for varying periods, surpluses between current production and consumption (Swift, 1989).

Box 2.1. Livestock as an asset and income portfolios in rural Ethiopia

In the 1970s and 1980s, the rural economy of Ethiopia was subject to a number of controls which affected the range of possible activities and the returns to them. Private land ownership had been abolished, many agricultural outputs were heavily taxed, and restrictions on trade and wage labour limited non-farm income opportunities. Livestock markets were relatively unrestricted, however, and this, together with the lack of other investment opportunities, increased the incentives for cattle ownership.

A study covering five regions of southern and central Ethiopia was conducted in 1989. It collected household income and other data from 423 households in 6 villages. Table 2.1 shows the composition of household incomes found in each village.

Table 2.1. Income portfolios in rural Ethiopia

	Site of sample survey					
	Derbre Berhan	Dinki	Koro-degaga	Adele Keke	Gara-godo	Domaa
Size of sample (hhs)	67	54	89	60	56	97
Income per capita (Birr)	236	145	71	163	46	40
(US$)[a]	114	70	34	79	22	19
Income composition (%)						
Crops	43	78	54	51	66	73
Livestock products	14	0	0	8	4	0
Livestock live sales	26	4	6	13	2	10
Non-farm[b]	16	10	38	24	19	7
Remittances	2	6	1	5	10	8

[a] The exchange rate at the time of survey was 2.07 Birr = US$ 1.00.
[b] Non-farm income includes wages and business income.
Source: Dercon and Krishnan (1996: 856).

The most important source of income for all communities was found to be crops, mainly utilised for subsistence rather than sales. Villages differed in the importance of remittances and non-farm income, reflecting site-specific characteristics. Across all villages, there were significant differences between the income sources of the poorest groups, defined as the bottom third of households in terms of income per capita, and the richest. The clearest difference lay in ownership of livestock, particularly cattle, with almost three quarters of the better-off group owning cattle, compared to only 13 per cent of the poorest. The better off were also more likely to be involved in non-farm activities for which investment or particular skills were required, such as weaving or carpentry. The poorest tended to concentrate on off-farm activities with low entry constraints, such as firewood collection.

These findings lead to consideration of the obstacles which prevent the poor from engaging in livestock-rearing or more remunerative non-farm activities. The purchase of livestock is a substantial investment, and the funds required are not easily raised since credit is scarce in rural Ethiopia. This suggests that only those households that are able to raise funds through their own savings are able to purchase cattle. Analysis of the data confirmed that households with high income-earning potential, associated with more male adult labour and larger farm sizes, were more likely to be found in cattle-rearing. Higher return non-farm activities also require cash investment or special skills, both of which the poor are unable to supply.

The study concluded that although risk is likely to be a factor in explaining diversification into non-cropping income sources, observed patterns of diversification seem to be a reflection of different households' abilities to take advantage of opportunities with high entry barriers, which in turn reflect differences in skills and access to funds for investment. Human capital and financial capital dominate above risk as explanations of observed diverse income portfolios in rural Ethiopia.

Source: Dercon and Krishnan (1996).

Social capital. The term social capital attempts to capture community and wider social claims on which individuals and households can draw by virtue of their belonging to social groups of varying degrees of inclusiveness in society at large. Social capital is defined by Moser (1998) as 'reciprocity within communities and between households based on trust deriving from social ties'. This places the emphasis on localised reciprocity, as envisaged, for example, in ideas of moral economy and social insurance (Scott, 1976; Platteau, 1991). It also directs attention to personal or family networks, typically comprising near and remote kin, as well as close family friends, that offer spatially diverse potential means of support when past favours are reclaimed. Berry (1989; 1993) emphasises the time and resources that are devoted to extending and nurturing such networks, implying that they are very much seen as an investment in future livelihood security by rural households.

Swift (1998: 8) states that social capital 'is made up of both of networks of ascriptive and elective relationships between individuals, which may be vertical as in authority relationships, or horizontal as in voluntary organisations, and of the trust and expectations which flow within those networks'. Stated as such social capital would comprise the vertical claims, for example, on patrons, chiefs, and politicians that are expected to be met in times of crisis (Swift, 1989). Putnam *et al.* (1993) envisages social capital as consisting more of horizontal social groups such as associations, clubs, and voluntary agencies that bring individuals together to pursue one or more objectives in which they have a common interest (e.g. farmers' associations).

This fits less well with ideas of claims and reciprocity. Nevertheless some evidence suggests that a high level of this type of associational life as indicated by membership of religious, social and economic groups is correlated, at village level, by higher average village per capita income (Narayan and Pritchett, 1999). The latter study was undertaken in rural Tanzania in 1995, and involved collecting data on membership of groups as part of a larger participatory poverty assessment. Statistical analysis ruled out the reverse causation of income levels leading to higher associative activity.

Of all the assets described here, social capital is clearly the most difficult to describe in other than broad qualitative terms (Bebbington, 1999). A great deal of reciprocity is hidden, or is discovered only by time-consuming anthropological research, or emerges into the open only at times of serious livelihood crisis. The processes that create 'insiders' and 'outsiders' with respect to social capital are complex and difficult to unravel, but clearly such divisions do exist, and they sometimes result in the 'social exclusion' of particular individuals or groups within rural communities.

Mediating processes

All frameworks of this kind recognise that the translation of a set of assets into a livelihood strategy composed of a portfolio of income earning activities is mediated by a great number of contextual social, economic and policy considerations. Scoones (1998), for example, divides these between the two categories of contexts, conditions and trends, on the one hand, and institutions and organisations, on the other. The former category includes history, politics, economic trends, climate, agroecology, demography, and social differentiation. Similarly, D. Carney (1998) has the two broad categories denominated 'the vulnerability context' and 'transforming processes'. In this instance the vulnerability context comprises many of the same factors listed under contexts by Scoones (1998), while transforming processes include policies, institutions, laws, incentives (relative prices), and social relations. Yet another version of this idea of livelihood mediating processes is found in Reardon and Vosti (1998: 1497) where all such considerations taken together comprise what are called 'conditioning factors'.

The layout of Figure 2.1 draws on the insights of these and other sources to distinguish key categories of factors that influence access to assets and their use in pursuit of viable livelihoods. The primary distinction made in this framework is between social relations, institutions and organisations, on the one hand, and trend and shock factors, on the other. The former category consists of social factors that are predominantly endogenous to the social norms and structures of which households are a part, while the latter category consists predominantly of the exogenous factors of economic trends and policies, and unforeseen shocks with major consequences on livelihood viability. Of course, these broad categories are not watertight as far as the endogenous-exogenous distinction is concerned, since there are many social factors that may be endogenous at higher levels of scale, like the district or the ethnic group, but that are treated as exogenous as far as the individual or household is concerned. Nevertheless, it is considered that there is some utility in distinguishing external trends and events over which even countries may have no control (e.g. world prices of primary commodities), from contextual factors that are, in some sense, 'much closer to home'. Such factors include power, authority, and the social and political processes through which rules and rights for individuals and social groups evolve.

Different authors tend to use the terms 'institutions' and 'social relations' in different ways, and sometimes the entire social side of livelihoods is lumped together under the institutional label. In Figure 2.1, social relations are distinguished from institutions, and the latter from organisations (column B). Social relations refer to the social positioning of individuals and households within society. This social positioning comprises such factors as gender, caste, class, age, ethnicity, and religion. The significance of gender in creating constraints on individual courses of action is established later in this book (Chapter 7) and elsewhere (e.g. Davies and Hossain, 1997). Other factors such as caste or ethnicity may be of fundamental importance in some rural social settings, and not important at all in others. Class is an ambiguous social construct, difficult to generalise across different cultural contexts. While it has precise meanings for Marxist social analysis (the owners of capital or capitalist class vs. those who own only their own labour), its manifestation in rural societies may be by reference to partial indicators like overt differences in land ownership, personal wealth, and educational attainment across different rural social strata.

Following North (1990: 3), institutions are the formal rules, conventions, and informal codes of behaviour, that comprise constraints on human interaction. Examples of institutions are laws (e.g. criminal law), land tenure arrangements (property rights), and the way markets work in practice ('the market' as an institution). The role of institutions is to reduce uncertainty by establishing a stable structure to human interaction (North, 1990: 6). Institutions tend to change slowly and incrementally, rather than in discontinuous jumps, even during or following social upheavals. Organisations, as distinguished from institutions are 'groups of individuals bound by some common purpose to achieve objectives' (North, 1990: 5). Examples of organisations are government agencies (e.g. police force, Ministry of Agriculture, government veterinary service), administrative bodies (e.g. local government), NGOs, associations (e.g. farmers' associations), and private companies (firms).

Social relations, institutions and organisations are critical mediating factors for livelihoods because they encompass the agencies that inhibit or facilitate the exercise of capabilities and choices by individuals or households. Land tenure institutions, for example, comprise such determinants of access to land as the ownership structure at a particular moment (possibly highly unequal), whether this ownership is defined by private freehold title or by customary rights of access, the existence or not of a market in land, the various tenure contracts that may enable non-owners of land to gain access to land, the social mechanisms for resolving land disputes, and so on. These institutions may work more, or less, well. There is no guarantee that laws and customs with distant historical roots are efficient in the sense of optimal resource allocation, nor that they are fair in terms of the way access rules are applied to different types of people (North, 1990). As discussed in Chapter 7 below, for example, the ownership by women of property in land is comparatively rare worldwide, and may be deteriorating over time (Agarwal, 1994b). Nor is there any guarantee that the organisations that interpret institutions (e.g. village councils, local courts etc.) do so in an even-handed and consistent way across individuals, irrespective of their social positioning.

From the foregoing discussion of social factors mediating people's access to resources and activities, it is evident that social capital as an asset is closely related to such factors. Indeed, carrying out an evaluation of the social context of rural livelihoods is likely to yield information relevant both to the social capital status of individuals, households or communities, and to the constraints and opportunities represented by local level customs, rules, and organisations. A community low in social capital as manifested by weak networks and associational activities, poorly performing or perfunctory organisations, and little reciprocity occurring between households, seems also likely to be one that offers little scope for negotiating access to assets, and experiences weak management of common property resources.

The interrelationship between assets, mediating processes, and livelihood activities is a process that is unfolding over time. The manner of this unfolding, and the stresses and strains that result in new patterns of activity emerging, are influenced by trends and events that are in varying degrees exogenous to household and to local circumstances (column C). Some important trends are the rate of population growth (locally and nationally), the population density (locally), rates of out-migration from rural areas either to other rural areas or to urban centres, agricultural technology and its evolution over time, the growth of non-farm activities in rural areas and in the economy at large, relative prices, national economic trends, international trends, and macro policies that mediate the impact of these within the domestic economy. The relative importance of these trends for different rural locations is likely to vary tremendously. For example, the international economy is of direct importance to small farm producers of export crops like coffee, cocoa, or cashewnuts, but may be of indirect or negligible importance for producers of yams or bricks that are not internationally traded.

Trends may be fortuitous or adverse. In Indonesia, for example, in the period from the mid-1980s to the mid-1990s, there was a high rate of national economic growth based on labour-using technologies, combined with rapid uptake of new seed technologies in rice production, and a slow down in population growth rates. A mushrooming of economic activity occurred that significantly reduced the proportion of the rural population with incomes falling below the poverty line. Livelihood diversification was facilitated, and growth was fast enough for this to give way fairly rapidly to full-time occupations in new manufacturing and service industries. Trends on the other hand can be mixed or outright inimical to poverty reduction. In the latter case, livelihood diversification occurs more through necessity than choice (Chapter 3 below), and becomes a permanent, enduring, feature of rural survival.

Shocks represent a particular challenge to livelihood sustainability (Blaikie *et al.*, 1994). In Figure 2.1, events such as drought, floods, pests (of crops and animals), diseases (of crops, animals or humans), and civil war are listed as shocks. Shocks destroy assets directly; for example, crops standing in the field in the case of drought, houses and fields in the case of hurricanes or floods, animal numbers in the case of livestock diseases, human capital in the case of human diseases such as outbreaks of cholera. They also result in the erosion of assets indirectly, as a consequence of enforced sales and disposals made in order to maintain consumption during the sequence of responses that occur at times of disaster (more on this below). The latter shocks are events having widespread impacts on rural populations in particular localities; however, shocks can, of course, be individual as well as social in scope. Loss of access rights to land, accident, sudden illness, death, and abandonment are all shocks with immediate effects on the livelihood viability of the individuals and households to whom they occur.

Activities and livelihood strategies

The asset status of households, mediated by social factors and exogenous trends or shocks, results in the adoption and adaptation over time of livelihood strategies. Livelihood strategies are dynamic; they respond to changing pressures and opportunities and they adapt accordingly. In the case of shocks, households adopt coping strategies, that may result in an entirely different livelihood mix emerging from a crisis from that which obtained before. A more complete discussion of coping and adapting behaviours is contained in the next section of this chapter.

Livelihood strategies are composed of activities that generate the means of household survival. The categories and sub-categories of activities that are potential components of a livelihood strategy are given in column E of Figure 2.1. These are divided between natural resource and non-natural resource based activities. Natural resource based activities include collection or gathering (e.g. from woodlands and forest), food cultivation, non-food cultivation, livestock keeping and pastoralism, and non-farm activities such as brick making, weaving, thatching and so on. Non-natural resource based activities include rural trade (marketing of farm outputs, inputs, and consumer goods), other rural services (e.g. vehicle repair), rural manufacture, remittances (urban and international), and other transfers such as pensions deriving from past formal sector employment.

Activities in all categories represent potential contributions to the survival portfolio of rural households. Moreover, the composition of this portfolio has policy relevance. Households that depend mainly on gathering from the natural environment differ from those that derive their income mainly from cash crop cultivation, and they, in turn, differ from households that derive a small proportion of their livelihood from food production, but otherwise depend on non-farm activities as their means of survival. Also within the constraints that are described elsewhere in the diagram, substitutability is a prime consideration when thinking about livelihood diversification. For example, if a policy aim were to reduce pressure on a natural habitat for reasons of species conservation, then the requirement is to examine and facilitate the substitution options for the households or communities involved.

For some purposes of research or policy work, a classification of livelihood strategies between broad types may be useful. For example, Scoones (1998) identifies three strategy types, with respect to which different configurations of assets-mediating processes-activities apply. These strategy types are agricultural intensification or extensification; livelihood diversification; and migration. The first type corresponds to continued or increasing reliance on agriculture as a strategy, either by intensifying resource use in combination with a given land area, or by bringing new land into cultivation or grazing. The key asset here is land, and, for agricultural intensification, attention is directed towards the institutions and organisations that facilitate technical change in agriculture. The second type, within the restricted definition of diversification employed, directs attention to non-farm rural employment as a key policy issue. The third type directs attention to migration and remittances as a particular strategy adopted by members of rural households, with, as will become apparent in later chapters, particular implications for the asset status of those left behind, the position of women, and the utilisation or not of external resources to carry out productivity enhancing farm investments.

There are reasons to be cautious about such livelihood strategy typologies. They are prone to similar difficulties surrounding homogeneous policy domains as previous farm output-based policies were (e.g. supporting cocoa producers). A key problem is the exclusion from the ensuing analysis of those that do not fit the type. Diversification as a consideration notably cuts across livelihood typologies. Individuals and households may diversify on-farm, off-farm and non-farm, including, decidedly, migration as part of the diversification strategy. For poverty reduction purposes, it may be more appropriate to start off with who is poor in a village or locality, and see whether useful pointers for policy interventions can be derived from comparing the livelihood strategies of the poor with those that are better off.

The final two columns of Figure 2.1 point, in a provisional way, to indicators of the outcomes of livelihood strategies. Thus column F divides livelihood strategy outcomes between their livelihood security and environmental sustainability aspects. Livelihood security is defined in Figure 2.1 as containing some combination of attributes related to income level, income stability, reduction in adverse seasonal effects, and reduction in the overall risk profile of the income portfolio. This in turn leads to people becoming less vulnerable or more vulnerable in terms of their capability to manage adverse trends or cope with shocks. Likewise, environmental sustainability refers to changes in the resilience and stability of resources such as soils, water, rangeland, forests and biodiversity. Environments may improve, stabilise or degrade. These are difficult terms to pin down (see Chapter 6), however, they indicate that there are alternative paths by which environments stay the same, or become more able, or less able to sustain the outputs for human consumption that are the reason for their management by people.

Some extensions: substitution, crisis management, adaptation

There is wide agreement in the literature that secure livelihoods are closely connected to substitution capabilities amongst assets and activities. Low potential for substitution makes livelihoods more vulnerable, especially to shocks, since a sudden change in a single asset or activity cannot be compensated by redeployment or switches between them. Moreover, low substitution capabilities are likely to be associated with high sensitivity of livelihood systems to small disturbances, utilising a distinction between sensitivity and resilience made by Blaikie and Brookfield (1987) and Bayliss-Smith (1991) which is elaborated in Chapter 3 below.

Households vary not only in the profile of assets that they hold, but also in their capability to substitute between assets when confronted by change. The argument is made by Reardon and Vosti (1995) that identifying both the type of asset poverty (i.e. poor in what?) and the ability to convert one type of wealth into another are critical for poverty reduction and environmental sustainability policies. Asset substitutability depends in part on the existence and functioning of asset markets. Assets that can freely be converted into cash that is then utilised to purchase other assets provide considerably more livelihood flexibility than assets that cannot be substituted in this way. In an environmental context, an additional important factor is whether the value of an asset to the individual household is the same as its value to society at large.

Reardon and Vosti (1995: 1502) provide some interesting illustrations of these considerations. One example is that of frontier settlers in the Amazon rainforest. Here, rural households are rich in trees and biodiversity that are locally abundant but globally scarce. Poverty in all asset categories but forest cover leads farmers to convert forests into farmland by burning trees to generate nutrients to enhance soils. That is, farmers use biophysical processes rather than markets to convert an asset which for them has low value as a means of generating survival, to an asset, i.e. farmland, which has higher value for this purpose. Moreover, even as converted to farmland, this asset, due to its relative abundance, is regarded as cheap compared to labour which is in short supply. This results in the adoption of land extensive methods of production, for example, cattle ranching, which combines a lot of the inexpensive land asset with little of the scarce labour asset.

The authors of this example take pains to point out that the devastation of the Amazon cannot be laid at the door of small farm households that act in the way suggested (Reardon and Vosti, 1995: 1502). For one thing, the Amazon was opened up by the Brazilian government as a political response to land hunger elsewhere in the country, or for timber concessions; for another, many of the 'households' that managed to obtain land holdings at the forest fringe were not by any stretch of the imagination poor farmers.

Asset substitutions can occur within asset categories as well as between them. Moser (1998) contains an insightful discussion of substitutions that occur within the human capital category. These mainly take the form of re-allocating labour between domestic and outside earning activities according to changing circumstances, but subject to the well-known gender constraint on male involvement in domestic duties that seems to characterise most societies worldwide. For this reason, substitutions in deployment of household labour assets can have negative as well as positive effects on the well-being of individual household members. Women may find themselves as chief income earners, as well as chiefly responsible for domestic duties. In this way, asset adjustments that diversify household incomes may reduce the vulnerability of the household to shocks, while at the same time aggravating unequal burdens for women, or leaving them prone to lose male support in the future (ibid., pp.11–13).

Households can also split, combine, or change their demographic structure in other ways as a response to stresses and shocks. It is a mistake to view households in static terms, and also to think that units that become demographically non-viable for one reason or another are unable to pursue adaptive responses. Due to marital disintegration or to absent fathers, children are often looked after, and reside, in households different from those of their natural parents. Women who find themselves suddenly without male support and male labour will often restructure their households accordingly, by combining with other households or taking in male relatives from other families to assist with tasks that are regarded as in the male domain in that cultural context.

Assets both facilitate, and are facilitated by, diversification. Human and social capital facilitate diversification by increasing the range of opportunities from which choice can be made. Diversification may also be used as the instrument for acquiring or enhancing assets, for example, by generating cash income that is invested in children's education or improvements to farm physical capital. The easier it is for individuals or families to convert one type of asset into another, the more options are opened up for livelihood generation and the greater the substitutability that is then made possible between activities. For example, if natural capital (e.g. ownership of a farm) can be readily converted into human capital (education, health, skills), then this increases the range of livelihood options open to the household. Clearly, the most substitutable of all assets is cash in the form of savings or available credit. This can be used to build up or improve the quality of any of the other assets under household control.

A lot of work has been done on household responses to crisis, utilising approaches that are similar to the framework outlined here. When faced with a collapse in their regular sources of consumption, households tend to follow a sequenced response in which the conservation of assets that would permit them to resume their previous livelihood strategy is a key tactic (Watts, 1983; 1988; Corbett, 1988; Swift, 1989). A typical sequence might involve, first, the pursuit of new sources of income (diversification); second, drawing on reciprocal obligations (social capital); third, reducing the size of the resident household by temporary migration (see, for example, Toulmin, 1992: 51; Devereux, 1993); fourth, the selective sale of movable assets such as goats, cattle or farm implements; fifth, the sale or abandonment of fixed assets such as land, houses, grain stores and so on.

These sequences of response to crisis are usually referred to as coping strategies (e.g. Corbett, 1988; Davies, 1993). In principle, the observation of regularities in such sequences might make it possible to achieve an earlier diagnosis of an impending catastrophe, and enable relief agencies to target their support at coping with crisis, rather than picking up the pieces when livelihoods have totally fallen apart (Corbett, 1988). A key feature is household asset management. The order in which assets are unloaded, the overall erosion of assets that takes place in order to cope with an event like crop failure, and the process of building up assets after the crisis are all thought to be critical factors in improving policy responses to crisis situations. However, practical difficulties abound in this area, therefore also sounding a cautionary note as to what can and cannot be achieved by utilising this sort of framework. Monitoring household level assets to the degree of accuracy required of a predictive tool for forecasting the timing and depth of a disaster represents insuperable problems in practice. Moreover, the sequencing of disposals of different kinds of asset during a crisis varies across households, so that no generalised indicators based on asset types can be constructed (Devereux, 1993).

Davies (1993; 1996) makes the distinction between coping strategies, on the one hand, and adaptive strategies, on the other. Coping strategies are short-term responses to unplanned crisis. However, what Davies argues is perhaps more important as an entry point for assisting people to become less vulnerable to disaster is to understand adaptive strategies, that is, the way households respond over the long term to adverse events, cycles and trends. Successful adaptation means that households become less prone to crisis over time, that is, it implies improving the capacity to resist shocks. Building up assets, changing the asset mix, and diversifying income sources may all have roles in successful adaptive strategies. On the other hand, some paths of adaptation may be unsuccessful. Households may adjust their portfolio of assets and activities, but in ways that reduce flexibility and make them more vulnerable when the next crisis occurs. Households may, over successive difficult seasons, be unable to recover the level of assets that pertained in earlier times. Poverty and disaster policies should focus on identifying negative adaptation, and on taking steps so that more sustainable livelihood strategies are within reach of those caught up in such processes.

A case-study of Botswana summarised in Box 2.2 illustrates some of these points, and demonstrates the potential importance of policy for making possible positive rather than negative adaptations to disastrous events (Valentine, 1993).

The foregoing discussion shows that analysis of livelihoods according to an assets-access-activities framework has been going on for many years, even though in contexts where the framework is not as explicit as it has been made here. The key point is that understanding, and being able to act on, people's survival capabilities starts off first and foremost with the assets that they own, control, or can draw down on in good and bad times. Assets can be increased, temporarily diminished, eroded gradually over time, or destroyed at a stroke by a catastrophic event. A successful rural livelihood strategy is one in which the quantity, quality, and mix of assets are such that adverse events can be withstood without compromising future survival. This requires flexibility and substitutability between assets. It is a theme of this book that diversification, often, but not always for everyone, contributes to a successful livelihood strategy. This is due to its ameliorating effects on the risks and seasonality of rural livelihoods that are prone to unpredictable events and adverse trends.

Utilising the framework for livelihoods analysis

As already stated, a framework of this kind does not provide a set recipe for solving problems of causes and effects in rural poverty reduction. It does, however, suggest a way of organising the policy analysis of livelihoods that identifies main components (assets, mediating processes, activities), encourages thinking

Box 2.2. Livelihood strategies and diversification, rural Botswana

Since Independence in 1966, Botswana has sustained a high rate of economic growth. This is mainly as a result of earnings from diamond mining, but live-stock also made a strong contribution to foreign exchange earnings in the 1970s. The performance of the livestock sector was boosted by favourable cli-matic conditions and high export prices during most of that decade, leading to rapid expansion of the national herd.

In the late 1970s and mid-1980s a series of droughts hit Botswana. As a re-sult of these droughts, and adverse trends in the rural sector, real agricultural production fell by 38 per cent between 1974–75 and 1987–88. Many house-holds lost income and assets, including cattle, making recovery from the drought more difficult. The ratio of cattle to humans fell from 4-to-1 in the late 1970s to 2-to-1 in 1990, and livestock ownership became more unequal because the drought affected the poorest groups disproportionately. Crop production, which makes a vital contribution to the livelihoods of poorer people, was also hit by the drought.

These conditions of diamond-led growth and drought-induced decline in the agricultural sector might be expected to lead to increasing income in-equality, both between the rural sector and other sectors, and within the rural sector itself. The study described here investigated changes in income distribution within the rural sector using data from two national household surveys, the 1974–75 Rural Incomes Distribution Survey (RIDS) and the 1985–86 Household Income and Expenditure Survey (HIES). The surveys rep-resented two extremes, 1974–75 being one of the peak years for livestock ex-ports, and 1985–86, the height of one of the spells of drought experienced by Botswana in the 1980s.

Contrary to expectations, no significant difference in rural income distrib-ution between 1974–75 and 1985–86 was found. The findings can be ex-plained in terms of the diversification strategies undertaken by households in response to the droughts. Table 2.2 compares the composition of household income in the two years.

Even in good years, households diversify their income sources as a means of managing, spreading and sharing the risks associated with agriculture in Botswana's drought-prone climate. Households derived less than half their incomes from livestock and crop production in 1974–75, and had diversified into wage employment, small-scale enterprises, and temporary or permanent migration. The effect of the droughts was to further reduce the share of live-stock and crops in income, to less than a quarter of the total. Wage employ-ment, much of it provided through the government's drought relief programme, now constituted the largest proportion of income.

Table 2.2. Intertemporal rural household income portfolios in Botswana (%)

Source of income	1974/5	1985/6
Wage employment	21.5	34.5
Livestock farming	35.0	20.2
Crop farming	10.8	3.2
Other activities[a]	18.5	13.4
Private transfers (remittances)	14.2	23.8
Public transfers	—	4.9

[a] e.g. beer brewing, basket weaving, carpentry.

Source: Valentine (1993: 115).

The most significant change in income composition, however, was in income transfers (both private and public), which doubled between the two years of the surveys. Despite a shift from temporary to permanent migration, migrants maintained strong links with family in rural areas, and increased remittances in response to droughts. Public transfers, associated with the drought relief programme, were also important, more so than the figure of 4.9 per cent suggests. The poorest rural households benefitted most from public and private transfers, which provided 40 per cent of their income. Thus, in Botswana, transfer entitlements acted to redistribute the gains of export-led growth in favour of poor rural households, supplementing households' own rural diversification strategies.

Source: Valentine (1993).

about the critical links between them, and emphasises identification of constraints as a precursor to formulating, interactively with those concerned, policies to overcome constraints and allow assets to be utilised productively.

The apparent information requirements of complying with the framework in its entirety are, of course, much too large for project and policy purposes. Budgets would get swallowed up in information gathering, rather being used in direct or indirect support of improvements in livelihood system components. As Scoones (1998: 13) states: 'In work of this sort the principle of "optimal ignorance" must always be applied, seeking out only what is necessary to know in order for informed action to proceed.' The term 'optimal ignorance' used here is attributable, as far as can be ascertained, to McCracken *et al.* (1988). In practice, participatory rural appraisal (PRA) methods can quite quickly establish, at village level, the priority areas of community-wide concern, and, from there, a phased approach can zero in on the particular problems and constraints of sub-groups within the village, such as the lowest asset-holding third of the village population, or the different priorities of women compared to men.

Best practice rural development already does this, although not necessarily with such an explicit framework in mind. Once a broad set of priorities, or problem areas that need addressing, have been identified, the framework comes into its own, because it encourages the contextual constraints and opportunities to be explored rather than simply taking a stated priority at its face value. This may reveal more than one way of solving a problem, or, indeed, may result in an upstream prior constraint coming to light which means that the problem can be tackled in an entirely different way from that which first suggests itself.

The framework encourages attention to be directed at assets. This means identifying the assets that are weak or lacking under each category of assets, as well as those that are deteriorating over time due to adverse processes, either in the livelihood strategies of households individually, or in the collective community-level management and utilisation of natural resources. It is important that assets are viewed in a dynamic sense; it is not always the static level of a particular asset that is significant, it is more often the direction in which that asset is moving as a consequence of the impact of external pressures and trends on livelihoods. Moser (1998: 15) provides an excellent example, in an urban context, of using asset vulnerability as a tool for identifying promising solutions to people's problems. Emerging or existing asset problems are listed against the category to which they apply, for example, unemployed young male labour belongs in the category of human capital, while lack of piped water close to people's houses belongs in the category of physical capital, sub-category social infrastructure. Once a list of asset problems is agreed upon, priorities can be negotiated, and solutions sought to them.

D. Carney (1998) proposes a schematic approach to comparing the asset status of different social groups, differentiated according to the broad asset characteristics that the individuals or households within them share in common. The approach involves plotting asset status on a pentagon, with each corner of the pentagon representing one of each of the five major asset categories (see Figure 2.2 below). The pentagon is, in effect, a five axis graph on which the relative wealth in each category of assets can be plotted, with the centre of the pentagon representing zero level of an asset, while the outer perimeter would represent the maximum level of that asset, in terms of the particular community under study. It follows, then, that the overall asset status of the designated social group is represented by the central area bounded by the lines joining the agreed points on each axis.

The pentagon is intended as a descriptive rather than quantitative method for evaluating comparative asset status (however, see Chapter 10 below for a quantitative example). As proposed by D. Carney (1998), the axes are not calibrated in quantitative terms but represent rank orderings when broad comparisons

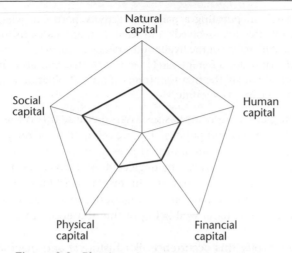

Figure 2.2. Plotting asset status on a pentagon

Note: The example displays a household that is high in social and natural capital, but low in human and financial capital, and moderately endowed with physical capital. For making comparisons between households, assets always need to follow the same order round the perimeter of the pentagon. Then the area of the pentagon gives an approximate 'view' of the relative asset endowment of the social units that are being compared.

Source: D. Carney (1998).

have been made across different groups. Provided that the same ordering of asset categories is maintained around the perimeter, the shape of the central area indicates the strengths and weaknesses of a particular group's asset portfolio; while its area enables comparisons to be made between strong and weak asset groups overall. The descriptive calibration of such pentagons would evidently take place in the context of a participatory appraisal, supplemented perhaps by more detailed investigation of some individual households.

Scoones (1998: 8) suggests a checklist for taking forward an asset-based analysis of rural livelihoods. This checklist, summarised here, consists of a series of key questions to be asked about household asset portfolios:

- *Sequencing*. What is the starting point for establishing a successful livelihood strategy? Is one type of asset more relevant than others for subsequently gaining access to other assets?
- *Substitution*. Can one type of capital be substituted for another? Or are different assets needed in combination to pursue a particular strategy?
- *Clustering*. Does access to one type of asset confer access to others? is there a clustering of particular combinations of assets associated with particular livelihood strategies?
- *Access*. What are the factors resulting in different groups having different access to particular assets?

- *Trade-offs.* In pursuing a particular activity portfolio, what are the asset trade-offs that are involved? And what do these trade-offs imply for the future sustainability of the livelihood strategy adopted?
- *Trends.* How are different assets being depleted and accumulated, and by whom? What are the trends in terms of access? What new livelihood assets are being created over time?

The foregoing discussion emphasises assets, because this is the widely agreed entry point for projects and policies that are oriented to poverty reduction and to long-term livelihood sustainability. However, an emphasis on assets does not mean that activity portfolios can be neglected. At a trivial level, lack of knowledge about activity portfolios can result in misplaced attention being directed to high-profile activities that may, on investigation, prove to make a much smaller contribution to the material well-being of the household than appears at first sight.

Export crops typify this occurrence. For historical and macroeconomic reasons, export crops like coffee, cocoa, tea, or cashewnuts are often assumed to be the predominant and critical source of survival of farm families that live in the geographical zones where such crops are produced. However, export crop producers have plenty of experience of being disappointed. World prices fluctuate, often wildly; governments tax, often erratically; diseases and pests strike, reducing yields unpredictably. For this reason, investigation will often reveal that export crop producers have many other survival capabilities in place, aside from the crop that is purported to be their predominant source of survival. It then becomes a debatable point whether the scarce resources available for trying to improve the sustainability of rural livelihoods should be directed into these traditional cash crops, or might be better deployed supporting other components of farm household survival strategies. Chapter 10 contains a case-study of coffee-growers in Tanzania that illustrates this point rather well.

The diversification theme of this book points to activities being jointly fundamental, with assets, as building blocks of livelihoods analysis. While assets focus on the potential to achieve sustainable livelihoods, activities focus on the realisation of that potential in the shape of a viable portfolio of income-generating activities. If that potential cannot be realised, then assets remain unemployed or underemployed, and an apparently robust asset portfolio becomes unable to generate a sufficient livelihood.

Summary

The livelihoods approach to rural poverty reduction comprises the three main dimensions of the assets of the rural poor (divided between five categories of capital), the mediating processes which influence access to those assets and the use to which they can be put, and the strategies adopted by the rural poor for survival (comprising a collection of activities made possible by the interaction of assets and opportunities). This assets-access-activities framework is iterative and is a process unfolding over time for individuals, households, and communities. Poverty reduction requires that particular attention is paid to the assets and activities that distinguish the poor from other members of rural communities. It also requires identification of those sub-components of the process of securing viable livelihoods that can be usefully strengthened with a view to enhancing their contribution and increasing the security and resilience of livelihoods.

This framework guides the discussion of livelihoods and diversification in downstream chapters of the book. The next part of the book looks at a number of key dimensions of diverse rural livelihoods, including factors that underlie diversification strategies; as well as poverty, agriculture, environment, gender and macro aspects of individual and household livelihood strategies. In all these aspects, attention is paid to the asset, activity and access issues that differentiate the poor from the better off in rural society.

— PART II —

Dimensions of Diverse Rural Livelihoods

— CHAPTER 3 —
Determinants of Livelihood Diversification

The purpose of this part of the book is to explore different dimensions of the livelihoods approach to rural poverty reduction, and of diversification as a key theme within the livelihoods framework. This chapter takes a disaggregated view of the reasons individuals and households pursue diversification as a livelihood strategy. Subsequent chapters examine poverty, agriculture, environment and gender aspects of the livelihood approach, in each case relating the diversification theme to the current body of livelihood-oriented knowledge in the area concerned. In some instances, it is found convenient to rehearse fairly standard concepts and debates in these areas, in order to place the livelihoods approach in an established context. The final chapter in this part of the book relates diverse rural livelihoods to macro policies and reform agendas under adjustment programmes in low-income countries.

Necessity versus choice

The reasons that individuals and households pursue diversification as a livelihood strategy are often divided into two overarching considerations, which are necessity or choice. This is sometimes posed as being a contrast between survival and choice (Davies, 1996) or between survival and accumulation (Hart, 1994). It corresponds in the migration literature to push versus pull reasons to migrate (Bigsten, 1996).

Necessity refers to involuntary and distress reasons for diversifying. Examples might be the eviction of a tenant family from their access to land, fragmentation of farm holdings on inheritance, environmental deterioration leading to declining crop yields, natural or civil disasters such as drought, floods or civil war resulting in the dislocation and abandonment of previous assets, and loss of the ability to continue to undertake strenuous agricultural activities due to personal accident or ill health.

Choice, by contrast, refers to voluntary and proactive reasons for diversifying. For example, seeking out seasonal wage earning opportunities, travelling to find work in remote locations, educating children to improve their prospects of obtaining non-farm jobs, saving money to invest in non-farm businesses such as trading, utilising money obtained off the farm to buy fertilisers or capital equipment for the farm enterprise.

In the literature, there is an implication, in part, with respect to this dichotomy that diversification for distress reasons is a bad thing. It results in household members undertaking casual and low productivity activities with poor prospects. Put another way 'it is a last resort rather than an attractive alternative livelihood' (Ghosh and Bharadwaj, 1992: 154). It may also lead to households adopting a more vulnerable livelihood system than they possessed previously (Davies and Hossain, 1997). Another less obviously stated implication is that poverty policies should focus exclusively on diversification born of necessity, since the ability to choose between alternatives places the household already in an enviable position that is above the margins of survival.

The division of the determinants of diversification into these two main types is descriptively attractive, but misleading concerning the range of experience it seeks to assign to one process or another. Choice, or the lack of it, does not obey some sort of definable breakpoint between two mutually exclusive states. There are many instances where individual choice may be socially circumscribed at standards of living well above the survival minimum, as occurs, for example, for women in some cultural settings. Hence, there can be no unambiguous mapping of household income or wealth to the exercise of individual opportunity. More generally, diversification obeys a continuum of causes, motivations and constraints that vary across individuals and households at a particular point in time, and for the same individuals or households at different points in time. Households and individuals can also move back and forth between choice and necessity seasonally and across years.

An alternative distinction that cuts across the necessity vs. choice divide is that between underlying trends and processes, on the one hand, and household level strategies, on the other. Trends and processes in the larger economy may create general conditions that provoke livelihood diversification as a response; however, individuals and households are likely to respond to these underlying changes in different ways, depending on factors that vary between households such as income levels and asset profiles. Some important underlying trends that create pressures leading to livelihood diversification are rural population growth, farm fragmentation, and declining returns to farming compared to other activities, which in itself may occur either due to rising real production costs or declining real prices, or some combination of both these factors.

One possible starting point for examining the motives for livelihood diversification is a farm household model (Singh *et al.*, 1986; Ellis, 1993). The limitations of this approach with respect to the social relations of the household have been alluded to in Chapter 1 and are not rehearsed here (Folbre, 1986; Hart, 1992; 1995). Its strengths are its predictive capabilities, especially concerning the interactions between household decisions and trends in the larger economy. Utilisation of this predictive capability does not preclude nor inhibit the modification or elaboration of its findings in the light of social and institutional factors.

The household economic model predicts diversification as a function of on-farm returns to labour time compared to off-farm earning opportunities. With a given asset base, that is, land plus farm infrastructure and equipment, and a given total amount of labour time, the household makes comparisons between the return to using more of that time on the farm or deploying it in off-farm or non-farm wage or other income-generating activities. Factors that increase the return to time spent on farm activities would tend to reduce the motivation to diversify. Two such important factors are an increase in the prices of farm outputs or a rise in farm productivity, obtained, for example, by cultivating a higher yielding variety. Conversely, a rise in off-farm or non-farm wage rates, or greater opportunities to undertake remunerative non-farm self-employment would increase the motive to diversify.

This basic logic can be elaborated in many different ways. For example, the existence of labour markets differentiated by gender or skills will affect the logic of diversification between different individuals within the household. The price and availability of consumer goods in rural areas affects the time allocated by household members to producing non-farm domestic consumption items compared to purchasing them in the market. Thus high prices and non-availability of consumer items are predicted to reduce diversification because the household will spend more time producing substitute items and services in the subsistence domain. Risk factors provoke both on-farm and off-farm diversification as ways of spreading perceived risk and reducing the adverse impact of failure in any single branch of household activity. On-farm, risk may cause the production of diverse food crops being preferred to specialisation in a single cash crop; off-farm, risk encourages the search for income sources with associated probabilities of failure which are not correlated with farm risks.

While the household economic model provides a useful entry point for examining the determinants of diversification, it is not always very good at capturing intertemporal dimensions of livelihood strategies, nor at describing the circumstances of survival under stress. This chapter divides the determinants of livelihood diversification between a number of key considerations, some of which are captured reasonably well by the household model, and others which require further ideas and dimensions that are not provided by such a model. These considerations are not mutually exclusive as determinants of diversification, they constitute distinct but overlapping forces and processes leading to diversification. They are seasonality; risk; coping behaviour; labour markets; credit markets; and asset strategies. In addition to examining each of these determinants in turn, the chapter also contains a separate discussion of migration as a component of household livelihood strategies.

Seasonality

All rural households confront seasonality as an inherent feature of their liveli-hoods (Chambers *et al.*, 1981; Chambers, 1982; Sahn, 1989; Agarwal, 1990). The production cycles of crop and livestock enterprises are determined by the onset of rains, their duration, the length of the growing season, temperature varia-tions across the calendar year, and so on. These seasonal factors apply just as much to landless rural families that depend on agricultural labour markets for survival, as they do to farm families, and they also have strong effects on activ-ity in agricultural supply and output services, such as fertiliser delivery and crop marketing. Trading activity is particularly cyclical along seasonal lines, and for some perennial crops with a single annual harvest (e.g. coffee), the harvesting and trading season may be very short indeed.

In economic terms, seasonality means that returns to labour time, that is, in-come that can be earned per day or week worked, vary during the year in both on-farm and off-farm labour markets. On-farm returns vary when periods of peak labour such as the cultivation and harvesting required in order to achieve farm outputs are compared to periods when little, if any, activity can be usefully undertaken on the farm. Off-farm returns vary as temporary labour markets spring into being, for example, to harvest a grain or tree crop, or to move re-cently harvested produce from farms into stores or distribution centres. Invoking the farm household model, seasonality causes changes in occupation to occur as labour time is switched from lower to higher return activities (Alderman and Sahn, 1989).

Labour markets may, or may not, provide solutions to the 'labour smoothing' problems of the farm household. In sub-Saharan Africa, labour markets are poorly developed in rural areas so that migration is a more common response to cyclical changes in farm labour needs than wage work secured locally. Labour smoothing is just one facet of the more general difficulty of matching uneven and unstable income flows to continuous household consumption needs, referred to as the 'consumption smoothing' problem (Morduch, 1995; Carter, 1997).

Note that seasonality provides a logic for diversification without necessarily having to invoke risk and market failures as considerations. While in practice risk and seasonality are closely related, conceptually it is useful for some pur-poses to separate them, and diversification that obeys different opportunities in different seasonal labour markets does not require risk as an explanatory argu-ment for its occurrence. For example, an opportunity to take temporary em-ployment in a mango juicing plant at the peak of the mango harvesting season does not need to be predicated on the risk status of the household to make sense as a diversification option.

Seasonality means that continuous household consumption needs are mis-matched with uneven income flows. To take an extreme example, a farm household producing a single annual crop of maize would effectively gain its entire annual income at the time of the maize harvest. It would be able to vary within limits the way output was translated into consumption by, for example, selling maize for different prices at different points of the year, but its entitlement to consumption occurs at a single point in time. In the hypothetical absence of risk and market imperfections, this would not place household survival in jeopardy provided that the maize harvest, via own consumption and sales, were sufficient to cover annual consumption needs, taking into account any lending or borrowing that occurs during the annual cycle. Crop storage, output sales and savings could be used to convert unstable income into stable consumption.

In practice, of course, both risk and market failures abound in the rural economies of developing countries (Alderman and Paxson, 1992). Consumption smoothing is a real difficulty for the rural household, made more acute the nearer the household is to a livelihood providing only the minimum for survival, and the higher the risks attached to the uneven income sources on which it depends (Lipton and Ravallion, 1995). For this reason an important motive for income diversification associated with seasonality is to reduce seasonal income variability. This requires income-earning opportunities the seasonal cycles of which are not synchronised with the farm's own seasons. Seasonal migration to other agricultural zones may be one option, circular or permanent migration of one or more family members to non-farm occupations another (Alderman and Sahn, 1989).

Under circumstances of barely sufficient survival from own-farm output, seasonal migration may occur not so much to supplement the incomes of the resident household, but to remove from it one mouth to feed (Toulmin, 1992: 51; Devereux, 1993: 53). Hence one or more household members may remove themselves from the farm in the lean season in order to ensure that food supplies remain sufficient for those left behind. In so doing, they must secure their own means of survival in a different location, and networks of contacts in particular trades in urban centres may be utilised to achieve this. The same behaviour has been observed as one of the early responses to the onset of drought. In these instances, livelihood diversification occurs, but is not accompanied by a change in the income sources of the resident group; rather the size of the group changes as an attempt to accommodate its potential inability to feed itself.

Seasonality can also, however, impose a limitation on options to smooth consumption, due to the labour needs of land preparation for the next crop season. It is well substantiated for semi-arid zones of West Africa, for example, that farm households are most vulnerable to insufficient levels of food consumption at the period when, through the onset of the rains, peak labour inputs are required in order to secure the next season's farm output. Under such conditions, the preceding strategy to cope with bare survival levels of consumption is not an option, and seasonal migration, if it is to assist at all, must occur in the period when food stocks are still available rather than after they have run out.

Risk strategies

Many researchers consider risk to be the fundamental motive for livelihood diversification (e.g. Bryceson, 1996). When definite outcomes in relation to income streams are replaced by probabilities of occurrence, the social unit diversifies its portfolio of activities in order to anticipate and to ameliorate the threat to its welfare of failure in individual activities (Alderman and Paxson, 1992). This is just another way of saying that families that are vulnerable to failure in their means of survival do not 'put all their eggs into one basket'. However, there are many different strands to the risk argument, and there is a lot of room for confusing risk arguments with coping arguments, and voluntary decisions with involuntary actions (Dercon and Krishnan, 1996).

From the economic perspective of the static allocation of labour time across different activities, it is the risk-discounted marginal returns to labour that determine the patterns of engagement and specialisation by household members. The higher the perceived risk attaching to a particular source of income, the more likely it is that the individual or the household will seek to compensate for this by having in place contingency income sources or fallback positions of social support in the event of failure.

Income diversification as a risk strategy is often taken to imply a trade-off between a higher total income involving greater probability of income failure, and a lower total income involving smaller probability of income failure. In other words, households are considered to be risk averse, and for this reason are prepared to trade lower total income for greater income security. Research into on-farm diversity has demonstrated that this is not always true; that diverse on-farm cropping systems such as mixed cropping and field fragmentation take advantage of complementarities between crops, variations in soil types and differences in micro-climates that ensure risk spreading with little loss in total income (Walker and Ryan, 1990; Blarel et al., 1992). The same is true of many types of off-farm and non-farm diversification. For example, wage work in the agricultural slack season may both diversify and raise total household income, and the same is true for the exercise by different household members of different skills in different labour markets.

Whether or not risk spreading involves a fall in income, one of the critical features of livelihood diversification for risk reasons is the achievement of an income portfolio with a so-called low covariate risk between its components. This means that the factors that create risk for one income source (e.g. climate) are not the same as the factors that create risk for another income source (e.g. urban job insecurity). A characteristic of rural livelihoods in developing countries is that many of the income-earning opportunities open to poor households, that is, own-farm production and agricultural wage labour, exhibit a high correlation between risks attached to alternative income streams; in other words, if there is a drought or flood in a particular locality, all income streams are adversely affected simultaneously. While on-farm diversity can take some advantage of differences in the risk-proneness of crops or crop mixes to adverse natural events, the protection this affords is only partial. Diversification into non-farm incomes, by contrast, can result in low risk correlations between livelihood components.

The amelioration of risk helps to explain much observed livelihood behaviour in rural areas of developing countries, including the economic strategies of occupational diversification and migration, and supporting social strategies of maintaining an extensive network of kinship ties. As already mentioned, in many African societies it is customary for families to establish and nurture strong links between urban and rural branches of the family, as well as to maintain a geographically dispersed spread of future reciprocal obligations that can be drawn on in time of need (Berry, 1993). In Africa, and elsewhere, ethnic patterns of affiliation are often observed in the locational and sectoral branches of activity that are utilised by members of rural families as seasonal or occasional means of obtaining additional support for survival. Thus, for example, dock workers in a particular port may all be from one village or group of villages, and they perpetuate their claim over this source of income by always ensuring that a full complement of labour is available from their community of origin.

Household risk strategies are prone to confusion with coping behaviour, since some researchers treat coping as an aspect of risk behaviour, as in the phrase 'risk coping strategies' (World Bank, 1990b: 90–91; Alderman and Paxson, 1992: 2). This blurring of risk and coping is imprecise as a guide to policy in areas such as poverty reduction or famine prevention (Davies, 1996). It confuses voluntary with involuntary actions; planned responses to potential threats to household well-being with unplanned reactions to unexpected livelihood failure.

Coping, vulnerability and adaptation

Household coping strategies were introduced in Chapter 2 where they were defined as the sequence of survival responses to crisis or disaster. The problem of the distinction between risk and coping is resolved by distinguishing *ex ante* risk management from *ex post* coping with crisis (Webb *et al.*, 1992). Risk management is then interpreted as a deliberate household strategy to anticipate failures in individual income streams by maintaining a spread of activities (Walker and Jodha, 1986); while coping is the involuntary response to disaster of unanticipated failure in major sources of survival. A complementary way that risk and coping have been distinguished is to interpret risk as *ex ante* income management and coping as *ex post* consumption management in the wake of crisis (Carter, 1997).

These distinctions imply that risk strategies comprise forward planning to spread risk across a diverse set of activities, in the context of subjective evaluations about the degree of risk attached to each source of income. Coping, by contrast, refers to the methods used by households to survive when confronted with unanticipated livelihood failure. Lack of anticipation may attach to gradual processes such as a deterioration in the capability of a given natural resource system to support human livelihoods. However, more often it is associated with natural and civil disasters including droughts, floods, hurricanes, pests and civil war (see Blaikie *et al.*, 1994). At a more individual level, it describes sudden shocks to the family such as illness, divorce or dispossession. Coping mechanisms, in so far as they result in diversification, therefore correspond quite closely to the notion of diversification through necessity with which this chapter began.

As suggested in Chapter 2, coping comprises tactics for maintaining consumption when confronted by disaster, such as drawing down on savings, using up food stocks, gifts from relatives, community transfers, sales of livestock, other asset sales, and so on. These sequences typically seek first to protect the future income generating capability of the household, even if current consumption is compromised. It is only as a last resort that assets critical for future survival are sold or abandoned to stave off starvation.

With respect to diversification, unplanned responses to crisis may involve searches for new income sources in the early stages, and, at a later stage, enforced asset sales can irrevocably alter the future livelihood patterns of the family. Therefore, the term coping can be used to encompass distress and crisis reasons for the emergence of new livelihood patterns, and these differ conceptually and in practice from risk management determinants of diverse livelihood patterns.

A concept in widespread use in discussions of risk, coping and survival is that of vulnerability. Vulnerability is defined as a high degree of exposure to risk, shocks and stress; and proneness to food insecurity (Chambers, 1989; Davies, 1996). It has the dual aspect of external threats to livelihood security due to risk factors such as climate, markets or sudden disaster, and internal coping capability determined by assets, food stores, support from kin or community and so on. The most vulnerable households are those that are both highly prone to adverse external events and lacking in the assets or social support systems that could carry them through periods of adversity.

Further concepts that are useful for refining the concept of vulnerability are those of resilience and sensitivity, which originate in the agroecology and natural resource management literatures (Blaikie and Brookfield, 1987; Bayliss-Smith, 1991). Resilience refers to the ability of an ecological or livelihood system to 'bounce back' from stress or shocks. Diversity is an important factor contributing to resilience in both natural and human systems. For example, food supply systems can be said to be resilient when a crisis in one source of supply can be easily overcome by switching to other sources. Sensitivity refers to the magnitude of a system's response to an external event, for example, if a small change in the price of rice rapidly causes widespread under-nutrition in a human population, then the livelihood system is acutely sensitive to even this minor shock. When applied to natural resource systems, sensitivity refers to the magnitude of the change in ecological systems set in motion by a particular process of human interference.

It follows from these ideas that the most robust livelihood system is one displaying high resilience and low sensitivity; while the most vulnerable displays low resilience and high sensitivity. However, other combinations of these attributes are possible. For example, livelihood systems in the Sahel in West Africa are highly sensitive, that is, prone to upset by changes in climate or ecology, but are also demonstrated to be resilient due to the ability of human populations to adapt to their natural environments (Davies, 1996).

Vulnerability has important social dimensions as well as those resulting from natural or economic risk factors. Social obligations such as dowry, bridewealth, weddings or funerals may result in an already precarious ability to cope with adverse events becoming even more so (Chambers, 1983). Likewise, insecurity of land tenure under rental or crop share tenancy, and insecurity of wage employment in agriculture, add to livelihood risks and increase vulnerability.

The further concept identified earlier that arises in the context of coping behaviour is that of adaptation. Livelihood adaptation has been defined as the continuous process of 'changes to livelihoods which either enhance existing security and wealth or try to reduce vulnerability and poverty' (Davies and Hossain, 1997: 5). Adaptation is evidently closely related to diversification but the two are not synonymous. Diversification explicitly draws attention to a variety of dissimilar income sources (farm, non-farm, remittances etc.) as its chief characteristic. This is one potential outcome of adaptation but not the only one; new ways of trying to sustain the existing income portfolio are also forms of adaptation. Adaptation may be positive or negative: positive if it is by choice, reversible, and increases security; negative if it is of necessity, irreversible, and fails to increase security. Negative adaptation results in the adoption of successively more vulnerable livelihood systems over time (Davies, 1996).

A case-study undertaken in Uganda in 1990 (Bigsten and Kayizzi-Mugerwa, 1995; see Box 3.1) illustrates a particular process of adaptation to social and economic crisis. In this instance, economic decline and civil insecurity resulted in a retreat into subsistence rather than in diversification of income sources. However, the subsistence solution was available only to those who had ownership or customary access rights to land, and others, principally the young, indeed had to diversify in order to survive, and they did so by creating small-scale self-employment opportunities for themselves.

A focus on coping, vulnerability and adaptation emphasises the limitations of comparative static economic models for describing the motivations for income diversification. In the zone of precariousness of survival and proneness to outright livelihood failure, many of the predictions of orthodox economic models are rendered blunt and inconclusive in the face of the multiple factors that

Box 3.1. Household responses to economic crisis in Uganda

Uganda's economy declined dramatically from the early 1970s, as a result of poor macroeconomic management, adverse terms of trade, and the effects of civil and external wars. The living standards of rural households fell, and although the decline began to be reversed in the late 1980s, there remains some way to go before earlier prosperity is regained. The economic decline disrupted previous rural livelihood patterns, lowering income from cash crops, mainly coffee, and reducing remittances from relatives in urban areas. Rural households were forced to find new ways of constructing their livelihoods.

A survey carried out in 1990 in Masaka district, southern Uganda, investigated the responses of rural households to the crisis, and to the economic recovery programme, begun by the government in 1987, which aimed amongst other things to revitalise the agricultural sector. The district has favourable weather and land endowments, and was previously one of the major food and coffee-producing regions in Uganda. Most land is now devoted to food crops, including bananas, maize, beans and cassava, and grazing for livestock.

Data was gathered from 220 households in 4 counties of Masaka district. Table 3.1 shows the composition of household income on average, and some household characteristics. Farming was observed to be by far the most important source of income, and was primarily subsistence-oriented, except in the highest income households. Low prices, poor infrastructure, and risk

Table 3.1. Income portfolios in Masaka district, rural Uganda, 1990

	Composition of average household income	
	U.Shs	%
Non-farm wages	3,397	6.0
Allowances	579	1.0
Remittances	2,211	3.9
Farm wages	2,597	4.6
Net farm income	36,110	64.2
Business profits[a]	11,314	20.1
Total household income	56,208	100.0
Household size	7.8	
Income per capita	7,188	

[a] The figure is based on estimates by respondents, and is probably on the low side.

aversion had prevented the recovery of cash crop production, mainly coffee. Wage income was probably an important income source before the decline, but this had fallen due to the collapse of the formal economy. Similarly, remittances from relatives in urban areas were reported to have declined, and, at the time of the survey, made up only 4 per cent of income. Small-scale businesses had become an important source of cash income, and they provided 20 per cent of total income, which was probably an underestimate of their true significance. A small quantity of coffee was also grown as a means of generating cash, and was preferred over food cash crops because food storage, processing, and marketing were not well developed.

Given the importance of farm income, landholding was an important determinant of welfare, and larger landholdings were associated with higher incomes. Seventy per cent of households in the sample held less than 2 hectares of land, and they were proportionately more reliant on wage income and business profits than were larger landowners. Human capital endowments, as indicated by the years of education of the household head, did not appear to be associated with higher incomes, perhaps because education does not contribute to greater agricultural productivity in the absence of technical innovation. Higher level education was however needed for formal wage employment. The life-cycle stage of the household, based on the age of the household head, also influenced its livelihood sources. Households with young heads had little access to land and derived a substantial proportion (76 per cent) of their income from business activities that had low barriers to entry. In contrast, households with older heads had higher farm incomes and lower business incomes.

In summary, many rural households retreated into subsistence production during the crisis in Uganda, as their opportunities to generate cash were constrained, and the flow of goods and services from urban areas declined. With limited opportunities in formal wage employment, and low returns from cash crops, households with smaller landholdings turned to private business activities to generate cash for goods and services, including health and education. However, this source of income was constrained by limited markets, poor infrastructure and low credit availability. Policy measures designed to facilitate small business would assist younger and poorer households with smaller landholdings, whilst improving food marketing channels would assist older and richer households.

Source: Bigsten and Kayizzi-Mugerwa (1995).

crowd in on household decision-making. Decisions that apparently make no sense for short-term optimal resource use, such as depleting the farm of able-bodied labour available for agricultural operations, may make sense in the context of previous experience of crises and the need to strengthen survival capabilities against future eventualities. Sudden catastrophes result in the loss or destruction of productive assets that then necessitate a new household strategy in order to secure future survival.

Labour markets

Seasonality and risk point to the role of labour markets in reducing the threats posed by unstable and insecure income sources in the construction of viable rural livelihoods. However, labour markets also offer non-farm opportunities for income generation differentiated by other considerations such as education, skills, location and gender. The economic motivation for diversification cited in relation to seasonality applies more generally, in that when the marginal return to labour time in farming for any individual falls below the wage rate or the return to self-employment attainable for that person off the farm, then, leaving aside for the moment intrahousehold distributional issues, the household as a unit is better off switching that individual into off-farm or non-farm activities. This is not to imply that intrahousehold distribution can be neglected, on the contrary, it is an important aspect of diverse rural livelihoods which is examined in a later chapter (see Chapter 7).

Work opportunities vary according to skills (e.g. in trading, vehicle repair, brick making), education (e.g. for salaried jobs in business or in government), and by gender (e.g. male wage work in construction or mines vs. female opportunities in trading or textile factories). Economic considerations of labour allocation may be overlaid and modified by social rules of access both within the family and in the community, and these rules may result in the 'social exclusion' of individuals and households from particular income streams (Davies and Hossain, 1997).

There exists a substantial literature on rural labour markets in developing countries, focused in particular on the working of labour markets in the agricultural sector itself. It has been observed for many African rural settings that the market for agricultural wage labour is poorly developed or non-existent. This has several effects including the well-known occurrence of seasonal labour shortages in agriculture due to the dependence of farm households on their own supply of labour. It also means that household members must go further afield to participate in active labour markets, and semi-permanent migration to distant work opportunities is a commonplace feature of rural livelihood strategies in African countries, especially notable in southern African countries, including South Africa itself (see Box 3.2). A further implication is that large family size be-

Box 3.2. Migration, remittances and household livelihoods in rural South Africa

The bantustans of South Africa were rural areas reserved for settlement by Africans during the apartheid era. Today, they are characterised by high population densities, low productivity agriculture, and high levels of migration to engage in wage employment in the non-rural economy.

A study carried out in the mid-1990s investigated rural livelihoods in the former bantustan of Lebowa, in the semi-arid Northern Province. The study collected income and other data from a total of 94 households in two communities, Mamone and Rantlekane. Mamone is a long established, close-knit community with a fairly strong commitment to agriculture, despite increasing pressure on land. Rantlekane is more typical of rural settlements in the region. About one-third of households are long settled in the area, but the remainder arrived in the preceding 30 years, having been displaced from white-owned farms, and many of them lack access to land. As a result, the community relies much more on external income sources than does Mamone.

Table 3.2 indicates the importance of remittances for households in both communities. However, this source is much more significant in Rantlekane,

Table 3.2. Income portfolios in two semi-arid communities, South Africa (mean household incomes)

	Mamone		Rantlekane	
	Rand/month	%	Rand/month	%
Remittances	263	37.1	477	66.1
Pensions	104	14.6	118	16.3
Transfers	83	11.7	23	3.2
Formal wage	29	4.1	24	3.3
Informal wage	5	5.0	20	2.8
Informal non-wage	0	7.0	33	4.6
Business	45	6.3	3	0.4
Crops	65	9.2	3	0.4
Livestock	26	3.6	6	0.8
Other	9	1.3	14	2.0
Total income	710	100.0	721[a]	100.0

[a] Although mean household income is higher in Rantlekane, income per resident is lower due to larger household sizes.

Source: Baber (1996: 297).

where it constitutes two-thirds of household income, and is an income source for 93 per cent of households. In contrast, in Mamone it provides just over one-third of total income, and 66 per cent of households have migrant members.

Mamone has a stronger local economy, as is demonstrated by the proportion of income it derives from local sources; approximately one-third of income compared to about an eighth in Rantlekane. This partly reflects its larger size and higher incomes, which generate more opportunities in building and other local businesses. Farming, though relatively limited in both communities, also accounts for a considerably greater proportion of income in Mamone (10.8 per cent of income compared to only 1.2 per cent in Rantlekane), and this generates other income from agricultural support services, such as tractor ploughing. The small contribution of farming in Rantlekane is partly due to the high level of landlessness, but also reflects the low returns to agriculture in this arid area. Pension income, predominantly from the state, is relatively large in both areas, since migrants return to their rural homes on retirement. Many pensioners transfer income to poorer daughters and daughters-in-law in other households, and these make up the majority of transfers.

The importance of different income sources also varies across income strata. In Rantlekane, the poorest third in terms of income per household resident relies most on income from remittances, whilst the richest third supplement this source with income from pensions and local business. In Mamone, the middle group is heavily reliant on remittances, which account for over 50 per cent of their income. The poor, on the other hand, derive less than 20 per cent of their income from remittances, and a greater proportion (about 25 per cent) from agriculture, whilst the rich pursue more profitable business enterprises.

Although the two communities have very different income patterns, farming makes up a relatively small part of rural livelihoods for most households. There is much scope for improving the productivity of farming, and a strong local market for agricultural products, but the climate is a limiting factor. Policy makers may be better advised to support the development of higher return local enterprises. Better health and education services would also help households to improve the returns to their labour in the wider economy.

comes an advantage, both to ensure that labour is always available for agricultural tasks, and to facilitate diversification into non-farm activities (Toulmin, 1992).

The lack or near absence of a wage labour market in agriculture may affect the economic logic of labour allocation on the family farm, as hypothesised in the

Chayanov theory of the farm household (Thorner *et al.*, 1966; Ellis, 1993: Ch.4). According to this, the lack of an objective measure of the value of labour time, as would be given by a rural wage, means that the labour and land committed to production will vary according to the size and age structure of the farm family, and how this changes over time. In other words, the level of farm output is determined by the demographic cycle of the farm family, not by the opportunity earning criterion of comparing returns to labour on the farm with the off-farm wage rate.

While in the past some empirical support has been found for a Chayanovian logic in African agriculture (e.g. Hunt, 1979), it seems unlikely that this explanation of cultivation decisions would apply when cultivable land becomes scarce and livelihoods more difficult to construct. More plausible is the argument that both the area cultivated and labour inputs are determined by how farm activities fit into a diversified livelihood strategy composed of participation in non-farm labour markets, leaving only certain members of the household behind on the farm to carry out agricultural tasks.

Unlike in Africa, rural wage labour is ubiquitous and plentiful in South and South East Asia. This stems from high rural population densities, endemic land shortages, and significant inequalities in land ownership. These factors bring about the existence of large numbers of landless or near landless families for which wage labour on other farms is the chief means of survival. In consequence, the literature on rural labour markets in Asia has different preoccupations from that on the African case. Here the focus has been on imperfections in labour and land markets, resulting in the emergence or persistence of institutions like sharecropping that seek to overcome so-called 'supervision' and 'moral hazard' problems associated with hiring labour (e.g. Bardhan, 1989; Taslim, 1989).

Looked at from the viewpoint of landowners, reliance on wage labour to carry out agricultural activities carries with it the cost and difficulty of monitoring the amount and quality of the work performed, in other words, 'shirking' for them is a potential hazard. Sharecropping as an agrarian institution is thought to overcome this problem by locking together land and labour markets in such a way that the sharecrop tenant is motivated to apply quality labour inputs to the production process.

Another facet of labour market debates in the Asian context has been differences in how labour markets work for households operating small farms with potential labour time to hire out, compared to households operating larger farms needing to hire in labour. Labour is thought to be used more intensively in small farms, because market wage rates are discounted by job search costs such as the risk of not obtaining a day's work and the travel time to the site of work; therefore individuals will continue to work on the small farm up to the point where the return to an additional day's work is lower than the apparent opportunity wage obtainable off the family farm. Conversely, larger farmers

wishing to hire in labour must add to the market wage rate the costs of supervision, as already mentioned above, and of compliance with government regulations related to the hiring of wage labour. Therefore they will tend to use less
labour than is indicated by the opportunity cost of labour time, and be motivated to substitute capital, such as tractors, for hired labour, and this is not efficient in social terms. Thus differences in the way labour markets work for small
and large farms lend support to the proposition that small farmers represent a
more socially efficient use of resources in labour-abundant economies, and thus
strengthen the argument for pursuing a small-farm rather than large-farm agricultural development strategy (Berry and Cline, 1979; Ellis, 1993: Ch.10).

These literatures on the working of farm labour markets in Africa and Asia in
the end shed surprisingly little light on the adoption of multiple occupations by
rural families, whether these are families characterised as landless agricultural
labourers, food-deficit small farmers, or farm households that manage to produce a surplus above their basic consumption requirements. The reason for this
is the preoccupation of much of the theorising in this area with the small-farm
enterprise as the core of a rural development strategy. However, diverse rural
livelihoods suggest that this point of departure may be faulty for poverty reduction policy. Perhaps what is becoming more relevant is gaining a better understanding of what types of labour market, in what branches of activity, can
provide the rural poor with greater scope for constructing a resilient livelihood.
Case-studies provided in several text boxes in this book, for example Boxes 2.1,
4.4 and 4.5, are pertinent in this regard.

Migration in livelihood strategies

Migration is included as a topic in this context, not because it constitutes a determinant of diversification, but because it is an important type of diversification that links up with labour market factors in household and individual
decision making for survival (see Box 3.2 for an example of the significance of
migration and remittances in a semi-arid rural location in South Africa).
Migration means that one or more family members leave the resident household for varying periods of time, and in so doing are able to make new and different contributions to its welfare, although such contributions are not
guaranteed by the mere fact of migration. Some different types of migration are
described briefly as follows:

1. *Seasonal migration.* This refers to temporary migration that occurs in corre-
spondence to the agricultural seasons, and is typically associated with movement away in the slack season and the return of migrants for the peak periods of
labour input in the agricultural calendar, mainly land preparation and harvesting. Seasonal migration may also occur within the rural economy to take advan-

tage of seasonal peaks in the labour requirement of harvesting annual or perennial crops. For example, a crop like coffee experiences a major annual peak in labour demand for the short period during which the ripe coffee is ready for harvesting; likewise the harvesting of paddy rice is characterised by notable seasonal peaks in labour demand in many Asian countries.

2. *Circular migration*. This refers to temporary migration that is not necessarily tied to seasonal factors in agriculture, and that may be for varying durations, sometimes dictated by cyclical needs for labour in non-farm labour markets. Circular migration implies that migrants routinely return to the resident household and regard that as their principal place of domicile; in other words, they do not set up permanent living arrangements in the places they go for temporary work.

3. *Permanent migration (rural–urban)*. This implies that the family member makes a long duration move to a different location, typically an urban area or a capital city, and sets up domicile at destination. In this instance the contribution to the rural resident household takes the form of regular or intermittent remittances back home. Clearly the capability to remit depends on the type and security of the livelihood secured by the migrant in the urban environment.

4. *International migration*. The family member moves either temporarily or permanently abroad. There are many variants of international migration corresponding to the distance travelled, the permanence of the movement, the type of work obtained in the destination country, and so on. Some international migration is a cross-border extension of circulatory migration, in which temporary movement occurs to take advantage of work opportunities in an adjacent country. Some corresponds to contract work opportunities further afield, such as occurs with migration from rural areas of South Asia to the Middle East, typified by one- to three-year periods of work in the destination country. Some is distant and permanent, and involves the family member taking up residence abroad.

In terms of economic decision-making, migration decisions have been viewed variously as individual choices (Todaro, 1969; J. R. Harris and Todaro, 1970) and as intertemporal family contracts (Stark, 1980; Stark and Bloom, 1985; Stark and Lucas, 1988). The former interpretation focuses on income differentials between rural and urban areas adjusted for job search probabilities as the prime determinant of migration, and this version continues to receive support (Bigsten, 1996; Larson and Mundlak, 1997). The latter interpretation emphasises risk spreading (Stark and Levhari, 1982; Katz and Stark, 1986) and imperfections in rural capital markets (Stark, 1980; Collier and Lal, 1986) as reasons to migrate. Remittance income exhibits the key attribute that it is not correlated with either seasonal cycles or risk factors in agriculture.

Critical to these propositions is that migrants maintain a flow of remittances to their families, and several reasons to do with migrant self-interest are advanced to explain why this occurs; namely, the need for a fall-back position if urban income sources collapse, and the protection of land and other assets to which the migrant has claim back home, including assets expected at inheritance (Lucas and Stark, 1985; Hoddinott, 1994). Empirical studies generally show that the majority of migrants (between 80 and 90 per cent) do indeed send remittances home, although the proportion of income sent and its frequency display wide variation across individual migrants (Rempel and Lobdell, 1978; Hoddinott, 1994). In the family contract model, remittances are part of a long-term implicit contract between parents and children that includes investment in education, migration, remittances and inheritance (Hoddinott, 1994).

The migration literature has dwelt on both 'pull' and 'push' reasons for migration to occur. Income differentials are seen as the major 'pull' factor; while seasonality, risk, market failures, erosion of assets (e.g. land subdivision at inheritance), landlessness, and disasters leading to livelihood collapse are seen as 'push' factors. Evidence supporting both forces are found in the literature, for example, Bigsten (1996) finds that the pull of high wages is more important than the push of land scarcity in explaining migration decisions in Kenya; while Adams (1993) finds the reverse in a study of the factors explaining international migration from rural Egypt (see Box 3.3).

Box 3.3. Push vs. pull factors in migration, an Egyptian case-study

---

A survey carried out in 1986–87 investigated the determinants of international migration in rural Egypt. Data on the incomes and assets of migrant and non-migrant households, as well as on individual migrants, was collected from one thousand households in three villages in Minya Province, about 250 km from the capital city, Cairo.

Remittances accounted for a substantial proportion of household income in the study area, about 12.5 per cent overall, and 30 per cent for migrant households. Almost 40 per cent of the sample households reported that a household member had worked in another country in the ten years prior to the study, and about 10 per cent still had a member overseas. All were men, since it is considered unacceptable for women to work outside the household in rural Egypt, and most went to Iraq, which had no restrictions on the entry of Egyptian workers at the time of the survey. Wages were considerably higher for migrants than those available in rural Egypt, for example, an unskilled agricultural labourer could earn on average LE350 (US$255) per month in Iraq in 1986–87, compared to only LE90 (US$65) locally. Migrants were generally able to find work within one or two months, and most work was of an unskilled nature, for example, agricultural labour or construction work. This suggests that provided he could meet the travel and related costs of migration estimated at LE500 (US$356), practically any rural man could migrate. At the time of this study one Egyptian LE was equal to US$0.73.

Analysis of the links between various individual or household characteristics, and the propensity of an individual to migrate produced two main findings. First, the prediction of the human capital model that those with more education would be more likely to migrate because they enjoy higher expected income-earning opportunities in destination areas, was not borne out in this study, as migrants did not have significantly higher levels of education than non-migrants. This result reflected, however, the nature of the international labour market for rural Egyptians, which consisted mainly of unskilled positions.

Second, individuals from middle-income households (in terms of income per capita, excluding remittance income) were more likely to migrate than those from the poorest and richest households, although there was only a small difference between the middle- and low-income groups. However, when the area of land farmed, both owned and rented, was considered along with income, so that both the wealth and current income of households were taken into account, the men of the poorest, landless households were most likely to migrate. Rural Egyptians who were both richer and wealthier seemed to feel less of a 'push' to work abroad, and a greater 'pull' to stay at home and enjoy the economic opportunities associated with ownership of land.

The study concluded that 'push' factors provided a better explanation of international migration in rural Egypt than 'pull' factors. It also emphasised that focusing only on household income, rather than income and assets, may give misleading results when analysing the economic determinants of migration.

Source: Adams (1993).

The notions of push and pull are similar in descriptive intent to the earlier juxtapositions of involuntary vs. voluntary and necessity vs. choice as ways of broadly categorising alternative sets of circumstances resulting in livelihood diversification. To reiterate a point made before, while it is on occasions useful to dichotomise cause and effect in this way, the ease of so doing should not be confused with the accuracy of the description thus achieved. In practice, individuals and households are influenced by a multiplicity of factors determining the livelihood changes they undergo. While rarely a single factor may dominate over all others for an entire village or location, more often a cumulative combination of factors will represent variable pressures and opportunities for different individuals and households within rural communities.

Migration is often viewed negatively in policy terms (de Haan, 1999). This reflects unease about urbanisation rates and labour movements across national boundaries. However, a livelihoods approach points in an opposing direction, namely that 'policies should be supportive of population mobility' (ibid. 1).

Credit market failures

The availability of funds to carry out timely purchases of cash inputs into agricultural production, as well as to buy capital equipment like ploughs or water pumps, has long been regarded as one of the critical constraints inhibiting rising productivity in small-farm agriculture. The severity of this constraint is typically thought to reside in the poor functioning of rural financial markets in developing countries (Hoff *et al.*, 1993; Besley, 1995). In particular, private markets in loanable funds, or credit markets, operate unevenly, if at all, in rural settings.

There are many reasons for this market failure, amongst which the high costs of setting up banking operations in rural areas, the difficulty and cost of securing adequate information on potential borrowers, the risk of default on loans, and the absence of collateral to put up against loans, are amongst the most frequently identified. In rural Africa, there remains a generalised problem of low rural credit availability (Bigsten and Kayizzi-Mugerwa, 1995). In rural Asia, private money lending exists, but tends to be associated with personalised transactions in interlocked markets that can place the borrower in a permanent state of obligation to the lender (Bhaduri, 1986; Basu, 1994). Governments and NGOs have, of course, for decades tried to overcome these market failures (Johnson and Rogaly, 1997), but their success at doing so has tended to be intermittent and uneven.

Credit market failures provide another motivation for diversifying livelihoods (Binswanger, 1983; Reardon, 1997), in this instance with the aim of utilising cash funds generated outside agriculture in order to purchase agricultural inputs or make farm equipment purchases. This strategy has the potential to overcome the absence of lending facilities in rural areas, to avoid paying high rates of interest on such funds as may be available from public or private sector financial institutions, and to avoid also placing the individual or the family in a subordinate social relationship with a private moneylender. The use of off-farm income to purchase recurrent farm inputs has been noted in several sources (e.g. Evans and Ngau, 1991; Meindertsma, 1997).

Asset strategies

Rural households take a longer term view of livelihood security than merely taking advantage of currently available income-earning opportunities. Therefore an important additional motive for diversification, not covered by consumption, security, or purchase of recurrent farm inputs, is that of making investments in order to increase income-generating capabilities in the future.

Investing in order to enhance future livelihood prospects is described here as the household's asset strategy. Assets in this respect refer to the five main types of capital identified in Chapters 1 and 2 as constituting the platform upon which livelihood strategies are constructed. To recapitulate, these are natural capital (land, water, trees); physical capital (irrigation canals, implements, roads); human capital (education, skills, health); financial capital or its substitutes (cash savings, jewellery, goats and cattle); and social capital (networks, associations).

Some of the sub-categories of assets listed here fall outside the capability of the individual rural household to control directly. Thus rural infrastructure (roads, power) and rural services (health and education) are typically provided as public goods by the government, and investment in their improvement requires an outside agency such as government, donors or NGOs. Nevertheless the quantity and quality of such assets makes a big difference to the viability of rural livelihoods. Other assets are under household control, and investment in them is made in order to improve future livelihood prospects. It has been observed, for example, that rural households in sub-Saharan Africa devote considerable attention to personalised networks, setting up complex, but informal, systems of rights and obligations designed to improve future livelihood security (Berry, 1989; 1993). This is a form of social capital (Putnam *et al.*, 1993), and is regarded by households as an asset requiring investment with a view to securing potential future returns.

The distinguishing aspect of asset strategies as a motive for diversification is their intertemporal nature. The process is one of diversifying in order to achieve greater livelihood security in the future. Diversification for this reason may be temporary. For example, once a particular objective, such as buying more land, is achieved by it the household income strategy may revert to reliance on own-account farming. On the other hand, diversification undertaken to improve human capital (e.g. to finance the schooling of children) may result in even more diverse sources of household livelihood in the future.

Summary

Within the livelihoods framework, various forces and motives can be identified that tend to result in diversification as a household strategy. The distinction is often made between necessity and choice as causal factors in diversification, although it is argued here that these categories are in practice less readily distinguished from each other than may on first consideration seem the case. Diversification out of necessity, due, for example, to personal misfortune or natural catastrophe, is often interpreted as leading to unfavourable outcomes because it may result in livelihoods that are less sustainable than they were before.

Seasonality, risk, labour markets, credit substitution, and asset strategies are factors identified as constituting voluntary motives for the adoption of diverse livelihoods; and these same factors demonstrate the benefits of diversification for the household in the form of consumption smoothing, labour smoothing, risk spreading, and the generation of resources for investment in assets as well as for consumption. Involuntary reasons for diversification are associated with coping strategies, and this leads into further discussion of coping, adaptation, vulnerability and resilience as livelihood attributes.

Determinants of livelihood diversification can be grouped according to key features that they possess in common. For example, risk, coping and necessity vs. choice are connected via adaptation, with diversification being seen as one particular way of adapting for survival under high levels of uncertainty. Seasonality, labour markets, migration, and credit market failures may be grouped as providing practical reasons for diversification in response to economic factors. It may be noted, however, that migration is not always a diversification strategy; it can also be a decision to relocate in order to obtain a full-time occupation in a different place.

— CHAPTER 4 —

Poverty and Income Distribution

The purpose of this chapter is to link the livelihoods approach put forward in Chapter 2 to the wider body of knowledge concerning poverty and inequality in rural areas of low-income countries. After providing a brief overview of poverty concepts and policy agendas in this section, the chapter goes on to relate poverty measurement to the livelihoods context, and to consider arguments and case-study evidence that have been put forward linking livelihood strategies to income levels and to income inequality. As elsewhere in this book, diversification is utilised as a key theme helping to illustrate the interactions between livelihood strategies, poverty and inequality.

A useful first step is to consider the characteristics of being poor, since these in themselves may shed light on the role that the livelihoods approach can play in reducing poverty. Poverty is fundamentally to do with lack of well-being (Dasgupta, 1993). Here a positive state of well-being may be thought of as an expression of the human capabilities of doing and being, where doing involves agency, choice and freedom, and being involves welfare and happiness. Lack of well-being therefore implies some combination of inability to act and enforced misery, which taken together imply severely curtailed human capabilities (Sen, 1993; 1997). All writers in this area concur that poverty signifies the inability of people to realise their potential as human beings.

The human capability properties of doing and being are not themselves measurable, even though attributes of their lack such as hunger, under-nutrition, physical weakness, illness, lack of shelter, being dressed in rags, and so on, are recognisable as descriptions of the many facets of being poor. For this reason, economists and others approach well-being, or the lack of it, indirectly, via indicators that attempt to capture important dimensions of poverty which are measurable within inevitable time and cost constraints. Some of these indicators go straight to the human physiology effects of destitution and hunger, such as comparing individuals in relation to expected values of their height-for-age and weight-for-height. Others measure poverty by reference to income and consumption. Still others do so using participatory techniques to discover which individuals or households are considered, or consider themselves, poor in the social context of their community or village.

The preferred method of economists for distinguishing the poor from the non-poor is the level of per capita consumption that just permits the individual to satisfy basic nutritional requirements expressed in calories, given the measured share of food in the per capita expenditure of the poor. This constitutes a poverty line, consumption levels below which are regarded as inadequate to achieve a minimally acceptable material standard of living. Levels of consumption falling below this poverty line correspond to what is called 'personal consumption poverty' (e.g. Lipton, 1996).

Studies of poverty using poverty line methods have in the past consistently shown that the majority of those in poverty live in rural areas of developing countries. For example, the World Bank (1990b: 31) provided data that suggested that between 65 and 95 per cent of the total numbers living in poverty in selected African and Asian countries were located in rural areas. Proportions of the same order of magnitude were cited in an International Fund for Agricultural Development (IFAD) study on rural poverty (Jazairy *et al.*, 1992: 37). However, it must also be recognised that the absolute number of people living in urban poverty is rising steeply in many low-income countries. In sub-Saharan Africa, for example, the income gap between rural and urban areas has been shrinking in the wake of structural adjustment policies (Jamal and Weeks, 1993). This is due to declining real wages in the formal sectors of the economy, especially government, and the retrenchment of urban-based state employees due to budget cutbacks. The decline in relative urban living standards is one of the factors provoking greater interdependencies between rural and urban branches of families in the construction of their livelihoods (Moser, 1998).

Poverty research has revealed much about characteristics that are widely shared by poor people and families. Perhaps the most fundamental of these is lack of assets, meaning lack of ownership or access to land, other productive assets, skills, education and good health. In a rural context, landlessness is observed to be a highly accurate predictor of poverty. So too is low human capital resulting from poor health and inadequate education provision in rural areas. The proportion of rural people in poverty rises markedly in locations that are marginal in terms of agricultural productivity, remote from services, and prone to natural disasters. Large rural households tend to be poorer, in per capita terms, than small rural households, although no direction of causality can be inferred from this finding. Large families often play an important social security role for their members, especially the elderly; however, they also have more difficulty meeting the nutritional and educational requirements of each individual child from limited resources.

In terms of the livelihood framework given in Chapter 2, therefore, the expectation is that variations in asset holding will provide fairly accurate predictors of relative levels of poverty. The task then becomes one of identifying those assets that can be made more accessible to the poor, perhaps through group formation that raises the social capital of the poor, or that can provide the basis of savings and credit (improving their financial capital status), or creating training oppor- tunities to assist the poor in acquiring skills that can enable them to make more effective use of their labour resource (enhancing human capital).

The 1990s saw the emergence of a broad consensus, certainly amongst econo- mists, regarding the priority to be accorded to poverty reduction, and the means to pursue that end. The World Bank played a key role in the derivation of this consensus, beginning with its 1990 World Development Report (World Bank, 1990b) and continuing with the funding of a large body of policy research on poverty in the mid-1990s. In this period, most industrial country donor agencies placed poverty reduction as the priority objective of their aid policies (e.g. UK Department for International Development, 1997). What was called for a time the 'new poverty agenda' (Lipton and Maxwell, 1992; Lipton and Ravallion, 1995) was a three-prong strategy for reducing poverty comprising the promo- tion of labour-intensive economic growth; access by the poor to social services; and the putting in place of safety-nets targeted at those unable, for one reason or another, to secure a minimally acceptable survival level of living.

The first of these components required an enabling environment for the rapid growth of small-scale, labour-intensive production and service activities in both rural and urban areas. In many countries, the spread of such activities was previ- ously, and still often is, inhibited by state regulatory regimes with which it was impossible for all but formal, large-scale, enterprises to comply. In the liveli- hoods framework, these inhibitory institutions are part of the 'mediating processes'. Hence market liberalisation, deregulation, and labour-intensive growth are closely related. So too, in practice, are livelihood diversification and labour-intensive growth, since success at achieving the latter clearly makes a big difference to the ability of the poor to pursue the former as a strategy.

The second component of the 1990s poverty agenda was improved provision of health and education services in locations, and under conditions, that im- prove their accessibility to the poor. The intention of this was to enable the poor to enhance their human capital, thus giving them greater prospects of partici- pating in available economic opportunities, as well as creating their own oppor- tunities. A central role for the state was envisaged in this provision by some commentators (Lipton and Maxwell, 1992), while for others indirect provision via the private sector and the introduction of user fees to compensate for dimin- ishing state resources appeared attractive alternatives (Jimenez, 1987; 1990).

The third component was for countries to put in place targeted safety-nets to ensure that minimum survival standards of living were achievable for groups that for one reason or another are unable to secure a viable livelihood in the pre- vailing circumstances they confront. These may relate to sudden shocks, such as drought or floods, for which mechanisms need to be in place to protect food security and to prevent the destitution or death by starvation of those most ad- versely affected. They may also relate to more recurrent difficulties, such as sea- sonal deficits, or resource-poor locations, that need more permanent safety-net arrangements to be put in place. The state evidently has an important co-ordinating role in this provision, although execution may be largely devolved to non-governmental organisations or to local communities themselves.

The livelihoods approach to poverty reduction represents a deepening of the ideas surrounding the 1990s poverty agenda. It is less dependent than the latter on objective economic measures of poverty of supposedly wide application across a country, or an entire region, and it focuses more on people's survival strategies in local and specific contexts. It places its emphasis on a holistic understanding of the relationship between assets, mediating processes, and strategies, with a view to identifying those parts of the process of constructing a livelihood that can be facilitated with a view to strengthening individual or household survival capabilities. As argued elsewhere in this book, diversification options are thought to play an important role in this regard, because a diverse livelihood is more resilient than an undiversified one, and this is a critical attribute for people living at the margins of survival.

Poverty measurement and diverse rural livelihoods

Whether poverty can be satisfactorily described for policy purposes by measurements that assign people into poor and non-poor categories continues to be a debated question that is unlikely to be resolved definitively one way or another. Recently, there have been two main contending bodies of thought on this question, with plenty of variation in interpretation within each of them, and certain facets of poverty that are not addressed very well by either of them. At issue is whether such a complex social phenomenon as poverty lends itself to objective measurement, or whether, in contrast, its prevalence is best assessed by reference to multiple criteria amongst which the subjective views of those living in poor communities are the most appropriate points of reference. The latter does not require a measurement of poverty, rather it seeks to identify at community level, by a participatory process of consultation, those that are most at risk of destitution.

The conventional economic approach has been to seek an objective criterion for measuring the magnitude of poverty in society at large, and in major subgroups of society such as rural versus urban areas, or remote areas compared to those more favourably placed in relation to infrastructure and services. Poverty in this context is *absolute poverty*, in other words it corresponds to people who fall below some fixed measure that represents the minimum material necessities for healthy survival.

By contrast, a lot of poverty research in industrial countries concerns *relative poverty*, meaning people whose income may be significantly below the average incomes of the country, and who are therefore excluded from participating in the customary activities of the majority of citizens. People can be in relative poverty, yet their consumption levels may be well above the minimum physiological needs of survival. Although relative poverty is not really a concern in this book, it is worth noting that it invokes subjective criteria for determining who is poor and who is not, that is, social perceptions about what constitutes a minimum acceptable standard of living, and this also arises with respect to participatory approaches to poverty in a developing country context.

The measurement of absolute poverty is by no means straightforward and in practice trade-offs are involved between the accuracy, complexity, cost, and logistics of measurement. In principle, an objective poverty line might be constructed by adding together the costs of minimum food needs and other basic necessities that are regarded as essential for realising human capability. However, agreeing on this list of basic needs proves too difficult in practice, and multiple problems arise concerning the valuation of such needs given the different prices for them in different locations.

Therefore the short-cut is taken of specifying the minimum nutrition, in calories, required to sustain a healthy existence. The level of consumption defining the poverty line is then that level that permits the purchase of the minimum acceptable amount of food, given the share of food in total consumption in the vicinity of the line. This means, for example, that if the share of food in total consumption were 85 per cent, an allowance of 15 per cent is implicitly being made for non-food necessities such as shelter and clothing. This method recognises that the poor themselves make trade-offs between food and other needs, thus individuals defined as poor in this way may not in practice consume sufficient food to achieve the minimally acceptable diet defined on nutritional grounds.

In addition to the absolute poverty line defined above, some poverty researchers advocate the derivation of a lower poverty line based on the cost of the minimum acceptable amount of food on its own, in order to identify the ultra-poor, that is, those at chronic risk of under-nutrition. In addition, a higher poverty line may be set, for example at 50 per cent of average per capita consumption for the country as a whole, so that dimensions of relative as well as absolute poverty are captured in the poverty analysis. Once one or more poverty lines are established, a number of poverty measures can be calculated (see Box 4.1). These are the head-count measure, that is, the number of people in poverty and their proportion of the total population, the poverty-gap index measuring the depth of poverty, and the poverty-gap squared index measuring the severity of poverty.

The source of data on poverty is typically large-scale sample surveys of households undertaken by national statistical offices in each country. Such surveys may collect data on income sources as well as expenditure, but it is the expenditure data that is used for poverty calculations. As discussed later in Chapter 9, income data is regarded as an unreliable guide to material standards of living for

Box 4.1. Alternative measures of poverty based on poverty lines

Once one or more poverty lines have been decided upon, typically based on personal consumption expenditure calculated from household income and expenditure surveys, there are several different measures of the prevalence and severity of poverty that can be derived from the data. The three main measures are the headcount index (P_0), the poverty-gap index (P_1), and the poverty severity index (P_2). These are often referred to as the prevalence, depth, and severity measures of poverty respectively, and they are described each in turn below.

Headcount index

This is the simplest and most frequently encountered measure of poverty. It gives the proportion of the total population (n) for whom consumption (y) is less than the poverty line (z). If the number of people found to be below the poverty line are denominated as q, then the headcount index is stated simply as:

$$P_0 = q/n.$$

This is a straightforward and easily understood measure of poverty, and can be used, for example, to compare at two different points in time for a particular country whether the prevalence of poverty has increased or declined in the intervening period. Its drawback is that it is insensitive to changes in the depth of poverty. For example, if someone goes from having an income 30 per cent below the poverty line to an income only 5 per cent below the poverty line, this change is not picked up by the headcount measure.

Poverty gap index

The income shortfall, or *poverty gap*, measures the amount of money required to raise the income of a poor person (y_i) to the level of the poverty line (z). The aggregate poverty gap involves summing individual poverty gaps across the total number of poor people (q). This represents the total income transfer that would be needed to raise the incomes of the poor up to the poverty line level. The poverty gap index expresses the poverty gap as a proportion of the poverty line, averaged over the total population (n), both poor and non-poor:

$$P_1 = 1/n \sum [(z - y_i)/z].$$

In this expression the $(z - y_i)$ are the individual poverty gaps. These are expressed as proportions of the poverty line, e.g. 0.05 of the poverty line, 0.30 of the poverty line etc., and these proportions are summed across all poor people (q). The resulting figure is then divided by the total population (n). This measure is regarded as a good indicator of the *depth* of poverty, i.e. how far below the poverty line, on average, are the incomes of poor people. It also yields an indicator of the minimum cost of eliminating poverty using targeted transfers to the poor, given by $\sum(z - y_i)$.

The reason for dividing by the total population rather than by the number of poor (q) is that when an individual poor person moves out of poverty (reducing q by 1), the poverty gap index would display an increase rather than a decrease. This problem is overcome by dividing by the total population, and also, mathematically, this brings all three poverty measures discussed here into consistency with each other.

Poverty gap index squared

A defect of the poverty gap index measure is that it fails to capture variations in income distribution amongst the poor. For example, two populations, one exhibiting relatively equal poverty gaps from the poverty line, and one exhibiting highly unequal poverty gaps, might give rather similar levels of the poverty gap index, due to the simple averaging involved in its formula. In other words, the poverty gap index fails to capture the *severity* of poverty, as contrasted to its average depth. This defect can be overcome by squaring (or indeed applying any power above 1) the individual poverty gap ratios $(z - y_i)/z$ before they are summed, thus ensuring that the larger poverty gaps of the extremely poor count more in the calculation than the smaller poverty gaps of the less poor:

$$P_2 = 1/n \sum[(z - y_i)/z]^2.$$

This measure of poverty is considered potentially useful for comparing populations that have differing experiences with respect to the severity of poverty, and also for examining policies targeted to reach the very poorest in society rather than all poor people. However, in practice, policy documents rarely get beyond headcount measures of poverty, with income gap measures being used to supplement this in some instances.

Sources: Ravallion (1992); Lipton and Ravallion (1995).

several reasons, the principal ones being annual income instability, seasonality, recall, and measurement (Glewwe and van der Gaag, 1990; Lipton and Ravallion, 1995).

By contrast to these difficulties, household expenditure tends to be more even over time. The basic necessities of the household, plus the small items of discretionary consumption that the household may be able to afford, occur on a daily and weekly basis. Data on them can be collected by going through a checklist of routine expenditure items with household members, or by leaving a diary in the household for one or two weeks, in which all items of expenditure are recorded. Separate questions in the sample survey can then be utilised to discover the daily consumption by the household of produce from its own farm or garden, and these items are then valued at prevailing market prices. Household recall of irregular and large items of purchase tends to be rather better than distant recall of irregular income receipts; moreover, such items are likely to be present in the homestead at the time of interview. Finally, consumption is considered a better measure of well-being than income because it reflects the household's ability to buffer its standard of living through saving and borrowing despite income fluctuations (World Bank, 1990b).

For these reasons expenditure is considered a better measure of material living standards than income. However, expenditure data is invariably collected at household level, so for poverty comparisons, aggregate household consumption must be converted to a per capita basis. This is done by dividing aggregate consumption by the adult equivalent size of the household, derived by summing the adult equivalents of each member of the household, for example, adult males—1.0; adult females—0.8; children under fourteen—0.5. The measure of welfare thus obtained is the adult equivalent adjusted average per capita consumption, and this is considered the most accurate measure for the analysis of poverty (Lipton, 1996). Note that this may still, rather confusingly, be referred to as an income measure of poverty, in the indirect sense that it defines the level of income needed in order to achieve the minimum required bundle of per capita consumption (Greeley, 1994). However, for purposes of discussion in this chapter and elsewhere in this book, investigation of income and its composition is distinguished from the measurement of consumption and its level.

Given that any measure of comparative living standards is likely to remain fairly rough and ready, several researchers have investigated how much difference is made to estimates of the number of people in poverty by using different indicators, some of which may be less costly or more timely in their data collection or analysis compared to other indicators. For example, Glewwe and van der Gaag (1990) utilised data from a living standards survey undertaken in the Ivory Coast to compare the lowest 30 per cent of people defined by per capita income, household consumption, unadjusted and adjusted household per capita consumption, proportion of budget spent on food (called the food ratio), calory intake, physiological data, and a basic needs index. Those identified as poor were found to differ significantly between these indicators. Moreover, the easiest definitions to apply, for example, the food ratio, were found to be least accurate by comparison to the authors' preferred indicator of adjusted per capita consumption. Income data as a guide to identifying the poor was found to be particularly problematic, thus reinforcing the conclusion that income information is an inferior guide to discovering who is in poverty.

An implication of the shift from income to consumption-based measures of welfare is that collection of income data and its analyis has tended to receive progressively less attention over time in poverty studies. Indeed, some large-scale, donor-assisted household surveys in the 1990s, such as for example a Human Resource Development Survey undertaken in Tanzania in the early 1990s (World Bank, 1993b), left out the income side of household welfare alto-gether and focused exclusively on expenditure and access to public services. The paradox thus arises that the pursuit of accuracy in measuring standards of living has resulted in the increasing neglect by economists studying poverty of the means by which those standards of living are attained. It is rare, indeed, for poverty studies to say very much about income or its sources, and the livelihood strategies being pursued by the poor compared to the better off do not very often emerge out of the analysis undertaken in such studies.

This relative neglect of the livelihood patterns of people at different levels of per capita consumption is a significant defect of consumption-based poverty studies from the viewpoint of the livelihoods framework and its utilisation for improving the effectiveness of poverty policies. This is not, however, the only defect that has been noted concerning that approach (Baulch, 1996b). Also im-portant is that its static nature yields no information on the trajectories of indi-viduals and households as they move in and out of poverty. For example, when families respond to deepening crisis by sending members away to obtain income in other locations, the resident household may not even be categorised as poor in a sample survey using the adjusted per capita consumption methodology. Another flaw is that gender differences in access to the necessities of material welfare are obscured by a methodology that calculates per capita living stan-dards from household level data (Kabeer, 1996).

An alternative set of ideas rejects the objective measurement of poverty as telling us little either about the experience of poverty or about ways of enabling the poor to improve their circumstances. For example, Chambers (1983) distin-guishes five attributes of poverty and deprivation including 'poverty proper' meaning lack of income or of the assets to generate income; physical weakness due to under-nutrition, sickness or disability; isolation in the sense of being mar-ginalised either locationally or socially from access to goods and services; vulner-ability meaning, as already noted in Chapter 3, proneness to risk, stress and hunger; and powerlessness within social, political and cultural structures. There may be trade-offs between these in terms of people's priorities, for example, an individual may trade lower income against being able to escape from a patron-client relationship in which they are powerless.

Participatory methods of poverty assessment seek to capture these multiple facets of poverty by facilitating the poor themselves to identify the factors that militate against an improvement in their circumstances. This may be accom-plished by asking diverse persons within the community to rank households along a poverty-wealth scale, and in the process listing the reasons given for placing individual households in one category or another. Other methods include self-wealth ranking by household members, and focus group discussions composed of people sharing common attributes (such as women, or the landless). These methods are predominantly subjective and local in scope. Their strength lies in demonstrating the multiple social reality of poverty, and they may prove more useful than conventional methods for identifying promising poverty reduction initiatives at the local level.

In some ways, the division of poverty research between these two distinct and opposing approaches is a false one in that they tend to operate at different scales, with different purposes in view, and, therefore, on different levers of poverty reduction policy (Baulch, 1996a). The consumption measurement of poverty utilising large-scale household surveys is designed to give a national aggregate picture of the incidence, depth and severity of poverty, useful also for international comparisons, and for influencing the aid allocation decisions of large bilateral and multilateral donor agencies. The participatory assessment of poverty is designed to discover the locally complex characteristics of the poor, the best way of addressing poverty in its local manifestations, and ways of involving the poor themselves in setting agendas for change. These are complementary rather than conflicting approaches over a wide range of intentions to reduce poverty in low-income countries.

Having said this, there is some evidence to suggest that when both types of method are applied in local contexts, they can yield strikingly different outcomes for the individuals within communities who are identified as being poor. In a comparison of four different methods for identifying the poor, drawing on household data sets for villages in rural Ethiopia, it was found that while different participatory methods came up with more or less similar poverty rankings, the consumption measurement of poverty was quite at odds with the others, and in opposing ways for different locations (Bevan and Joireman, 1997; see Box 4.2). The consumption measurement was heavily influenced by the two factors of seasonality (i.e. when the data was collected) and the timing of food aid deliveries to villages with direct effects on consumption levels, whereas participatory rankings incorporated numerous factors such as land access, livestock ownership, housing quality, social links, and family size that would not have been so influenced by the precise timing of the investigation.

While livelihood diversification is in principle more likely to arise as a consideration in participatory poverty assessments than those based on per capita consumption, nevertheless a review of participatory studies suggests that this phenomenon, while being recognised as important in survival strategies, is rarely investigated beyond its mere mention in group discussions. As a generality, in relation to poverty measurement and poverty assessment, livelihood diversification lurks in the background as a phenomenon recognised as important in passing, but about which not very much is known or said. With local level work, this may be explained because distant livelihood sources fall well outside

Box 4.2. Poverty is an elusive concept

Although poverty involves very real and material deprivation, no universally accepted definition exists. Understandings vary widely from culture to culture, and may embrace a range of variables which are not always correlated. Despite this, in most research it is assumed that 'the poor' can be identified using a single measure, and questions about what is actually being measured, or whether a different measure, drawing on other criteria, would produce the same result, are rarely addressed. Bevan and Joireman (1997) deconstruct the concept of poverty, identifying three main issues which arise in relation to different poverty measures.

First, there is the question of *what* is measured since there are at least five distinct categories of variables which could be included:

1. assets, including economic capital, such as land and labour, social capital, e.g. social networks, and environmental capital
2. outputs, including food, commodities and services
3. capabilities, which provide the freedom to achieve desired levels of well-being, e.g. income and access to resources
4. expenditure, e.g. on food, commodities, savings
5. well-being, e.g. health and nutritional status, education and community participation.

Second, there is the question of *who* decides what is to be measured. Many economists favour a universal or 'objective' measure, such as a minimum level of per capita consumption or income, which allows comparisons across space and time. In participatory approaches, a 'subjective' measure is preferred, based on community definitions of poverty or wealth, which takes account of local realities and cultural differences.

Third, there is the question of *when* to measure, or the reference period which should be used. In rural Ethiopia, for example, many individuals have periods of being poor and non-poor during their life-cycle, so that a decision must be made as to how long someone must be poor before they are classified as such. Seasonality and climate changes in a single year also affect measurement, especially where there is a relative lack of institutions for income and consumption smoothing; and annual variations, particularly in communities which are heavily dependent on agriculture, create problems when attempting to make comparisons across years.

Using data from three villages in rural Ethiopia, Bevan and Joireman compared four commonly used poverty measures: personal wealth ranking, community wealth ranking, sample survey of household wealth and consumption poverty, considering how each deals with the 'what', 'who' and 'when' questions identified above, and the extent to which the four measures identified a single group of poor households. The results of this exercise are shown in summary form in Table 4.1.

Table 4.1. Alternative measures of poverty in three villages, Rural Ethiopia (proportion of households identified as poor, %)

Poverty measure	Shumsheha	Yetmen	Gara-godo
Consumption poverty	15	12	76
Personal wealth ranking	71	38	64
Community wealth ranking	78	53	63
Asset cluster index	65	61	71

It can be seen from the table that these measures differed considerably in the proportion of the households they identified as 'poor'. Indeed only 30–40 per cent of the households surveyed in each village end up classified consistently as poor or non-poor across all measures. Amongst the measures, consumption poverty is seen as being wildly adrift of the other measures in two out of the three villages; while the other measures tended to produce results that were more consistent with each other overall. However, even between these other measures, a sizeable number of households are not assigned unequivocally to the poor or non-poor categories.

The reason for the poor performance of the consumption measure was identified as food aid deliveries to the two villages coinciding with the timing of the consumption survey. This had the effect of greatly reducing the number of households that were observed to fall below the poverty line. This illustrates, perhaps in rather an extreme way, the dependence of the consumption measure of poverty on timing for the results that it generates.

Source: Bevan and Joiremann (1997).

the limited locational scope of enquiry and action. For national level studies, it results, as we have seen, from scepticism about the validity of data collected on household incomes, and the focus of poverty studies therefore being directed to the expenditure side of the household income-consumption equation.

Diversification, poverty and income distribution

Poverty is not the same as inequality. A highly unequal income distribution can coexist with relatively low levels of absolute poverty, as is evidenced by poverty and income distribution data in many industrialised countries. However, in poor countries, a highly unequal income distribution is often accompanied by a high incidence of poverty, and a challenge to rural poverty policies is to find means of reaching the rural poor that do not inadvertently merely add to the incomes and wealth of the rural rich. Box 4.3 provides a brief account of measures

---

Box 4.3. Measures of income inequality

Inequality can be measured statistically in several different ways. A common one is to rank all the individuals in a sample or population in descending or ascending order of per capita income, then divide them into equal groups, e.g. quintiles or deciles, and calculate the average income level for each group, and its share of the total income generated over the whole sample. For example, it might be found that the bottom one-fifth of the population has a per capita income of US$200 per year and obtains only 3 per cent of the population's total income, while, conversely, the top one-fifth of the population attains an average per capita income of US$3,600 and obtains, as a group, 32 per cent of total income. In this instance, the income ratio between the top and bottom income quintile is 18.0, an order of magnitude that is not uncommon in real cases (see Deininger and Squire, 1996). Income equality in this method occurs when each income group displays the same average income and therefore has the same share of total income.

Closely related to the foregoing approach is the measure of inequality known as the Gini coefficient. The Gini coefficient varies from a value of zero, representing perfect equality, to a value of 1, representing maximum inequality. Therefore, the higher the value of the Gini coefficient the more unequal is the distribution. In income distribution studies, values of the Gini coefficient in the range of 0.25 to 0.35 are considered to describe a reasonable degree of equality. Income distribution in Sri Lanka, for example, has been calculated to have a Gini coefficient between 0.30 and 0.35 in several studies. On the other hand, values of the Gini coefficient above 0.50 display high inequality. Brazil, for example, has the dubious notoriety of having one of the most unequal distributions in the world, with a Gini coefficient of 0.57 (Deininger and Squire, 1996.).

of inequality that are utilised in several of the empirical case-studies summarised in text boxes in this book.

There are broadly two opposing camps concerning the effects on income inequality of the diversification of income sources. The first camp considers that diversification is likely to have an equalising effect on rural incomes. The reason for this, at the household level, is that poor households are unable to employ fully the assets at their disposal—predominantly their own labour—in farming alone, and that therefore non-farm activities and income sources constitute a fuller employment of resources and a net addition to household income. Many of the features already noted regarding diversification fit into this explanation, namely the role of non-farm income in reducing risk, seasonality, credit market failures, and so on. According to this hypothesis, the share of non-farm income in total income should decline steadily as farm size increases; therefore income distribution would be more unequal in the absence of diversification than in its presence.

This position receives support from several quarters. An important strand of thinking which is examined more fully in the next chapter of this book is the rural growth linkage approach which sees non-farm rural income generation being stimulated by agricultural innovation (Haggblade *et al.*, 1989; Haggblade and Hazell, 1989; Hazell and Haggblade, 1993). This is thought to raise the incomes of the rural poor because a greater share of income of the poor compared to the better off is derived from labour-intensive, non-farm artisanal production such as weaving, pottery, brickmaking, and food processing. The same ideas also result in the advocacy of rural non-farm enterprise (Saith, 1992; Fisher *et al.*, 1997) and rural small-scale industries (Chuta and Sethuraman, 1984; Liedholm *et al.*, 1994).

The inability to diversify incomes due to remoteness is cited as one of the reasons that distant rural areas tend to exhibit a disproportionately high incidence of poverty, as conventionally measured (World Bank, 1990b). In a case-study in semi-arid Burkina Faso, the capability of households to maintain food security in the face of recurring crises of agricultural subsistence was found to rest significantly on diversification as a livelihood strategy (Reardon *et al.*, 1992). Indeed, in that study, the zone most prone to food security risk at the onset of drought was the one typically regarded as successful at agriculture in which households exhibited the least diversified incomes.

Other researchers concur in the idea that income diversification enhances the survival capabilities of the rural poor (Matlon, 1979). Since poor households cannot use assets such as livestock to buffer their standard of living when confronted by adverse events, they rely on diverse income sources to do this instead (Dercon, 1998; see also Box 4.4). In similar vein, a research study undertaken in Paraguay in South America found that farm households with insufficient land to achieve food self-sufficiency relied on urban labour markets to compensate for their food deficit status (Zoomers and Kleinpenning, 1996).

Box 4.4. Assets, incomes and livelihood portfolios, a Tanzania example

The rural households studied here live in the Shinyanga District of Shinyanga Region, a semi-arid area in western Tanzania. The main crops in the area are cotton, sorghum, millet, maize and sweet potatoes. Livestock, particularly cattle, are important for ploughing, livestock products and manure, as well as being valued as relatively liquid assets. Non-farm activities are quite common, particularly casual labour in the surrounding areas.

A survey in Shinyanga District in 1990 collected income and other data from a random sample of 80 households. Mean incomes per adult equivalent and income sources for the poorest, middle and non-poor groups are shown in Table 4.2. The differences between mean income and mean consumption are likely to be due to survey errors rather than high savings rates, and they reverse the usual experience of household budget surveys in which income is typically underestimated compared to consumption.

Table 4.2. Income portfolios in Shinyanga, Tanzania

Mean adult-equivalent values	Consumption terciles			
	Poor	Middle	Non-poor	All
Total income (TShs.)	9,478	21,345	57,828	29,447
Total consumption (TShs.)	7,752	17,340	47,988	24,264
Income composition (%)				
Crop income	43.7	32.9	20.2	25.9
Livestock products	5.4	14.0	31.9	25.0
Livestock live sales	10.7	25.8	32.4	28.2
Non farm income	36.9	26.4	15.3	20.3
Off-farm wage income	3.4	0.9	0.1	0.7

Source: Dercon (1998).

As the table shows, the poorest households differ from the non-poor in the composition of their incomes. They rely proportionately more on crops (44 per cent as against 20 per cent for the non-poor) and on non-farm income sources (37 per cent compared to 15 per cent for the non-poor). In contrast, the non-poor derive a significant proportion of their income from livestock (64 per cent compared to 16 per cent for the poorest group).

Mean income and consumption are six times higher in the richer house-holds than in the poorer, and income from livestock represents about 74 per cent of the difference in these means. As in the preceding Ethiopia study (Box 2.1), the factors that prevent poorer households from owning livestock are the scarcity of credit, and the inability to accumulate savings from other sources, as well as smaller household size and lower land holdings.

The survey also shows that the poorest group derives a larger proportion of its income from non-farm sources than the middle and non-poor groups. This is an unusual result compared to other case-studies described in this book, and is due to the role of livestock in the asset strategies of households in this area of Tanzania. Relatively high return non-farm opportunities are available, for example shop-keeping, tailoring and carpentry, but the poorest mainly participate in activities which require little investment and few skills, for example casual labour. It is probable that entry constraints in the form of skills or capital investment prevent the poorest group from participating in higher return activities.

Risk is also a factor in explaining the income portfolio of the poor. Livestock provides a form of insurance for its owners because it is a relatively liquid asset which can be used to meet consumption shortfalls. Since the poorer, non-cattle owning groups do not have this form of insurance, they resort to low risk, low return non-farm activities to reduce their overall risks. Non-cattle owners were also found to grow more low return, low, risk crops—sorghum, millet and sweet potatoes—which may again point to a risk man-agement strategy in the absence of liquid assets to smooth consumption.

Source: Dercon (1998).

The case-study of Botswana reported by Valentine (1993), demonstrates that national level policies can, under certain circumstances, harness diversification in order to reduce income inequality (Box 2.2 above). According to Valentine's results a fall in the Gini coefficient for rural household incomes from 0.52 to 0.48 occurred in Botswana between 1975 and 1986, a period in which house-holds diversified their incomes markedly. In this, households' own survival strategies were supported, in part, by state transfers that worked with diversifica-tion rather than seeking to hinder it or prevent it from occurring.

A second camp pursues an opposing argument that diversification has a dise-qualising effect on rural incomes and wealth. The principal reason for this is that better-off families are able to diversify in more favourable labour markets as compared to the poor. The poor tend to possess low human capital in the form of skills and education levels that effectively disbars them from more highly re-munerated labour markets. In contrast, the better off are well placed to over-come entry barriers to activities and income sources, especially those, like the issuing of licences, that require knowledge of bureaucratic procedures and ways of surmounting or avoiding them. According to this hypothesis, the share of non-farm income is most likely to rise as either farm size or income rises; therefore income distribution will be more unequal in the presence of diversification than in its absence.

A paper by Reardon *et al.* (2000) compiles and compares a wide range of empirical evidence concerning the income distribution attributes of non-farm income sources. Support for both the foregoing hypotheses can be found from empirical studies conducted across developing countries in the 1980s and 1990s, and quite a few studies yield results consistent with neither hypothesis. Essentially, three main experiences are observed. In each of these, a more diverse income portfolio is taken to mean one in which non-farm income sources feature more, and agriculture features less, in the overall composition of rural incomes.

The first is that there is a linear negative relationship between non-farm income share and either total household income or landholding. In other words, rising income levels are associated with less livelihood diversity. This relationship is upheld mainly by case-studies undertaken in rural Asia and Latin America, with only one example from Africa. These case-studies correspond to situations where land ownership or the lack of it is the chief asset factor separating the rural better off from the rural poor. Those owning land can continue to obtain the majority of their income from agriculture, while those lacking land must seek survival in other activities.

The second is that there is a linear positive relationship between these same variables, and this characterises most recent studies of the composition of incomes in rural Africa, as well as a few studies from other regions. Here, then, rising income levels are associated with more livelihood diversity. These case-studies correspond to situations where livestock and human capital are the assets that separate the rural better off from the rural poor. High human capital, in particular, enables the better off to obtain subtantially higher returns to labour allocated to non-farm activities than is possible for the rural poor.

The third is a U curve relationship, where the non farm income share is rela tively high for small farms and poor households, declines in the middle income or farm size range, and rises at the higher end of farm sizes and total incomes. Case-studies corresponding to this finding occur in rural areas where the poor are landless, the better off own or have access to land from which they derive most of their income, and the rich are large landowners that gain high incomes from many different sources.

An important point made by Reardon *et al.* (2000) is that patterns in these relationships differ between income shares and income levels. In quite a large proportion of the studies looked at, the ratio between the level of non-farm income of the highest and lowest income group is much greater than the ratio of the non-farm income shares between them. For example, a Vietnamese case-study is cited by Reardon *et al.* in which the top quintile displayed twice the non-farm income share of the bottom quintile (82 per cent against 41 per cent), but the level of non-farm income of the top quintile was 9 times that of bottom quintile. This finding supports the notion that there are substantial entry barriers (e.g. licence fees, equipment purchase, skills acquisition) for activities that yield high returns to labour. Hence, the low-asset household can spend a large share of its time in non-farm employment, but the absolute level of income thus obtained remains low.

Many of the text boxes utilised as illustrative material in other chapters of this book are insightful about the relationship between assets, income levels, and income distribution. For example, in societies where livestock ownership is a measure of economic success and a store of wealth, the poor are distinguished by low livestock income and low capability to acquire livestock (Dercon and Krishnan, 1996; Dercon 1998; see Boxes 2.1 and 4.4). By contrast, in societies where land ownership confers wealth through crop production, poverty is defined by lack of land, and livestock ownership in this instance may be an indicator of poverty rather than wealth (Adams and He, 1995; see Boxes 1.1 above and 4.5).

These studies support the contention that human capital makes the difference between diversifying in favourable labour markets and diversifying in intermittent, part-time, low paid and unskilled work. Finally, these and other studies identify significant barriers-to-entry that distinguish the livelihood options of the poor from those of the better off. These 'invisible barriers' are largely to do with navigating officialdom, in which lack of literacy, numeracy, knowledge of procedures, and contacts diminish the access to opportunities of the rural poor.

In a Kenya case-study cited in the next chapter (Box 5.1), Evans and Ngau (1991) provide a clear-cut illustration of the rising non-farm income share as income rises that characterises the majority of empirical studies undertaken in sub-Saharan Africa. In this instance, the richest quartile of households obtained 52 per cent of their income from non-farm sources, while the corresponding share for the poorest quartile was 13 per cent. At the same time, the absolute level of non-farm income of the richest quartile was over 100 times that of the poorest quartile; and the farm income was 16 times greater between the richest and poorest quartile.

The sample survey of three villages conducted over a three-year period in rural Pakistan described by Adams and He (1995) is further instructive on the income distribution question (Box 4.5). This demonstrates how some income sources have equalising, and others disequalising, effects on rural incomes. Specifically, livestock, non-farm wages, non-farm self-employment, and domestic remittances were found broadly to have an equalising impact on rural income distribution; while agriculture (crop production), rental income and international remittances have disequalising impacts. This occurred in large part because crop income was correlated with highly unequal land ownership, while livestock income was not correlated in this way. Note also that international migration

Box 4.5. Sources of inequality in rural Pakistan

The Adams and He (1995) survey data cited in Box 1.1 above was used to analyse the effects of different income sources on poverty and income inequality. Overall, inequality in the survey area was moderate, with a Gini coefficient of 0.381 for three-year average total per capita household income. This is higher than figures calculated from national government surveys, which may reflect the restricted geographical focus of the survey, or differences in the definition of income used in the surveys.

Table 4.3 shows the importance of the five income sources for the different income groups. It illustrates the considerable differences between the income sources of the poor and the rich; for example, poor households, defined as those in the bottom income quintile, obtain almost 50 per cent of their income from non-farm sources and less than 10 per cent from agriculture, while households in the top income quintile obtain 36 per cent of their income from agriculture and only 17 per cent from non-farm sources.

Table 4.3. Income portfolios by income quintile, rural Pakistan

Income quintile	3-year average income (Rps)	Percentage of mean per capita income from:				
		Non-farm	Agri-culture	Transfer	Livestock	Rental
Lowest	1,008	49.9	6.8	13.9	24.5	4.9
Second	1,818	48.4	9.3	13.4	23.5	5.3
Third	2,537	43.6	14.3	15.1	18.3	8.7
Fourth	3,639	42.7	21.4	12.7	15.6	7.6
Highest	7,354	16.8	36.5	17.1	8.8	20.8
Total	3,271	40.3	17.7	14.4	18.2	9.4

Note: Income is calculated by averaging per capita household income over the three years.

Source: Adams and He (1995: 19).

Statistical analysis showed that agriculture is the biggest contributor to overall income inequality, accounting for between 35 and 45 per cent of inequality, depending on the year. Moreover, additional increments of agricultural income with all other factors held constant are predicted to increase overall inequality. At the other end of the scale, additional increments of non-farm and livestock income reduce inequality. In between are transfers and rental income, both of which increase inequality.

The main explanation for these findings lies in the highly uneven distribution of land in Pakistan. Agricultural income is strongly correlated with land, but the Gini coefficient of land ownership is very high (0.769), and more than 37 per cent of households surveyed owned no land. There is, however, an active rental market so that in fact the lower figure of 17 per cent of households were entirely landless. The direct benefits of Pakistan's high agricultural growth have gone to richer, land-owning households. Livestock and non-farm income are poorly correlated with land ownership, which accounts for their favourable impact on income equality.

involves barriers to entry, notably travel and visa costs, that make it more accessible to better off than to poorer households, hence the difference in income distribution effects between domestic and international migration.

On a rather different tack, some researchers would argue that poor rural families are often forced into low return income diversification by to the actions of the rural rich in pursuit of their own livelihood strategies (Ghosh and Bharadwaj, 1992). This is, of course, a variant of the diversification out of necessity class of determinants discussed in Chapter 3. However, the angle taken on it here differs because it invokes unequal power in rural social relations as the explicit reason for diversification to occur. The type of situation envisaged here is one, for example, where a tenant family is ejected from its farm so that the landowner can consolidate his or her landholdings, and, perhaps, thereby use more capital-intensive methods on a farm of sufficient size to permit the substitution of mechanised for labour-intensive methods. In such circumstances, rural inequality may widen—the landowner gets richer and the previous tenants get poorer—while at the same time the previous tenants must adopt an income diversification strategy in order to survive.

Summary

The livelihoods approach is linked in this chapter to relevant parts of the body of knowledge surrounding poverty, its measurement, and rural income inequality in low-income countries. Poverty studies have long recognised the role of assets in determining the capability of individuals or households to construct livelihoods that are above the poverty line. The measurement of poverty throws up some critical issues in a livelihood strategy context. One of these is the lack of consistency that can occur between poverty measures utilising different methods for identifying who is poor. Another is the preoccupation of conventional poverty studies with consumption and expenditure measures of poverty, resulting in relative neglect of the income and livelihood strategies of the rural poor.

Opinion and evidence is divided on the question of whether livelihood diversification is associated with less or more income inequality. While diversification is often a strategy that enables the poor to survive in the absence of ownership of assets like land and livestock, the form of this diversification is typically in low-paid, casual, and unskilled types of employment. The strongest empirical result of numerous case-studies is the difference between the diversification alternatives of the poor and those of the rich, who are able by virtue of their assets to diversify in high wage labour markets or high return self-employment.

Education and skills are shown to be critical factors distinguishing the livelihood strategy options of the poor from those of the rural better off. Linked to these human capital attributes, the poor are less able to navigate officialdom and bureaucracy in pursuit of alternative livelihood sources than the better off. This begins to point to a conclusion that is reinforced in other contexts later in this book, which is that the 'mediating processes' dimension of rural livelihoods, that is, rural social relations, institutions and governance at local levels, play a key role in determining the differential success of individuals and families in securing viable livelihoods that can provide higher material standards of living.

— CHAPTER 5 —

Agriculture and Farm Productivity

It was observed earlier that by far the most dominant approach to rural development of the last three decades of the twentieth century was what has been referred to as the 'agriculture first' strategy (e.g. Saith, 1992). This consisted of a variety of supports, some direct and some indirect, to small, poor, farmers in order to achieve simultaneously both growth and poverty reduction objectives. Direct supports included subsidies on fertiliser, irrigation, and credit, and the funding of international and national agricultural research. Indirect supports included funding of rural infrastructure such as rural feeder roads, the creation of state and parastatal agencies to provide services to agriculture, and integrated rural development programmes comprising multiple components within supposedly unified frameworks.

Notwithstanding these resource transfers to small-farm agriculture, many researchers considered that this sector was still discriminated against by public policy. Arguments along these lines included (1) pervasive bias of public policy in favour of urban and industrial interests, that is, urban bias (Lipton, 1977), (2) capture of the benefits of subsidies and other supports by richer rather than poorer farmers, (iii) incompetence, corruption and waste by state agencies resulting in a deteriorating institutional environment for small-farm growth, and (4) price and exchange rate policies resulting in artificially low returns to agricultural production (Krueger *et al.*, 1992). One response to these factors was to advocate that growth and equity objectives in small-farm agriculture might be better served by liberalised markets than by government controls. Another was to emphasise the capabilities of small farmers themselves to set agendas for change. Farming systems research (FSR), indigenous technical knowledge (ITK), and participatory rural appraisal (PRA) were all manifestations of the switch from top-down to bottom-up thinking about poverty reduction in small-farm agriculture (Richards, 1985; Chambers *et al.*, 1989; Scoones and Thompson, 1994; Chambers, 1997).

The recognition of diversification as a widespread strategy within a livelihoods approach to rural poverty necessitates moving away from the previous preoccupation with the small farm as the sole or main platform for rural poverty reduction. However, agricultural performance and diverse rural livelihoods relate to each other in complex ways, and it is the objective of this chapter to identify and examine some of these. In fact, three dimensions of this relationship are explored here. The first is the association at rural sector level between farm performance and non-farm economic activities in rural areas. The second are the impacts at farm level of household strategies that allocate labour and other resources to non-farm sources of income. The third is the role of on-farm diversification within the overall picture of livelihood diversification.

The first dimension directs attention to what have been called in the literature 'regional growth linkages' or 'rural growth linkages', meaning the backward and forward linkages from agriculture that result in the formation and growth of non-farm enterprises in rural areas. The existence of the rural non-farm enterprise (RNFE) sub-sector, its dynamics and its technology, has been an important strand of rural poverty reduction policy for many years, predicated on its labour-intensive character and its potential to generate jobs and skills in rural areas other than in agriculture. A focus on this sub-sector directs attention to sectoral level diversification of types of economic activity away from agriculture within rural areas of developing countries. The point has already been made (Chapter 1 above) that sectoral level diversification need not be synonymous with household level diversification; it all depends on the degree to which households and individuals straddle different types of activity rather than commit themselves sequentially to moving wholly from one to another.

The second dimension comprises the effects on agriculture of household-level diversification. While agriculture as a sub-sector may benefit from improving input and output linkages in the rural economy, it is not quite so clear that it gains when the principal resource of labour is withdrawn from the farm in order to engage in other activities both nearby and in distant locations. The gains and losses here depend in part on who leaves the farm, how far away they go, for how long they go, whether they remit or bring back cash resources that can be used for farm investment, and so on. The arguments and evidence here are mixed, and are worth examining in order to shed light on the patterns of interaction that can occur between farm level performance and engagement in non-farm activities.

In something of a change of gear, the third dimension of diversification looked at in this chapter is that of on-farm diversification. On-farm diversification of crop and livestock enterprises may constitute a different means by which the household satisfies some of the objectives of diversification away from the farm, that is, reducing the adverse effects of risk and seasonality. It may also be a means of raising farm income, by intensifying the use of land as a resource, or taking advantage of niche markets for high-value farm outputs such as fruit, vegetables, spices, and dairy products. In considering rural livelihood strategies for reducing vulnerability and raising incomes, on-farm diversification certainly has its place alongside the non-farm diversification that is the chief theme of this book.

The rural growth linkages approach

One particular approach has governed a large proportion of the policy discussion for the past twenty years concerning the relationship of farm to non-farm rural activity. This is the rural growth linkages model, originating in the mid-1970s in the work of certain influential writers on rural development (Johnston and Kilby, 1975; Mellor, 1976), and applied to the study of rural growth, employment and incomes in Asia and Africa (Bell *et al.*, 1982; Hazell and Roell, 1983; Haggblade *et al.*, 1989; Delgado *et al.*, 1994). A critical attribute of this approach is that it retains an agriculture first strategy at its core, while at the same time invoking the prospect of a diverse and dynamic non-farm rural sub-sector providing employment opportunities for those rural dwellers who are not able to participate directly in farm growth.

The starting point of the growth linkages model is that growth in agriculture itself provides the stimulus for the growth of rural non-farm activities in developing countries (Haggblade and Hazell, 1989; Hazell and Haggblade, 1993). This is said to occur due to the rising expenditure of farm households on locally-produced non-farm commodities and services, including consumer goods and services (expenditure linkages), inputs and services to agricultural production (backward linkages), and processing and marketing services related to farm outputs (forward linkages). The significance and magnitude of these linkages have been explored in a number of sources (Ranis and Stewart, 1987; Ranis, 1990; Bagachwa and Stewart, 1992).

Expenditure linkages comprise consumption by farmers of items such as locally processed food (e.g. flour, bean curd, jaggery); clothing and textiles (e.g. hand-woven materials); and utensils (e.g. clay pots). Backward linkages comprise purchases by farmers of farm inputs and services such as fertilisers, implements, water pumps, and machinery repair. Forward linkages refer to downstream activities related to farm outputs such as trading, storage, transport, wholesaling, food processing, packaging and so on. The essence of the approach is captured by Mellor (1983) as follows:

> The strength of the growth linkage multipliers and their concentration on labour-intensive goods and services produced within rural areas for local household consumption suggests that agricultural growth has the potential to significantly enhance rural non-farm employment, thereby broadening the participation of the poor in the benefits of growth and generating a greater market for agricultural output.

Some important assumptions are required for rural non-farm growth to occur in this way (Sanghera and Harriss-White, 1995). In particular, the rising demand by farmers enabled by farm income growth must be mainly directed towards rurally produced consumer and input commodities, for otherwise expenditure and backward linkages are not rurally concentrated; instead they may occur predominantly outside rural areas. An earlier contribution on this topic was sceptical of this assumption and predicted opposite outcomes (Hymer and Resnick, 1969). According to the latter, farm-led growth would tend to decimate preexisting, low technology, non-farm cottage industries in rural areas. This was because demand from rising agricultural income would tend to be spent on modern consumer goods imported into rural areas from urban centres or from abroad. These goods would be higher quality, and cheaper, than the artisanal items they replaced, thus outcompeting local production and leading to its decline. The same would also be true for forward and backward linkage activities, for which previous reliance on local supplies and artisanal methods would be replaced by increasing demand for modern inputs (e.g. fertiliser) and output processing (milling, canning, packaging), the production processes of which are located in towns and cities rather than being truly rural in character.

Thus for the rural growth linkage model to work, the conditions required are that rising farm-led demand calls into being new rurally-located, labour-intensive, small factory production in the consumer, supply and output markets of the farm sector. The key feature of this new small-scale production is its rural location, taking advantage of low labour costs, lower cost sites of production compared to urban areas, and proximity to the source of demand in terms of farm family spending power. Under this scenario, the artisanal rural non-farm sector will certainly decline, but only in the context of growth in new labour-intensive, non-farm activity that replaces it. These conditions are thought to be facilitated by relatively egalitarian income growth in agriculture, since this militates in favour of demand for locally-produced, labour-intensive goods, rather than the imported capital-intensive goods favoured in the consumption patterns of the rural rich.

Empirical studies utilising the growth linkages approach have appeared to demonstrate big multiplier effects in the rural economy resulting from growth in agricultural output. Studies in Asia concluded that every $1 extra value added in agriculture created $0.80 in additional non-farm income (Bell *et al.*, 1982; Hazell and Ramasamy, 1991); while a review of evidence for sub-Saharan Africa suggested a lower multiplier of the order of $0.50 growth in non-farm income for each $1 extra agricultural income (Haggblade *et al.*, 1989). However, by altering certain assumptions in the models concerning the items that can legitimately be classified as locally-produced, non-tradable goods, some researchers have estimated higher multipliers, ranging between $0.95 and $1.90 non-farm growth per $1 farm growth, for selected sub-Saharan African countries (Delgado *et al.*, 1994; 1998). In a Zambian study, for example, Hazell and Hojjati (1995) estimated a rural growth multiplier of around $1.50 per $1 extra farm income, but this resulted from including local foods as rural non-tradable commodities; the multiplier for non-food items was only $0.30.

Studies of rural growth multipliers mainly concur that consumption linkages tend to dominate forward and backward linkages in explaining total linkage effects (Hazell and Haggblade, 1993). In other words, labour-intensive, non-farm output growth is purportedly stimulated especially strongly by consumption expenditure, reflecting demand by farm households for locally-produced products and services. Controversially, some studies found that these consumption linkages were higher for larger farmers than for smaller farmers (Hazell and Roell, 1983; Haggblade and Hazell, 1989), leading to the potential policy inference that larger farms should be favoured above small and poor farmers in promoting higher farm productivity in order to achieve balanced growth within the rural sector.

The direction of causality in the growth linkage model is always from farm growth to non-farm growth, not the other way round. This implies that the primary focus of anti-poverty policies should remain growth in farm output. This helps to explain the continued emphasis on technological change in agriculture in much writing on rural development in the 1980s and 1990s. It also explains the preoccupation of some authors in the 1990s with the purported 'failure' of the green revolution in Africa; the logic being that unless farm yields and output rise steadily in African agriculture, the growth linkage multipliers will fail to occur and the non-farm rural economy will stagnate as well (Mellor *et al.*, 1988; Delgado *et al.*, 1994). Concomitantly, the rural non-farm sector according to this viewpoint has little dynamic of its own and would be unlikely to take a leading role in employment and income growth in the rural economy. In the succinct words of Saith (1992: 114) 'the tail cannot wag the dog'.

The empirical methods of the growth linkage approach have been criticised for relying on unrealistic assumptions about the responsiveness of local non-farm output to increasing demand by farmers, and for their ambiguity in the definition of what constitutes local supply and tradables, allowing for wide variation in multiplier results according to the definitions adopted (B. Harriss, 1987a; Hart, 1989; 1993). Specifically, non-tradable goods produced in rural areas enter these models under an assumption of perfectly elastic supply; in other words they are supposedly abundantly available at static prices irrespective of the growth of demand for them. In addition, such items are classified as originating in the rural economy when they are wholesaled and retailed there. These assumptions, as well as other internal characteristics of the models, can result in substantial exaggeration of the multiplier effects of agricultural growth in the local economy (Haggblade *et al.*, 1991; de Janvry, 1994).

In a case-study utilising a different methodology from that of the chief proponents of the rural growth linkage model, undertaken in North Arcot district of the state of Tamil Nadu in India, B. Harriss (1987b) found, first, the overwhelmingly urban location of industries supplying farmers with consumer or producer goods; second, the weakness of local commodity linkages in both farm and non-farm production processes; and, third, variable labour-intensity over a wide range in non-farm linkage industries.

Furthermore, a study of intertemporal employment and output patterns in India concluded that diversification into non-farm activities was more likely to have occurred as a result of stagnation in agriculture or post-green revolution shedding of labour by farmers who are substituting capital for labour than from farm yield growth itself (Chandrasekhar, 1993). In other words, the existence of an excess labour supply unable to secure agricultural jobs may have been a stronger stimulus to non-farm investment than farm growth. In similar vein, the location and vigour of rural non-farm activity may be due to its own cost and competitiveness characteristics rather than to farm output growth. Fisher *et al.* (1997) demonstrate that the most dynamic growth areas in the rural non-farm sector in India rely heavily on urban and export demand, and possess negligible links to agriculture. Similar findings are also reported for Taiwan (Hart, 1994). These studies reinforce the more sceptical view of growth linkages outlined above.

This seems to bring us back full circle to the necessity vs. choice determinants of diversification discussed in Chapter 3. It is possible that rather than being stimulated by rapid agricultural growth, the rural non-farm sector expands due to the lack of employment opportunities in agriculture (Unni, 1991). In other words, distress and impoverishment may be the driving forces of non-farm growth (Vaidyanathan, 1986; Shukla, 1992). Several researchers have used the expression 'sponge effect' to describe the rural non-farm sector, meaning that it absorbs excess rural labour, but only in low-productivity petty and casual types of employment (e.g. Livingstone, 1991). The rural non-farm sector has also been described as a 'bargain-basement' sector promoted by the international donor community and by NGOs in order to avoid confronting difficult policy choices on issues such as land reform in agriculture (Saith, 1992).

In summary, one important dimension of the relationship between agriculture and livelihood diversification is the role of rural non-farm activities in providing alternative sources of employment and incomes in rural areas. A popular narrative in this regard is the rural growth linkage model which proposes that rapid farm growth will bring into being a dynamic rural non-farm sector, responding to the local linkages of agriculture. This leaves the priority emphasis of public policy squarely fixed on agriculture, while invoking an escape hatch for landless families and others that are unable to participate in agricultural prosperity. However, the empirical foundations of this model seem controversial and ambiguous, and where rural industry is indeed thriving, this seems to follow more the logic of industries locating in rural areas because of the presence there of cheap labour and other cost advantages than to be necessarily due to links with the farming community.

Livelihood diversification and farm output

A focus on the household within a livelihoods framework rather than the sector results in preoccupations that are different from the growth linkage emphasis on the leading role of farm output growth in local employment creation. One of the features of the growth linkage approach evident from the foregoing description is that it seeks to show how rural employment opportunities are created for individuals and families who are unable to participate directly in rising agricultural prosperity, presumably because they are landless or near landless. An implication is that they become wholly involved in new trades and skills offered by rural non-farm employment. However, household level diversification points in different directions: the inadequacy of farming as a sole means of survival; the adoption of a diversified income portfolio for risk and seasonal reasons; long-distance migration as a key feature of household survival strategies.

The impact of household level diversification on farm productivity and output depends on numerous factors relating to the allocation of farm family labour, the strategic perspectives of household members concerning the future livelihood role of the farm, inheritance effects on the viability of holdings due to farm size changes, and processes of social and economic change in the larger economy. Some of these factors can be reasonably well captured using a short-term economic analysis; others require a deeper understanding of long-term social processes. There is little doubt that different factors will predominate at different times and places, so it is likely to prove difficult to generalise about the agricultural side-effects of diversification. Nevertheless some patterns of cause and effect can be identified that are informative for policy discussion.

Taking land as a resource first, one of the most commonly observed relationships between land and diversification is that involving land subdivision and fragmentation that occurs at inheritance. Land subdivision in densely settled areas can create farm holdings that are insufficient to provide their owners with a means of subsistence. This corresponds to a 'push' reason for diversification (see Chapter 3 above). It may also result in a decline in the productivity of land due to sub-optimal field sizes, scattering of plots, and changes in access to inputs (e.g. irrigation water) due to the manner in which subdivision was carried out. Eventually, subdivision can cause the relationship between land ownership and cultivation to become increasingly tenuous. Absenteeism by owners of tiny plots results in a patchwork pattern of tenancies and sub-tenancies that are scarcely viable as sources of survival for tenant families, and that are unlikely to provide a sound basis for maintaining or raising farm productivity and output.

Some economists would argue, and this is a policy issue to which we return in the next chapter, that the problems of declining agricultural productivity caused by land subdivision at inheritance could be ameliorated by instituting private land tenure, and in other respects creating conditions of security and trust for private land markets to operate. Having moved to predominantly non-farm sources of livelihood, families would then sell their parcels of land, enabling reconsolidation of land holdings to take place. This argument has several flaws. One is the presumption that those with customary or legal rights to land will voluntarily enter land markets to make sales. There is scarcely any historical evidence to support this, enforced evictions rather than voluntary sales being a much more common reason for land consolidation to take place. Moreover, the precariousness of urban livelihoods in many developing countries means that urban branches of rural families have excellent reasons to hold onto their rural land rights indefinitely, whether under private tenure or not. Agriculture then becomes a fallback position for insecure non-farm means of survival, rather than the primary means of livelihood on which so much 'agriculture first' writing is predicated.

Secondly, diversification involves labour as an asset. Specifically, it involves re-allocating labour from farm to non-farm activities. In some instances, this may have no adverse effects on the viability of farm operations, because non-farm work is undertaken in the agricultural slack season, or because the individuals who take up non-farm opportunities are not required in farm operations. However, it has been argued that distant migration is detrimental to agriculture in these respects (Lipton, 1977; 1980). This is because it is typically the younger, more innovative, better educated, and male members of farm families that leave the farm to undertake distance migration. In so doing they deplete the farm of physical labour capacity and farming skills. Migration also weakens the capability of small-farm rural communities to stand up for themselves politically (Lipton, 1980). In a study in Indonesia, written up under the title 'too busy to farm', Preston (1989) found that the non-farm occupations of farm household members resulted in the gradual withdrawal from cultivation of the less productive arable areas on farms.

The labour market aspects of migration have been examined using a farm household model to study the effects of household members confronting different non-farm job prospects and wage rates, as well as the impact of the market price of food on labour allocation decisions (Low, 1981; 1986). If it is assumed that all family members make roughly equivalent contributions to farm output when they provide an additional day of labour to the farm, that is, they generate equal on-farm marginal returns to labour time, then the pattern of migration will be determined by which household members are able to obtain a higher return than this in non-farm labour markets. Further than this, a key consideration for a food-deficit farm household is the relationship between wages and the market price of essential foods. Low food prices mean that the purchasing value of non-farm wage income is increased, and this may make it even more attractive to send household members off the farm to the neglect of own-farm output.

Applying this model to southern Africa, Low (1986) found that it provided a plausible explanation of agricultural stagnation in countries bordering South Africa in the 1970s and 1980s. A booming market for unskilled male labour in mines and factories, coupled with low retail prices for maize, meant that it made sense for households to send able-bodied males to distant labour markets and to purchase food deficits from the market. Both the ability and the incentive to raise farm output and productivity were diminished. In this context, the farm productivity of adult women may well be as high as that of men, but women have other obligations in household reproduction that constrain the hours they can spend on farm work.

These effects would of course work out quite differently under other labour market conditions. For example, if the buoyant labour market were for women in textile or electronic factories, then men would presumably stay on the farm. Also, high food prices compared to non-farm wage rates would increase the incentive for home food production above market purchases.

Thirdly, there is the use made of the cash resources that are generated from migration. Several different circumstances can prevail here. On the optimistic side, remittances from migrant family members may be used for agricultural investment (Lucas and Stark, 1985). In doing this, they can be interpreted as relieving a credit constraint caused by credit market failures (Stark, 1982; Savadogo et al., 1994; Taylor and Wyatt, 1996). In similar vein, non-farm income can be viewed as a substitute for insurance, enabling the farm household to carry out risky innovations that it would not otherwise contemplate (Evans and Ngau, 1991). As such, it may contribute to agricultural intensification and rising farm productivity (see Box 5.1). One well-known Kenya case-study appears to demonstrate massive long term benefits arising from the investment of urban earnings in environmental recovery and agricultural innovation (Tiffen and Mortimore, 1992; Tiffen et al., 1994).

On the pessimistic side, remittances may simply fail to happen. The resident household, having made an investment in the job prospects of the migrant (education, clothes, transport, job search, seed money), may fail to obtain a return to such outlays if the migrant fails to secure remuneration above bare survival or establishes urban domestic obligations that prohibit rural transfers. If the survival prospects of the farm household are precarious, then this might make it even more so, due to the double squeeze of loss of cash savings and loss of an able-bodied person to work on the farm. Cash generated from working in mines or factories might be utilised to invest in non-farm activities rather than the home farm (e.g. Pottier, 1983). Alternatively, remittance income may be utilised by the farm household primarily for consumption purposes or unproductive investment rather than productive investment (Rempel and Lobdell, 1978). For example, it may be used to build and furnish a new house, rather than to get farm terraces repaired or to buy fertiliser.

A fourth argument is that in the sub-Saharan African context, investment in the social and kinship networks required to support diverse livelihoods diverts resources from investment in agriculture (Berry, 1989: 46–51). The link here is between the precariousness of dependence on agriculture in many African rural settings, and the need for viable fallback positions in the event of adverse trends and crises. In many African countries, decades of uncertainty caused by erratic and unpredictable government policy implementation towards agriculture have been followed by equally unpredictable market contexts following structural ad-

Box 5.1. Diversification, farm output, and incomes:
a Kenya case-study

Kutus town, in the Kirinyaga District of Kenya, is situated at the foot of Mount Kenya, about 100 km from Nairobi. The area is relatively prosperous, with coffee as the major cash crop, supplemented by tomatoes for the Nairobi market, and french beans for export. Maize and beans are the main food crops grown for home consumption.

A survey carried out in the late 1980s collected income and farm budget data from 111 households, selected randomly from the rural hinterland within a 7 km radius of Kutus town. The composition of annual incomes by income quartiles is shown in Table 5.1. Overall, households derived just over 50 per cent of income from farming. Another quarter came from non-farm business, with just under a quarter coming from wages and salaries, and a negligible amount attributable to remittances and other transfers. This latter finding may be due to remittances from non-resident members being reported as wage income, since the figure is substantially less than has been reported for other areas of Kenya.

Table 5.1. Rural household income portfolios, Kutus, Kenya

	Income quartile				
	I	II	III	IV	All
Total income (KShs)	3,815	14,766	35,150	114,305	41,358
Net farm income (KShs)	3,301	8,997	19,144	54,417	21,168
Share total income (%)	86.5	60.9	54.5	47.6	51.2
Non-farm income (KShs)	515	5,769	16,006	59,889	20,190
Share total income (%)	13.5	39.1	45.5	52.4	48.8
Land cultivated (acres)	3.4	4.9	5.0	7.1	5.1
Coffee output (kg/acre)	348	923	1,648	2,899	1,916
Maize output (bags/acres)	3.5	4.7	6.0	8.7	6.1

Source: Evans and Ngau (1991: 525).

There were considerable differences in income patterns across quartiles. Households in the poorest quartile obtained 87 per cent of their income from farming, compared to only 48 per cent for the richest quartile. Non-farm sources thus accounted for over 50 per cent of the incomes of the rich, compared to only 13 per cent of those of the poor. These findings were confirmed by two other measures of income diversification: number of income sources and number of household members in non-farm revenue-earning activities. The majority of poor households earned income from a single source, while richer households tended to rely on three sources: wage labour, non-farm business and farm income. In addition, only 18 per cent of poorer households had members in non-farm activities, compared to 67 per cent of richer households. Thus, greater diversification was found to be associated with higher incomes.

The study also considered the effects of increasing non-farm income on farm productivity. As Table 5.1 shows, as the proportion of income from non-farm sources rises across quartiles, farm income in absolute terms increases, as does agricultural productivity. Households in the top quartile produced 2.5 times more maize per acre and eight times more coffee per acre than those in the lowest. An explanation for these results is that households which had more non-farm income were more willing to undertake high return but risky production activities than those with less income from these sources. This was supported by other findings, for example, as households' income sources become more diversified they engage more in riskier activities, such as growing larger areas of high value crops, and purchasing more inputs. Thus, diversification may enable small farmers to raise agricultural productivity.

Finally, the study considered the factors that caused or enabled households to diversify their income sources. A number of factors were considered; however, the key variable was found to be education, both in terms of the number of household members with 5 or more years of education, and the years of education of the household head.

The study suggested that narrow sectoral approaches to raising agricultural productivity are likely to be less successful than more broadly based approaches which encourage the growth of small-scale businesses, and generate non-farm employment. Attention should also be paid to the provision of primary education, which is a key factor enabling households to diversify, as well as itself being associated with higher farm productivity.

Source: Evans and Ngau (1991).

justment and market liberalisation. These market uncertainties are compounded by natural and political catastrophes, especially droughts and civil wars. It is argued that many families, both rural and urban, devote an increasing proportion of their energies to securing future means of survival through social networks, at the expense of paying attention to current farm production.

From the foregoing it is clear that the impact of livelihood diversification on agriculture depends on a complex conjuncture of factors operating within household, rural, and economy-wide contexts. Some factors giving rise to recognisable negative patterns are as follows:

1. Dynamic non-farm labour markets, whether rural or urban located, cause withdrawal of labour resources from the farm; therefore, depending on how many and which members of the household leave for distant labour markets, farm output may stagnate or even decline;

2. The fundamental insecurity of urban as well as rural livelihoods means that families are reluctant to dispose of their access rights to land, even when these have become so small as to be unviable due to successive subdivisions at inheritance; therefore the land market is unable to consolidate or enlarge holdings and this may also contribute to agricultural stagnation as a concomitant of diversification;

3. When rural livelihoods are permanently precarious, family members will devote a considerable proportion of their time and energy to maintaining and consolidating social networks in order to ensure future fallback positions in the event of crisis; and this too may detract from agricultural investment.

Offsetting these broadly negative connotations for agriculture are circumstances in which the prospects of high returns from agricultural investment cause a reverse flow of funds from income generated in rural non-farm or urban activities. The operative factor here must be perceptions about returns to farm rehabilitation, innovation, or the introduction of new farm enterprises. In other words, this reverse flow of resources generated outside agriculture will not occur by happenstance; it will be driven by prices and markets that make new farm investment a viable proposition for the diversified rural household. It is also in this sense likely to occur differentially between households, and may therefore exacerbate rural income inequalities.

Note that the logic of the growth linkage model is reversed if non-farm cash resources are utilised for farm growth, because here, indeed, the 'tail wags the dog'. Non-farm income sources become the agent of positive change in agriculture, rather than agriculture being the agent of rural non-farm growth. Furthermore, whereas in the growth linkage model it is rising farm productivity that enables labour to be released to the non-farm sector in a virtuous circle of rural growth, in the reverse instances cited it is the prior release of labour from a stagnant agriculture that sets up a reverse chain of causality in which the alleviation of capital constraints becomes the catalyst of farm output growth.

These apparently irreconcilable interpretations of the relationship between farm productivity, agricultural growth, intra-rural diversity, and household level income diversification reflect the distinct temporal and spatial contexts to which they apply. The growth linkage approach is associated with the period in Asia when green revolution technologies were achieving unprecedented increases in yields and output for the food grains, rice and wheat. The approach was formulated in part as a rebuttal of earlier pessimistic prognoses about the distributional impacts of the new technologies (e.g. Griffin, 1979). The context of the models was agrarian economies containing many landless or near land-less labour and rural labour markets offering an elastic supply of labour at the going wage rate.

Sub-Saharan Africa has been unable to reproduce anything like the farm out-put growth of that era in Asia, and nor is it likely to do so given that climate, cropping systems, soils and so on are vastly more heterogeneous and risk-prone than in the Asian case. Nor, with few exceptions, do sub-Saharan African coun-tries possess rural labour markets of the type prevalent in Asia; on the contrary, rural Africa is much more widely characterised by seasonal and locational labour shortages in agriculture than is typically the case in Asia. Most income diversifi-cation in Africa has been not just non-farm but non-rural in character (Bryceson, 1996).

The different findings concerning the impact of diversification on farm out-put are spatially and temporally specific. The stagnation of farming in the south-ern African periphery in the 1970s and 1980s was due to the adjacency of a booming labour market and low food prices (Low, 1986). These conditions are unlikely to be replicable on the same scale at other times in other places. Likewise the 'greening' of Machakos District adjacent to Nairobi as a result of the reverse investment of urban earnings (Tiffen and Mortimore, 1992; Tiffen *et al.*, 1994) may not possess the generality it tries to convey. In the end, the direction of resource allocation by family members will reflect real comparative returns to different activities in different locations, modified by considerations of risk and the long-term livelihood security of the rural family.

In summary, the livelihoods framework causes the focus of rural poverty analysis to switch from an agriculture-centred, sector-level, viewpoint, to a household or individual-level viewpoint in which diversity of income sources is likely to be a key feature. Unlike the sector-level rural-growth linkages model, the livelihoods approach is unable to offer a single chain of causality linking sec-toral growth to rural poverty reduction.

The conventional assumption that there is always a continuous, positive, two-way relationship between household incomes and farm performance is shown not to hold automatically, and the way the household deploys its assets (land, labour, financial capital) becomes contingent on strategic livelihood decisions in which agriculture is only one out of multiple possibilities that are, in practice, considered. This does not mean that the livelihoods approach results in weak and inconclusive results for rural poverty reduction. What it does mean, is that the strategies and options of the rural poor need to be understood before decid-ing the most appropriate means to support their efforts. The livelihoods ap-proach embraces complexity, and requires that poverty reduction policies are adapted to the local circumstances to which they are applied.

On-farm diversification and agricultural intensification

While much of this book is about diversification away from agriculture as the primary means of survival of the household, on-farm diversification deserves attention as a complementary or alternative livelihood strategy. Moreover, resource flow reversals of the kind discussed in the preceding section, can take the form either of diversifying the farm away from its previous lines of specialisation, or of intensifying resource use by adding new enterprises into existing farming systems. An example of the former would be growing tomatoes for commercial sale in urban areas on land previously used to cultivate maize. An example of the latter would be adding a zero grazing dairy enterprise into an intensive mixed cropping farming system.

Some definitions are in order. On-farm diversity refers to the maintenance of a diverse spread of crop and livestock production activities that interlock with each other in various ways. This may involve cultural practices that are specifically designed to spread risk or to take advantage of complementaries between crops in their use of soil nutrients, sunlight and other resources. Thus intercropping and mixed cropping are diverse farm systems, as also are cultivation practices that take spatial advantage of different microclimates within the land resources to which the household has access (Blarel *et al.*, 1992). The opposite of on-farm diversity is monoculture, for example, specialisation in sugarcane or tea production. In view of these attributes, diversification evidently implies resource use decisions to move from a position of less to one of greater diversity in on-farm production.

The meaning of intensification in an agricultural context is the utilisation of a greater amount of non-land resources for a given land area. Extensive and intensive agriculture are opposites, with the former meaning low resource use combined with lots of land to produce low output per hectare, while the latter means high resource use combined with a small land area to produce high output per hectare. Intensification may or may not coincide with diversification, depending on the route taken to deploy resources more effectively and the use made of complementarities in input use and between outputs.

The orthodox route to intensification involves specialisation rather than diversification. This occurs by emphasising only those outputs for which agroecological conditions seem especially well suited (e.g. wheat growing on the great plains of North America) and then continually refining, over time, the cultivars, input combinations, and cultural practices that result in output per unit area rising over time. High yielding varieties of food crops, such as wetland rice and wheat, correspond to this route to intensification, even though they are labour-intensive, small-farm crops, in contrast to the capital-intensive crop specialisation of the industrial countries. So, too, historically have the major estate and plantation crops like coffee, tea, cocoa, and sugarcane, although nowadays more flexible production systems are found for most such crops.

Intensification does not have to follow the specialisation route. A wide variety of agricultural practices, for example, mixed farming, mixed cropping, alley cropping, sequential cropping, inter-cropping, crop-livestock systems and so on, represent, in varying ways, intensification based on multiple farm activities rather than just one or a few. This occurs for sound agronomic and economic reasons. Input use is intensified when better seasonal use is made of available labour time; sequential cropping makes better seasonal use of land; and various mixed cropping and crop-livestock regimes exhibit significant complementarities between inputs that raise the overall productivity of land. Diversification in these instances goes hand-in-hand with intensification, and there are several African case-studies that demonstrate this for places where increased population density and the closing of the land frontier have caused spontaneous intensification processes to arise (e.g. Netting *et al.*, 1989; Netting, 1993: Ch.9; Adams and Mortimore, 1997; see also Box 5.2)

As already observed in relation to off-farm and non-farm diversification, sectoral level events and trends need to be distinguished from farm or household level ones. Agricultural sector diversification has in the past quite often been identified as a sectoral policy priority in developing countries, but this need not coincide with on-farm diversity since different farms may choose to specialise in a small range of outputs. Sector level diversification usually arises in the context of a perceived national disadvantage due to undue reliance on one or more major crops. Many examples arise in relation to export crops such as coffee, bananas, sugarcane and tea where long run declines in real world prices provoke a search for alternative farm enterprises into which farmers can be encouraged or assisted to move (e.g. Wyeth, 1989; Stewart, 1994a).

External trade considerations can also invoke diversification as an issue for food crops. For example, diversification became a policy issue in Indonesia in the late 1980s after the country had become self-sufficient in rice, due to the overwhelming dependence of farmers on paddy cultivation, the existence of national deficits in many other commodities that could be grown on paddy land, and poor prospects for exporting rice surpluses for reason of the inferior quality of domestic rice according to world rice trade standards. In this instance, sectoral level efforts to promote diversification were unsuccessful since rice production continued to yield the highest returns to farmers under a wide range of relative crop prices (Pearson *et al.*, 1991). An example with some similarities and some differences pertains to Sri Lanka, where efforts to persuade farmers to diversify out of low-return rice production and into high-value fruit and vegetables for export have been mainly unsuccessful (Dunham, 1993).

In these instances, the aim of government policy is often to stimulate farmers to switch from one main output to another, in other words, to swap specialisations. This is clearly different from on-farm diversification where farmers choose

Box 5.2. Intensification and flexibility in North-East Nigeria

Research undertaken in north-east Nigeria during the 1990s sought to shed light on the role of agricultural intensification in livelihood systems across a gradient of differing demographic and environmental circumstances (Adams and Mortimore, 1997). The research located itself within the major debates about population density and survival, and particularly with respect to the Boserup proposition about a positive relationship between agricultural intensification and population density.

For the purposes of the research a definition of agricultural intensification offered by Tiffen *et al.* (1994: 29) was taken as the starting point, namely 'increased average inputs of labour or capital on a smallholding, either on cultivated land alone, or on cultivated and grazing land, for the purpose of increasing the value of output per hectare'. This was then elaborated to comprise increased labour inputs, creation of land enhancing capital such as irrigation canals, and land management changes such as the proportion of land cultivated, the crops selected, the integration of crops and livestock, and the management of rangeland and trees.

The research used the term 'indigenous intensification' to describe intensification that takes place in the absence of intervention by external agencies, and four observations are made about such processes of intensification in Africa. First, that they are historically uncommon but becoming more prevalent as population density increases; second, that they can be risky and costly; third, that they are driven by economic factors but these do not cause the same outcomes at different places or at different times; and fourth, that there is no reason to expect simple relationships between intensification and sustainability.

The study examined intensification relationships, especially those related to allocation of labour time, in four villages in the Nigerian Sahel. These villages were purposively selected to lie along a gradient of declining rainfall, population density, intensity of farming, and biological productivity. The proportion of total available land that was cultivated was found to decline, broadly, along this gradient, as also was land-use intensity.

A livelihood management attribute designated as flexibility was designated for the purpose of making comparisons with agricultural intensity. Flexibility comprised six criteria: labour use on the farm, crop diversity, tree diversity, grazing resource use, field location, and non-farm livelihood activities. Three of these flexibility attributes—on-farm labour deployment, crop diversity, and tree diversity—were found to be common across all sample sites. However, an inverse relation was found between intensity and the other three flexibility attributes, i.e. field location, grazing and non-farm activities. Essentially, the least intensive agricultural systems were characterised by more shifting cultivation, greater flexibility in grazing regimes, and higher reliance on non-farm income sources.

There are several implications of these observations. One is that intensification possibly carries with it some cost with respect to livelihood flexibility and adaptability. This is because both land and labour become fully committed to the intensive farming systems adopted. On the other hand, on-farm diversity can substitute for non-farm diversity, especially when it is associated with income-increasing farm intensification. A key finding of the study that is echoed in many different sources was that livelihood adaptation is a social and economic process that works out differently across different households within and across different locations.

to maintain or to increase the diversity of farm outputs for strategic reasons to do with the survival and food security of the farm household. A primary reason for such diversification is, of course, to reduce risk, and in this sense it plays the same role for livelihoods as non-farm diversification undertaken for risk reasons.

Many studies have demonstrated that traditional cultivation practices such as mixed cropping reduce the adverse impacts of events such as unseasonal temperatures or rainfall failure because different crops in the mixed stand possess different degrees of resilience to unstable climatic outcomes. Such practices do this without necessarily sacrificing output per unit of area, due to complementarities in resource use between outputs. On-farm diversification may be actively promoted as a policy objective in rural development projects for the same reasons. Thus a small-farm sugarcane project may incorporate an area on each farm assigned to household food and vegetable production, in order to offset the livelihood risks for families of natural or market-induced declines in the returns to sugar production.

Recent experience in sub-Saharan Africa shows that on-farm diversification can be combined with intensification to provide new and higher income sources for rural households (Jaffee and Morton, 1995). This process is predominantly market driven, although the identification of markets, if they are international, and the facilitation of marketing are important enabling roles for NGOs and governments. One example is the spontaneous growth of milk production based on stall-fed dairy cattle that has occurred in urban as well as rural locations in sub-Saharan African countries. In rural areas it tends to occur in densely settled farming zones where dairy farming is added to the intensive cultivation of export crops like coffee or tea, along with horticulture and grain production. Another example is the domestic demand-led cultivation of vegetable crops like tomatoes, onions, shallots and aubergines. Yet another is the export oriented production of horticultural crops, typically undertaken as contract farming linked to agribusinesses engaged in the international trade of such commodities.

These examples are cited because they relate to livelihood diversification in sometimes unexpected ways. A first point is that they represent increased farm output and incomes driven by markets for different outputs rather than by rising yields in existing outputs, which is the conventional route to increasing farm incomes. A second, and related, point is that the participation of urban branches of rural families is often observed to be the catalyst of such changes in the pattern of farm output. Indeed, in some cases, it is young unemployed urban dwellers that have rented land from villagers in order to produce items like tomatoes or shallots. A third point is that on-farm diversification that also involves intensification can be a substitute for non-farm diversification (Adams and Mortimore, 1997). This is because the increased labour requirements of intensive, diversified, small-farm systems reduce the scope and the incentive for family members to seek income earning opportunities away from the family farm.

Summary

This chapter confronts the implications of a livelihoods approach for conventional rural poverty reduction models centred on small-farm agriculture. The mainstream economic approach known as the rural growth linkages model is summarised. This sees rural poverty reduction as predominantly being achieved by rising productivity in small-farm agriculture, happily resulting also in growth in labour-intensive rural non-farm activities due to the linkage effects of rising farm incomes. The livelihoods approach, however, provokes a switch in focus from the sector to a household or individual level. It then becomes plain that household strategies may conflict with agricultural productivity considerations. Households must deal with multiple options for achieving improved livelihood security into the future, in which farm investment is only one of diverse uses of household resources that they consider.

Pursuing the diversification theme in an agricultural context, the strategic alternative of diversifying on-farm is also considered. Where conditions provide the motivation to do so, on-farm diversification can satisfy many of the same criteria for achieving resilient livelihoods as non-farm diversification does, and there exist several case-studies demonstrating this, especially in locations with access to urban or export markets for diverse, high-value, horticultural crops or livestock outputs, including dairy products. In these instances, agricultural intensification and diversification coincide, thus satisfying the conventional criterion of productivity growth in agriculture alongside other livelihood considerations.

Previous approaches to farm-led rural development have sought patterns of cause and effect thought to have universal applicability as a means to identify and prioritise poverty reduction policies and projects. The livelihoods approach neither seeks nor requires such universality since it considers that poverty reduction initiatives should be adapted to support the poor's own livelihood strategies, as they are observed in different settings. On occasions, this may involve patterns that are more, rather than less, widely applicable, but this is not a prior requirement. On occasion, it may mean that support directed to rising farm productivity is the most promising route to poverty reduction, but again, this outcome is dependent on first reaching an understanding of the strategies of the poor in a particular locality, not from the imposition of a prior blueprint.

CHAPTER 6

Environment and
Sustainability

This chapter considers the relationship between rural livelihoods, diversification and the environment in developing countries. For this purpose, the environment is taken to mean the land, water and vegetation assets that are utilised either directly or indirectly to provide means of survival for human populations. The chapter is not concerned with urban and industrial environmental problems that are mainly about waste disposal and pollution. Nor is it concerned with the behaviour of natural ecosystems in the absence of human disturbances. It touches only lightly on global environmental issues such as large-scale deforestation or loss of biodiversity.

Environmental resources that are utilised by rural populations can be broadly categorised between those that are gathered, such as non-food forest products, wild fruits and vegetables, medicinal plants and so on, and those that are organised by human agency to produce managed outputs as in pastoral and farming systems. However, there does not exist in practice a neat separation between resources that are managed and those that are not; rather there is a continuum between intensive resource management at one end of a spectrum and minimal management at the other. It is rare for there to be literally no human management at all, for one of the features of rural communities is that everyone knows what everyone else does, so that socially undesirable resource extraction does not pass unnoticed. Nevertheless, customary means of regulating the use of certain resources may break down due to exogenous events or trends, and it is then that some of the problems associated with adverse resource trends tend to arise.

The topic of environment and rural livelihoods is a vast one on which an enormous amount has been written during the past two decades. For this reason, it is necessary to be rather selective regarding the aspects that seem to be most central to the topics of livelihoods and diversification. The chapter examines three such aspects, and then draws together the threads between them with a view to providing an overview of the current state of knowledge in this area. The next section considers, first, the relationship between rural poverty and the environment, a contentious area of enquiry displaying marked differences of interpretation concerning causes and effects. This is followed, second, by an examination of the concept of sustainability in a livelihood context, arriving eventually at a definition and discussion of the notion of sustainable rural livelihoods. The third aspect of livelihood diversification and the environment treated here is that of resource management institutions, specifically the tenure regimes that determine the access to and ownership of environmental resources by rural households. The chapter concludes with an attempt to set out the balance of current thinking in this area.

Poverty and environment interactions

A prevalent view in the decade from the mid-1980s to the mid-1990s was that poverty and environmental degradation were intimately connected, so that poverty was seen as both a cause and an effect of natural resource depletion, in a downward spiral (e.g. Leonard, 1989). An early statement of this view captures the line of thinking that it involves: 'Those who are poor and hungry will often destroy their immediate environment in order to survive: they will cut down forests; their livestock will overgraze grasslands; they will over use marginal land; and in growing numbers they will crowd into congested cities. The cumulative effect of these changes is so far-reaching as to make poverty itself a major global scourge.' (Brundtland, 1987: 28). Alternatively, and more succinctly: 'The relationship between poverty and environmental degradation is close and complicated, with a built-in potential for escalation.' (Pinstrup-Andersen and Pandya-Lorch, 1994: 8).

The rationales for an adverse poverty-environment connection have been spelt out in numerous documents (Leonard, 1989; World Bank, 1992). Population growth is seen as a critical factor because it diminishes farm sizes in densely settled areas, results in a growing class of dispossessed rural dwellers, and creates pressure for people to push into marginal zones that cannot sustain permanent cultivation. It also directly increases the rate of extraction of environmental goods such as firewood, building materials, and fodder for animals. Lack of land as an asset means that the rural poor tend to display a higher reliance on gathering activities from the environment than do those rural dwellers who are able to meet their subsistence needs mainly from own-account farming (Jodha, 1990). The same combination of increasing population density and landlessness causes the cultivation by the poor of steep slopes, accelerating soil erosion, and the prevalence of 'slash-and-burn' conversion of land to farming at the forest fringe.

The downward spiral occurs because environmental degradation such as soil erosion, over-grazed pastures, and loss of watershed protection further intensifies the degree of poverty experienced by marginal groups, and drives them to ever more intensive exploitation of the resources that are accessible to them. Important in these explanations is a purported 'survival calculus' of poor families that are on the brink of destitution, in which desperation leads them to consume the capital that could form the basis of future survival because no other choices are available to them. In addition, property regimes are sometimes cited as having key significance. The poor tend to move into areas where neither modern legal nor customary property institutions are operative, and they are therefore purported to behave in the mode of open access resources where the collective effect of each individual effort to survive results in overall unsustainable use of the resource in question. The lack of a stake in land occupied with no legal title or recognised tenancy further reinforces the adoption of perspectives prioritising short-term extractive rather than a long-term investment viewpoint.

Several conclusions arise from this interpretation of rural poverty and environmental change. One is that damage to local environments cannot be effectively halted unless poverty itself is addressed. This is turn requires a pace and pattern of economic growth that includes the poor, and a labour-intensive pattern of growth is the strategy advocated to achieve this goal (World Bank, 1990; 1992). Other elements of the 1990s poverty agenda discussed in Chapter 4 are also considered to make valuable contributions in this regard. The critical factor is to provide the poor with alternative sources of livelihood that reduce their reliance on gathering activities in the local environment, and diminish their motivation to initiate cultivation in environmentally sensitive locations. In this way, livelihood diversification appears on the scene as a potential solution to the poverty-environment trap. Changes in property regimes are also advocated, especially regularising the ownership or tenancy status of settlers in frontier areas or on marginal lands where legal ownership often rests with the state.

There are many writers, however, who regard the adverse poverty-environment proposition as a highly selective and therefore misleading interpretation of environmental change (e.g. Duraiappah, 1998). The problem is partly one of focus and scale (Broad, 1994; see also Box 6.1). By focusing attention at the micro level on the behaviour of the rural poor in pursuit of their livelihoods, the interpretation fails to capture the large-scale disturbances that set off new patterns of behaviour at local levels. Such large-scale events include timber concessions that are accompanied by sudden, unprecedented changes in road access into previously inaccessible forests; deliberate policies of new frontier settlement and transmigration carried out by governments and donor agen cies in order to satisfy domestic pressure groups or for other, primarily political, reasons associated with control over national territory; enforced relocation of rural inhabitants for dams and hydroelectric schemes; alienation of land to ranches, estates, plantations and national parks; diversion of rivers for irrigation schemes, and so on. The large-scale effects that events such as these have on ecosystems and rural livelihoods dwarf the trivial, even in the aggregate, effects that individual action might have on natural resource systems in the absence of such disturbances. In other words, making the poor the scapegoat for environmental deterioration merely lets off the hook the commercial and state behaviours responsible for the really big changes that result in switches in the dynamics of the interaction of people with local environments.

Box 6.1. The poor and the environment: a Philippines case-study

The paper from which this example is taken (Broad, 1994) sets out to challenge the 'poverty as the cause of environmental degradation' proposition, utilising fieldwork in rural communities across the Philippines undertaken in the period 1988–91. The author points to numerous documented instances worldwide in which the poor have been observed to protect the environment, for example, by replanting trees, opposing logging operations, fighting enclosure of communal lands, and seeking greater autonomy in community resource management. These grassroots actions often occur in opposition to large-scale environmental despoliation being contemplated or undertaken by commercial operators, typically licensed and supported by central governments.

Research was conducted across several sites in rural areas of the Philippines, a country characterised by severe poverty rates, significant ecosystem damage, and a highly organised civil society. The research found that large numbers of poor people in the areas studied had been transformed into environmental activists, and it sought to discover the preconditions for this activism to take root. These preconditions were found to reside both in people's relation to their ecosystems and in the state of civil society. Specifically:

- the survival capabilities of the poor are directly threatened by the environmental degradation;
- poor people have lived in the threatened area for some time, and regard themselves as having a permanent stake in the natural resource base there;
- civil society in the country is politicized and organised.

Examples from the Philippines are cited with respect to each of these preconditions. In a particular rural area of the island of Mindanao, for example, tenant farmers growing rice and maize experienced a steady decline over many years in the quantity and quality of their water resources, including seasonal drying up of water courses, flooding after rains, declining length of the rainy season and similar events. The villagers came to connect these events with the widespread commercial logging taking place in the watersheds surrounding their cultivated areas, and this resulted in three direct actions against commercial loggers: first, sitting down in front of logging trucks locally, then blockading trucks in the provincial capital, and, subsequently, staging a 'fast for the trees' in the capital city, Manila.

This and other examples revealed the importance of length of residence in a location for people to become involved in environmental protest; new migrants into threatened areas are unlikely to adopt the same viewpoint as established residents, and may even contribute to the problem rather than work towards a solution. Also important is the variety and density of civil organisations such as unions, peasant associations, people's organisations, and non-governmental organisations (NGOs), in respect of which the Philippines had become richly endowed in the years preceding this research. For example, there were no less than 1,300 development NGOs operating in the Philippines in the early 1990s.

While the research identifies these three factors as critical in the Philippines case, the central point is that conditions can exist, or be facilitated to come into existence, that empower the poor themselves to protect the environmental resources on which they depend for survival.

Source: Broad (1994).

This counter argument brings some balance into the assessment of poverty-environment interactions. The highly visible environmental changes that greatly worry people in industrial countries, for example, the rate of deforestation in Borneo or the Amazon, have almost nothing to do with rural poverty in developing countries and a lot to do with power struggles over valuable resources (tropical timber, oil, valuable metals) between the large players in national and international business and government. Subsequently, the poor, along with others, may be found to exploit the new opportunities thus opened up for survival, but this hardly constitutes the basis for a general argument about the poor's custodianship of environmental resources. Where large scale disruption to previous ecosystems has occurred, and where subsequent property rights are unclear or unenforceable, it is hardly surprising that a chain of irreversible environmental change is put in motion. Moreover, to the extent that the adverse argument depends on unusual examples at the fringes of normal behaviour, so, too, there are plenty of individual case-studies that offer the opposite evidence of poor rural people augmenting their environments in order to maintain and enhance their future survival capabilities (e.g. Tiffen *et al.*, 1994; Leach and Mearns, 1996; Mortimore, 1998).

Nor can inequality be ignored in any balanced assessment of links between poverty and the environment. The lack of assets of the rural poor is often a mirror image of the acquisition of assets by the rural rich, and the ownership of rural assets from land to crops, cattle, goats, and trees cannot be inferred by casual observation of rural habitats; absentee ownership of rural assets may sometimes be a significant feature of their misuse from a sustainability perspective.

These and related considerations have led researchers to advocate a more disaggregated approach to thinking through poverty-environment interactions which anticipate the livelihoods framework set out in Chapter 2. For example, Reardon and Vosti (1995) put forward a framework that seeks to distinguish different types of poverty and different types of environmental change, as well as the links that occur between them. Poverty differs according to the type or combination of assets that the household has at its command, or in which it is deficit. A household may be well endowed in one asset, for example, human capital, and poorly endowed in another, for example, land; the opportunities for converting one type of asset into another can vary considerably. For example, if access to a renewable environmental resource (e.g. firewood) could be converted via the market into land or education, then reliance on the first asset would reduce over time. On the other hand, if no such opportunity for conversion or substitution exists, then reliance on the original asset will be intensified over time. The importance of reaching an understanding of the asset basis of livelihood systems, in the environmental context, has also been emphasised by other writers (e.g. Dasgupta and Maler, 1995), and is of course a central feature of the livelihoods approach that informs this book.

Livelihood diversification enters importantly into the poverty-environment equation because it can directly switch the time allocation of the household from gathering activities in the local environment to off-farm or non-farm income generating activities, and, indirectly, it can improve the ease with which the household can convert one type of asset into another. As discussed in Chapter 4, access to non-farm income depends on relatively high levels of the human capital asset comprising skills, education and good health. In turn this access makes possible future increases in human capital for family members, and facilitates investment either in farm productive capacity (Chapter 5 above) or non-farm activities. The poor have particularly strong incentives to diversify incomes because of seasonality, risk and associated reasons; yet they may be least able to do so due to poverty in the assets needed to secure diversification options.

Economic factors and conservation

For natural resources that are under the direct management control of the farm family i.e. on-farm resources, the household economic model can provide some useful insights into the motives for conservation (Ellis, 1993). It is recalled that the general prediction of the household model is that labour time is allocated to different activities up to the point where the return to one more unit of time in an activity is equal to the opportunity value of labour, which is the market wage. Management of environmental resources brings a complication to this prediction because it involves a stream of costs and returns evolving over future time, rather than just a static comparison of returns to labour on and off the farm. For example, the decision whether to build a terrace to prevent soil erosion involves an interaction between the current opportunity cost of labour time and the expected future income gains from terracing.

A considerable proportion of resource conservation by farm households occurs as an intrinsic feature of farming systems, and is not separable from routine farming practices in terms of costs and returns. In ordinary circumstances farmers do not farm in ways that cause their yields to decline in successive years (Netting, 1993). Nevertheless, increased livelihood stress due, for example, to a severe downturn in the market price of the output of a cash crop, a labour shortage, or civil breakdown, may result in the neglect of routine conservation practices.

Non-routine conservation activities are deterred if the true opportunity cost of labour to the household is high. This may occur for several reasons, for example, (1) when the labour market is not well developed locally, (2) when able-bodied household members migrate long distances for wage work, or (3) when inflexibility in the gender division of labour causes women to experience absolute constraints on their availability of time. Due to these factors, even in a low-income country with widespread unemployment, farm households in particular locations can confront a high effective cost of labour time, curtailing their capacity to divert labour from recurrent survival activities into conservation activities.

On the benefit side of conservation, several reasons are commonly identified as reducing the motivation of the household to carry out specific conservation measures. These include: (1) severe livelihood stress, that is, extreme poverty and proneness to destitution or starvation, which corresponds to the 'survival calculus' already mentioned earlier; (2) insecurity of land tenure, typically resulting not from failures of customary tenure, but from failures by the state to institute workable tenure arrangements in newly settled zones; (3) high uncertainty surrounding future returns, resulting perhaps from civil breakdown; (4) low level of perceived returns due to falling real prices; and (5) high degrees of instability in market prices for farm inputs and outputs causing unduly high risk.

The conjunction of one or more of these adverse circumstances results in households having what economists call a 'high rate of time preference'. This means that future income streams are heavily discounted compared with current income; in other words, the achievement of current consumption is given high priority relative to future consumption levels. Insecurity and uncertainty are critical factors causing a high rate of time preference. Conversely, when households exhibit a 'low rate of time preference', future income streams are discounted less in household decisions, and more effort is likely to be placed in conservation activities (Pearce *et al.*, 1990).

A costs and returns framework at household level helps to dispel preconceived ideas that surround the custodianship of natural resources by poor farmers. It is not true that the poor are intrinsically prone to despoil and degrade their natural environments. It is much more common to encounter poor farmers carrying out resource conservation measures, such as ridging, terracing, rotations, mixed cropping, tree planting, and so on, than the reverse. However, an opposing mythology, that small farmers are always the good custodians of the environment, is not always true either. A variety of reasons arising out of markets or social dislocation can result in the balance of advantage being tipped in favour of neglecting conservation. It is evident that amongst the most significant of these is the withdrawal, erosion or decline of a stake in the future quality of the resource that is accessed or owned by the household. Institutional issues of land tenure and access to common property resources are important in this regard, and are examined below.

Livelihood diversification by rural households can evidently have different effects on local environments depending on the opportunities available and the strategies that are adopted to respond to those opportunities. In the livelihoods framework, this variability in cause and effect is to be expected. One trajectory is that growth of non-farm income sources, especially if accessible in remote rural areas, might reduce the need for landless rural dwellers to carry out extractive practices in local environments for their survival. This has been called the 'substitution of employment for the environment' and is quite a strong strand in the policy literature (e.g. Lipton, 1991). However, as discussed in Chapter 5, for settled agriculturalists it sometimes happens that the uptake of non-farm earning opportunities result in neglect of labour-intensive conservation practices due to the shortage of labour that ensues. An example of this is provided by Netting *et al.* (1989) in their discussion of different phases in the livelihood strategies of the Kofyar in Nigeria. Furthermore, in frontier areas, extensive methods of resource use (e.g. cattle ranching) are often adopted because land is extremely cheap compared to labour, and in such circumstances the availability of non-farm income earning opportunities may even reinforce rather than reduce the incentive to expand land holdings in order to undertake production on an extensive scale.

Sustainability, livelihoods, and diversity

Sustainability is a widely utilised but problematic concept that recurs in discussions about environmental resources and human livelihoods. Such are the problems concerning its usage that one respectable economics source is moved to comment that 'it would be difficult to find another field of research endeavour in the social sciences that has displayed such intellectual regress' (Dasgupta and Maler, 1995: 2393). Difficulties with the concept of sustainability arise from its objectives (what is it that is deemed desirable to sustain?), the level or scale to which it applies (species, ecosystems, biological zones, social systems, the planet?), and its objective or subjective character (does it describe the objective conditions for the persistence of certain attributes, or desirable outcomes that ought to be promoted according to widely agreed subjective goals?). The following treatment traces a particular path through this maze with no claim to its superiority over any number of other possible paths, but with the intention of arriving at some preliminary conclusions regarding the prevalent notion of sustainable rural livelihoods (D. Carney, 1998; Scoones 1998).

Sustainability attempts to convey continuity in the very long term of the capacity of a system to reproduce itself or expand over time. In an ecosystem context, this refers to biomass and species diversity, but in its application to human needs, it means sustaining outputs available for human consumption, and therefore the capacity of a resource or system to keep up the same or increase its contribution to human welfare and well-being. It is taken as obvious that this refers to a long-term trend, not to annual or cyclical variations around that trend. Variations around a trend describe a system's stability rather than its sustainability. In the ecological literature, the concept of resilience introduced in Chapter 3 above is an integral part of the larger notion of sustainability (Holling, 1973). Resilience refers to the capacity of the system to 'bounce back' in the context of stress or disturbance by natural events or human agency. Put another way, it means the system's ability to recuperate from natural and human perturbations (Altieri, 1995).

One scale to which the notion of sustainability has been applied is that of the human exploitation of renewable natural resources such as fisheries, forests, underground aquifers and so on. For example, the sustainable yield of a fishery might be defined as the annual catch that maximises long run output without causing an irreversible decline in the fish population. Likewise, the sustainable harvest of the rattan (used to make cane furniture) that grows wild in the forests of Borneo, is the level of harvest that allows plants to regenerate so that harvesting can be continued at the same or increased level in subsequent years. Used in this sense, it is clear that sustainability cannot apply to non-renewable resources like mineral deposits and oil reserves that are, by definition, depleted by human extraction.

Even at this apparently uncontroversial level, sustainability can soon run into difficulties of interpretation. This is because human agency causes indirect dynamic interactions in natural ecosystems with unforeseeable consequences. Harvesting of one resource (e.g. a particular type of fish) may result in large changes in the behaviour of allied species that exhibit complementary or predatory relations with the species being harvested. This may result in any one of a multiplicity of unknown outcomes such as, for example, larger catches of a different fish species also favoured in human consumption; the emergence to prominence of an inedible species; or the occurrence of a toxic plankton 'bloom' that kills a wide variety of living organisms in the surrounding lake or ocean.

More generally, sustainability specified in terms of the carrying capacity of natural resources has proved inaccurate as a description of the dynamic processes of adaptation and change that occur in ecosystems (Leach and Mearns, 1996). Carrying capacity presupposes equilibrium states for ecological or other systems to which deviations can be compared, for example, grass populations at sustainable levels of grazing compared with those associated with overgrazing. The 'new ecology' no longer accepts the existence of these equilibrium states, and prefers to recognise that all ecosystems are in continuous processes of adaptation to the perturbations and shocks that they confront, with or without human action being implicated.

Moving away from the scale of a single renewable resource, an important strand of the sustainability literature has been concerned with farming systems, typically under the rubric of 'sustainable agriculture'. Some authors have interpreted this as being principally about achieving steady rises in farm productivity over time (e.g. Lynam and Herdt, 1992). This requires technical change and intensification of resource use, including the substitution of chemical for organic inputs. However, other authors would profoundly disagree with such a definition, being more concerned with the interaction of the farming system with the adjacent environment, and the deleterious side-effects of the growing use of pesticides, herbicides and fertilisers on farms. On this latter tack, sustainable agriculture is more closely associated with the move away from chemical inputs, and has its purest manifestation in the advocacy of organic farming. Yet another view of sustainable agriculture derives from the notion of farming as an agroecological system, within which resilience is enhanced by system diversity (Altieri, 1995).

At an even more aggregate scale, but still within the realm of human-environment interactions, sustainable development has been defined in terms of the living standards of future generations not being compromised through environmental depletion by the current generation (Brundtland, 1987: 43). This raises philosophical issues about the moral obligations of the current generation to future generations that are far from clear-cut (Tisdell, 1988; Pasek, 1992). It also provokes economic questions concerning inter-generational comparisons of material welfare that give rise to some scepticism about its value as a guide to economic policy (Beckerman, 1992). Related points are that (1) the current generation cannot prejudge the tastes and preferences of future generations; (2) technology is changing continuously so that the necessity for conserving some types of resource now may become irrelevant in the future; and (3) when economic growth is occurring future generations will have higher income, and therefore more options, than the current generation.

A refinement of the Brundtland definition is to consider the environment as a gigantic capital stock, and then to define sustainable development as development that ensures that this capital stock does not decline over time (Pearce *et al.*, 1989). Some economists concur with the idea of treating the environment as a capital stock, that is, as a set of natural assets to complement physical, human and social assets (Dasgupta and Maler, 1995), and this is the position also taken in the livelihoods approach of this book. However, they would point out that almost any conceivable development path involves substitution occurring within and between different asset categories, so that sustainable human development does not necessarily require sustainability of individual natural assets.

The foregoing approaches to sustainability share a common entry point which is that the concept should apply to objective, preferably measurable, processes and outcomes. This is so whether the scale is the single renewable resource, agroecological systems (Altieri, 1995), farming systems (Lynam and Herdt, 1992), or overall social and economic development (Pearce *et al.*, 1989). A different approach is to pose sustainable development as a set of desirable attributes of environmental and social change. Reed (1996), for example, defines sustainable development as improving the quality of human life while living within the carrying capacity of supporting ecosystems. 'This definition of sustainable development is a normative concept that embodies standards of judgement and behaviour to be respected as the human community seeks to satisfy its needs of survival and well-being.' (ibid., 33). Reed's definition has economic, social and environmental dimensions, and includes factors such as labour-intensive growth, distributional equity, gender equity, provision of social services, full valuation of natural resources in development projects, and limiting the consumption of renewable resources to their regenerative rates.

Some serious flaws in the concept of sustainability emerge from this partial review of its attributes at different scales of aggregation and across different horizontal ranges of natural and social change (see also Box 6.2). One unresolved difficulty is that sustainability becomes progressively more difficult to describe as scale increases, due to the changing balance of endogenous *vs.* exogenous influences on system dynamics. Thus, for farming systems, for example, it is one thing to describe the farm-level agronomic interactions leading to plant growth and crop yields as sustainable, but quite another to describe the entire farm sector, the national market for farm outputs, or the world market in agricultural commodities as sustainable (Lynam and Herdt, 1992). In addition, sustainability is not transferable across hierarchies of scale (Goldman, 1995). For example, the achievement of sustainability at the scale of maize production using organic methods is no guarantee of sustainability in the higher order scale of the livelihoods of maize farmers. Meanwhile, the subjective definitions of sustainable development on the large scale are susceptible to such wide variation in prioritisation and emphasis, according to changing popular views on a wide range of development topics, that they become practically vacuous for policy purposes.

The notion of 'sustainable rural livelihoods' emerges in part from ecological definitions of sustainability, and in part from economic and social development preoccupations with poverty, vulnerability and food security. On the ecological side, it is based on the definition by Conway (1985), that 'sustainability is the ability of a system to maintain productivity in spite of a major disturbance, such as is caused by intensive stress or a large perturbation.' This definition was originally applied to describing the sustainability of agroecological systems (Conway, 1985; 1987). It distinguishes two different types of threat to the maintenance of system productivity, namely stress, which is defined as 'a frequent, sometimes continuous, relatively small, predictable force having a large cumulative effect', and shock, which is defined as 'a force that was relatively large and unpredictable' (Conway and Barbier, 1990).

The proximity of this terminology to ideas about livelihoods is immediately apparent. Livelihood systems likewise confront adverse trends and sudden shocks. Moreover, for poor rural people in remote locations, it may seem that these stresses and shocks coincide with those of the agroecological systems on which they depend for survival. Therefore, it is a relatively small step to define a sustainable livelihood as one that can cope with stress and shocks, and displays resilience when faced with adverse events. This is the definition of a sustainable livelihood found in several sources and already alluded to in the context of the livelihood definition given in Chapter 1 (Ahmed and Lipton, 1997; Scoones, 1998). In its favour, this definition has the virtue of being less ambitious than the all-embracing idea of sustainable development. It is also somewhat less susceptible to widely varying subjective interpretations, since describing the factors that enable rural households to maintain living standards in the presence of pressures and sudden shocks restricts the field of enquiry in some of its dimensions.

Diversity arises in several different branches of the sustainability literature, and is typically regarded as contributing to greater resilience. This is true, for example, of ecological interpretations of resilience in natural systems. Here, biological diversity permits complementarities between species in such processes as nutrient formation, nutrient uptake, and species reproduction; and, in addition, it confers reduced risk of irreversible ecosystem change from natural events such as frost or insect infestation. These same benefits recur with respect to farming systems in the agroecological literature (Altieri, 1995). Here, not only does crop specialisation greatly increase the susceptibility to disaster of monocrop production systems, but also intensive use of chemical inputs (fertilizers, herbicides, disease-control chemicals, pesticides) is required by monocrop systems in order to substitute for benefits that could have been achieved via system diversity. Note that varietal diversity does not necessarily prevent devastation of individual species by, for example, pests or disease; what it does do is contribute to system level resilience. This is a further example of non-transferability across scales of sustainability. Within a diverse system, an individual species or activity may not be sustainable while the sustainability of the system as a whole is assisted by diversity.

Following a similar line of reasoning, diverse livelihood systems might be expected to offer greater protection against erosion or catastrophe than undiverse ones. In this sense, livelihood diversification may be thought of as contributing positively to sustainable rural livelihoods. It is important to note, however, that non-transferability across scales of sustainability continues to apply. For a diverse rural livelihood to be sustainable it is not necessary for individual components of the livelihood to exhibit sustainability. For example, livelihood diversification that involves the migration of young, male labour to urban jobs

Box 6.2. Stress, shocks and sustainability in African agriculture

A paper by Goldman (1995) provides a critical review of sustainability with particular emphasis on its meaning as applied to farming and livestock production systems in sub-Saharan Africa. An empirical approach to sustainability is advocated which seeks to identify factors and processes that enhance or threaten the sustainability of agricultural activities, yielding three basic questions (p. 298): (1) What are we trying to sustain? (2) How do we know whether something is or is not sustainable? (3) What are the main threats to sustainability for the things we want to sustain?

For the purpose of addressing these questions, a working definition of sustainability is adopted as 'the continuance or persistence of an identified quality, activity, or system over a given period of time' (p. 301)

Having explored this definition with respect to crop, livestock and larger socio-economic systems in Africa, Goldman arrives at two main conclusions. The first is that 'The things we want to sustain comprise a hierarchy of attributes, components, and systems at increasing scales' (p. 291), and, moreover, the sustainability of higher order systems is not necessarily dependent on sustaining lower order component sub-systems due to substitutions that more complex or large-scale systems are able to make. The second is that extreme perturbations (i.e. shocks) are a more important source of lack of sustainability than is recognised in the literature, while adverse trends (i.e. stress factors such as soil erosion) are much less important.

Investigation of the causes of major crop declines and disappearances was used to test the nature of threats to crop system sustainability. Evidence on such events examined in Nigeria and Kenya covered the decline or disappearance of 25 crops in five different rural locations. The three main causes of these declines were found to be pests and diseases; substitutions due to changes in economic circumstances; and, least significantly, declines in soil fertility or land shortage. In other words, shocks were found to be more important than adverse trends in the majority of cases.

Many crops disappeared because they were devastated by pest or disease outbreaks, for example root rot disease of cocoyams in West Africa and aphid attacks on cowpeas in eastern Kenya. Others disappeared due to economic substitution factors that are rarely given due credence in the sustainable agriculture literature, for example, responses by farmers to changes in domestic or export prices, and changing consumption preferences within farming communities themselves.

Livestock debates about sustainability have been permeated by the notion of carrying capacity, implying incremental processes by which the capacity of the environment to support livestock populations would deteriorate over time. However, an examination by Goldman of 17 major events or phases of livestock decline in Africa during the twentieth century revealed that drought, famine, disease, locusts and civil wars (including ethnic conflicts and revolutions) were the principal reasons for drastic reductions in livestock numbers.

Goldman observes (p. 325) that 'The literature on sustainability and sustainable agriculture has focused on an increasingly holistic agenda of desirable objectives. Even if one concurs with the agenda, it is difficult to demonstrate that these desirable conditions have been functionally related to sustainability. Virtuous societies, admirable social attributes, and management systems that husband and conserve resources have not historically proven more sustainable than have less commendable societies, systems, or conditions. Neither have resource conserving practices necessarily conferred sustainability on human systems at a larger scale.'

Critically, most of the extreme events that have undermined sustainability 'had comparable effects on both well and poorly managed farms and on areas of both high and low land use stress' (p. 329). Moreover, 'household strategies to increase resilience [via diversifying income sources] may conflict with achievement of an optimal level of resource management.' It is important to acknowledge not just that this is what rural households are doing, but that this is an entirely sensible response 'given that the primary threat to survival of the household systems is from extreme events rather than from incremental resource or land degradation.'

may result in the abandonment of labour intensive forms of soil conservation such as terracing.

In the insightful study summarised in Box 6.2 above, Goldman (1995) examines crop-scale and livelihood-scale cases of system failure in sub-Saharan Africa, drawing on a wide range of empirical case-studies. The research leads to a rejection of the Conway and Barbier (1990) hypothesis that sustainability is compromised more by stress factors than by shocks. It is found that in almost all documented cases, the disappearance of crops from African farming systems was due to shock factors, principally pests, diseases, or sharp changes in relative market prices. Likewise, African rural livelihood failures are not due to the stress factors of resource degradation in soils, water, and rangeland. Rather, they are predominantly due to the shock factors of drought and civil strife, these two factors often coinciding to produce really catastrophic collapses in the livelihood strategies being followed up to that point.

It is probable that the capability of human populations to adapt to changes that occur gradually underlies these findings. The gradual deterioration of an individual livelihood component typically gives scope for substitutions to be made in resources, farm outputs or activities; whereas shocks do not permit such a process of adaptation. This may have some important implications for rural poverty reduction policies, in that increasing the scope for adaptation is perhaps more important than trying to prevent, at least by outside agency, underlying slow changes in the quality of environmental resources. Concomitantly, safety nets need to be in place that can be mobilised quickly when large-scale shocks occur in livelihood systems.

Resource management institutions and livelihoods

The discussion thus far has considered livelihood interactions with natural resources in the absence of the institutions that permit access to such resources. Institutions in this context mean the socially accepted rules that determine access to natural resources. Such rules may be written and formal, as for example, in the legally sanctioned ownership of private property, or in laws prohibiting the utilisation of certain resources (the outlawing of the ivory trade is an international example). Other rules may be customary but still relatively formal, such as the adjudication of land ownership disputes by village chiefs or councils. Still others may reflect socially acceptable behaviour, or its converse, deriving from belonging to rural communities. Institutions also include the rules of inheritance that can have a large impact on the evolution of access patterns to land over time.

Resource access institutions are important for describing rural livelihoods. Much writing in agricultural development appears to have in mind an ideal type of owner-occupier farmer, owning sufficient land for family survival, and, with technological progress, being able to increase living standards from farming alone. This stereotype is misleading on many counts, amongst which land tenure systems are certainly one. Private freehold tenure is prevalent in some regions (Asia, Latin America), but not in others (Africa). Where it exists, it is often associated with highly unequal land ownership structures, such that the majority of small farming households are agricultural tenants rather than owners. Where it does not exist in law, as in much of sub-Saharan Africa, *de facto* ownership deriving from well established local understandings of family and kinship rights over land is combined with a documented degree of flexibility over land access. In addition, common property is widely prevalent in developing countries, with collective access often overlapping and merging with private access in complex ways.

Research on land tenure and livelihoods in sub-Saharan Africa emphasises the significance of flexibility as an attribute permitting land access arrangements to adapt to changing pressures and circumstances in the rural economy (Shipton and Goheen, 1992). In this respect, it is usually inaccurate to portray land tenure as corresponding to fixed types of access, for example, private ownership or

common property. In many instances, even when private ownership is insti-
tuted in law as the formal mechanism of land ownership, flexibility of access is
maintained by a proliferation of different tenancy arrangements. Where private
ownership does not constitute the fundamental legal basis of ownership rights
in land, as in much of sub-Saharan Africa, customary land access systems are
characterised by their capability to adapt over time. Access to land for crop cultivation and grazing must then be seen as a process, evolving in a social context,
and one that involves renegotiation between interested parties concerning
rights of access, and reinterpretation of previous, current and future access patterns (Berry, 1997).

This flexibility is not only true of sub-Saharan Africa, although much of the
writing that underscores it utilises African case-studies. Appearances often de-
ceive where land access and ownership is concerned. For example, the densely
populated island of Java in Indonesia appears to have a relatively egalitarian size
structure of land holdings deriving originally from customary law and later in-
scribed in private ownership. The true picture differs from this, however, due to
subsequent land purchases by mainly urban-based property owners. In practice,
a highly complex array of tenancy arrangements abounds in the Javanese rural
economy, including share cropping, sub-tenancy, pawning, labour contracts,
and many other land access devices. These practices create a high degree of flexibility of land access on the small scale by rural dwellers, but they also obscure
underlying patterns of land ownership, and they are prone to give a false impression of the asset status of the rural poor.

The point has been made with respect to sub-Saharan Africa that land is not
very often interpreted by its users in a private ownership mode of thought. Land
access is inextricably bound up with social affiliations that provide both the
framework and the security of land utilisation for different purposes (Shipton
and Goheen, 1992). These social affiliations may be extended resident families,
kinship lineages, villages, chiefdoms, or ethnic groups. They may take the form
of tightly knit local groups, or networks involving geographically extended
links, or categories of people sharing common interests in the manner by which
they obtain a livelihood. Land access often involves reciprocal obligations with
respect to other aspects of livelihoods. For example, Toulmin (1992) shows how,
in a village studied in rural Mali, a resident ethnic group, the Bambara, allow seasonal cattle grazing on village lands by another ethnic group, the Fulani, in a
context in which the Bambara supply well water to the Fulani for their cattle in
exchange for cattle dung which is used to fertilise the millet fields of the
Bambara.

This type of unwritten interchange of resources, services and goods typifies
rural livelihoods in rural sub-Saharan Africa and elsewhere. A common mistake
of outsiders who observe such arrangements is to assume that they are fixed and
'traditional', and therefore likely to disintegrate when local pressures on land or
external factors causes them no longer to function according to previous cus-

tom. However, such land access arrangements are seldom fixed in that sense; they come into being under circumstances that make it beneficial for all parties to comply with them, and they are modified or abandoned when they no longer fulfil the livelihood role which has resulted in their adoption in the first place. A process of adaptation takes place in which arrangements that no longer work very well are replaced by ones that work better under the changing circumstances that individuals and communities confront.

There exists an influential view that land rights must eventually gravitate towards private property in the process of social and economic change. One strand of this view is that a combination of population pressure and increased integration into markets results in the emergence of a land market and, therefore, *de facto* private property, even while customary tenure in theory prevails. Another strand is that the institution of private property is the only effective way of avoiding the problems of over-utilisation of land and other natural resources associated with common property (e.g. Demsetz, 1967). According to this way of thinking, private property ensures a private incentive to conserve resources and carry out environmentally sustainable land management practices. It also provides the security to encourage long-term investment in enhancing the productivity of land. In the absence of private property, these incentives are missing, and environmental deterioration inevitably takes place.

Many researchers have questioned the validity of these claims for the superiority of private property in efficiency and intertemporal conservation terms (see e.g. Platteau, 1996). It is pointed out that any type of property regime has to be socially acceptable in order to work in practice, otherwise rural social conflict will for certain negate any supposed efficiency advantages of land privatisation. There are several reasons for thinking that in the African context, private land titling and registration might prove disastrous for livelihoods, and have severely adverse consequences for poverty reduction and equity goals. Some of these reasons are that:

1. private titling would freeze land ownership patterns at the point of registration, thus removing the flexibility and adaptation that characterise customary tenure;
2. disputes over ownership and the legitimacy of title claims would be rife, and a long period of extreme uncertainty would ensue while claims were debated in the customary and legal dispute settlement systems;
3. land registration would inevitably involve dispossession of individuals and families that hold customary access as part of complex social interchanges, but that are not part of the core social group by which ownership subsequently comes to be defined;
4. the position of women as land users is particularly problematic in this respect, and dispossession of *de facto* women landholders would inevitably be widespread in the context of most African legal and customary heredity systems;

5. land registration would without doubt exacerbate inequities of asset ownership and distribution: experiments in land titling have demonstrated
   unequivocally that the rich, the powerful, the educated, and the better-
   informed are those that are able to navigate the legal complexities of registration and are therefore those that are able to manipulate the registration
   process to their advantage;
6. the maintenance of land ownership records is a complex legal and administrative undertaking that is far beyond the capacity of already over-extended
   central and local administrations in Africa, and failures in recording ownership transfers, as also their falsification, would again tend to favour the ad-
   vantaged over the disadvantaged in land ownership disputes.

There is evidence from Kenya, an African country that has private freehold title
as its legal framework for land ownership, that freehold registration primarily affects land that had already been alienated from its customary access rights in the
colonial period. This is land that was owned by white settler farmers, and has subsequently been purchased and sold in a freehold land market. In rural areas where
land was not alienated historically in this way, registration of ownership title is
seldom used as a device for recording changes in land access, and research reveals
that land exchanges that are formally registered have a high likelihood of being
misrecorded or unrecorded in the land registration archives (Platteau, 1996).

In a study undertaken in Ghana, Kenya and Rwanda, Place and Hazell (1993)
investigated whether indigenous land rights systems inhibited the uptake of
new technology in the form of greater land improvements, input use, access to
credit, and crop yields. The authors discover that the widely varying land rights
observed in rural areas of these countries did not have any explanatory power regarding the adoption of agricultural improvements. They therefore concluded
that land registration and titling programmes should not be prioritised in rural
development policy in sub-Saharan Africa.

The outcome of these and related considerations is that the blanket imposition of private freehold property, as advocated by some enthusiasts, is a flawed
undertaking that underestimates the benefits of heterogeneity and misunder-
stands the adaptability of customary allocation procedures. It is widely agreed
by researchers who do not accept the private property advocacy that customary
access is not replicable by administrative command from above, and should be
left well alone, except, perhaps, in collaborating with local level institutions to
devise clearer and more timely methods for settling disputes.

Broadly similar arguments pertain in this context to common property resources. There is no unique way of defining common property as an institution,
except that it is characterised as lying somewhere within the spectrum that runs
from private ownership at one extreme to open access at the other. An earlier literature on the commons tended to confuse common property with open access,
and to advocate the privatisation of common property resources due to a perceived in-built economic logic for commons to be over-exploited (Hardin, 1968;

Ellis, 1993: 262–270). Common property is not, however, an open access resource. It typically exists in the specific locational context of villages and rural communities, and it comprises the land, water, trees, grazing etc. which are regarded as within the purview of village-level decision-making but are not allocated to the use of individual families or households. Land as a resource may switch back and forth between individual and common property according to season and the use to which it is put.

Common property has been shown to play a disproportionately important role in the livelihoods of the landless rural poor, by providing them with access to resources to which they would otherwise be denied due to their landless status (Jodha, 1990). In many locations customary common property has been eroded by privatisation, rising population density, road construction and so on; however, there are many instances of it arising anew when local communities confront a problem of regulating access to a resource that is broadly beneficial to the community as a whole (e.g. Ostrom, 1990). The common property solution to local resource access problems can only arise in the context of power devolved to district and village levels; it is inhibited by centralised state authority, and common property does not lend itself to regulation according to inflexible administrative rules devised outside its local social context.

Land tenure and property regimes play critical roles in the interface between livelihoods and the environment. On the one hand, flexibility of access to land and other resources contributes to the range of options that are open to livelihoods under pressure, and in that sense it can play a similar role in support of the incomes of the poor to widening the range of non-farm options for income generation. On the other hand, the environment is itself composed of property regimes, some of which encourage or facilitate conservation or enhancement of the natural resource base, and some of which have opposing effects. It has become increasingly clear that the state plays a pivotal role. This is because in most developing countries, it is the state that is owner of the land that has so far not been utilised for human settlement, or that is very sparsely populated, or that is in designated national parks, conservation areas and so on. It is the state that allocates forestry concessions, determines the conditions under which settlers can purchase or register private ownership of land, promotes or does not promote frontier settlement, and encourages or discourages devolved decision-making capabilities at local levels.

Diversified livelihoods and environments

It is clear at this point that there is no simple way in which livelihood diversification relates to environmental concerns in developing countries. As with other dimensions of the causes, effects, and attributes of diversification there are multiple processes at work giving rise to many different tendencies and outcomes.

Nevertheless, the preceding discussion has helped to clarify some significant aspects of this relationship. One important result is that sustainability of rural livelihoods is not the same thing as sustainability of particular ecosystems, even though a considerable amount of overlap might be expected between these two scales of sustainability. This is due to a phenomenon that is as much a characteristic of ecosystems as it is of livelihoods, namely, that sustainability of a lower order sub-component of a larger system is neither a necessary nor a sufficient condition for the sustainability of the larger system itself because of the complementarities and substitutions that the larger system is able to make in the process of ensuring its own sustainability. However, one result that seems to emerge quite strongly from sustainability considerations is that diversity is an important property of sustainable systems under conditions of high risk and uncertainty. This is because diversity increases resilience, the capability of the system to recover from adverse trends and shocks.

A second important finding arises from the examination of poverty-environment relations. Here, it was concluded that the responsibility of the poor for environmental degradation has been vastly overdrawn in some quarters. Nevertheless, poverty, livelihoods and the environment interact with each other, especially through the asset portfolio of the poor, and their ability to substitute between assets. The abundant asset held by the poor is their own labour. Where this asset can be combined with other assets, either through ownership or secure rights of access to obtain a viable livelihood, the poor are no more likely to despoil the environment than anyone else. The position in this regard improves the greater the substitution possibilities that exist between assets and activities, thus making livelihoods more resilient, as in the points made about sustainable livelihoods above. However, where no such access is available, or where future outcomes reach such a degree of uncertainty that only immediate survival becomes the imperative, then the poor may act in ways that diminish the future viability for human needs of certain environmental resources.

Property regimes are important in this overall picture. The latter responses tend to occur in situations where no viable common property regime is in place to regulate individual access according to local social priorities. This absence of common property rules, or their neglect, may occur due to active discouragement by the state, misplaced centralisation of local levels of management that could not possibly be organised by the state, social divisions at local levels resulting from widening disparities of wealth and income, abuses of power, and corruption by state or local officials. Private property is not necessarily a solution, and is widely discredited as a policy proposal in the sub-Saharan African context. The advent of devolved district administrations, set up so that the poor can participate in decisions that effect their livelihoods, possibly holds out better prospects for solving environmental difficulties at local levels.

Livelihood diversification into non-farm activities and income sources can have two rather different and, in some respects, opposing outcomes for the environment. On the one hand, it may take the pressure off those environmental resources that comprise collecting and gathering by rural dwellers. Collecting and gathering, for example, firewood collection, charcoal production, gathering wild fruits and vegetables, hunting wild animals, and so on are typically amongst the lowest return activities in the rural economy. Therefore the advent of alternative activities providing a higher return to labour is predicted to result in switches of labour time out of these activities. Moreover, access to higher cash incomes can result in substitutions in consumption, for example, between kerosene and firewood used for cooking.

On the other hand, diversification involves withdrawing labour from the rural household. It has been observed in some case-studies that this results in neglect of previous conservation practices on farms such as the labour-intensive maintenance of terraces and irrigation canals. However, counter examples to this exist, so that it remains a matter for investigation in differing circumstances, whether, in what circumstances, and in what sequence, earnings from non-farm activities become converted back into farm investment in the medium to long term.

Summary

This chapter situates environment and sustainability issues within the livelihoods framework, again paying attention to diversification as a livelihood strategy. The livelihood framework incorporates the environment under the rubric of natural capital, as well as via resource access institutions that are part of the mediating processes in the livelihoods approach.

Poverty-environment interactions are discussed, emphasising especially the weakness of superficial arguments about poverty as a cause of environmental degradation, and the need to achieve an understanding of people's substitution capabilities between assets and activities in order to explain the pressure placed on particular environmental resources by human agents in pursuit of their survival. Markets as well as social factors play an important mediating role, especially the way labour markets work in providing or failing to provide alternative means of survival, and the nearby or distant location of wage earning and self-employment opportunities.

The problematic concept of sustainability is examined, not just because the term tends to be utilised more in an environmental context than elsewhere, but also because the livelihoods framework used in this book is often presented as a 'sustainable rural livelihoods' approach. It is unclear, in the end, what additional depth of understanding is provided by the idea of sustainability over and above concepts such as stability, resilience, sensitivity, security, and adaptability also deployed with respect to the viability of rural livelihoods in the long run. Sustainability is especially prone to misunderstanding about the key role of substitution in complex systems, and this is shown by considering alternative scales of its application—e.g. from the agroecological system, to the livelihoods system, to the economic system at large—where it is manifestly not the case that sustainability of each successively larger and more complex system depends on the prior sustainability of all its component sub-systems.

The chapter considers land tenure institutions as one facet of mediating processes in the access of the rural poor to environmental assets. The case for private ownership often advocated as a means of ensuring natural asset conservation is shown to misinterpret the role of customary tenure in allowing flexible access to critical livelihood resources. Property regimes that protect or facilitate the husbandry of environmental assets tend to arise in the context of power devolved to rural communities; they are inhibited by central state authority and by inflexible administrative procedures that cannot adapt to local circumstances.

Enhanced options for substituting between low and higher return uses of household labour should reduce gathering activities that deplete certain types of environmental resource, for example, trees used for firewood, both through a direct labour allocation effect and through consumption substitution effects. The withdrawal of labour from farm households may have short-term negative effects on conservation activities, but in societies that prize rural land ownership (whether private or customary) not just as a short-term productive asset but as an indicator of social status, and as a social security fallback in the face of urban job insecurity, this effect is unlikely to persist in the longer term. There are also important gender dimensions to these relationships to which we turn in the next chapter.

— CHAPTER 7 —

Gender and Rural Livelihoods

It is often said that a book like this should not have a separate chapter on gender because gender ought to be fully integrated into all the relationships under discussion. Well, this may be ideally so, but pausing every two or three paragraphs to say 'and the gender implications of this are as follows' does run the risk of representing gender as merely an accessory to other concerns. Gender is, of course, an integral and inseparable part of rural livelihoods, but given that this book has not been written solely as a gender work, the next best thing, even though open to reproof, is to provide a space where the gender dimensions of livelihood diversity can be examined in a focused and reasonably integrated way. That is the purpose of this chapter.

Gender relations are defined here as the social construction of roles and relationships between women and men (e.g. Baden and Goetz, 1998). These socially constructed roles are usually unequal in terms of power, decision-making, control over events, freedom of action, ownership of resources, and so on. For this reason, gender is fundamentally about power, subordination and inequality, and it is therefore also about ways of changing these to secure greater equality in all its social manifestations for women. The gender approach recognises the vast diversity of relations between men and women across cultures, but nevertheless asserts the lessening of the social inequalities experienced by women as an overriding goal. In contrast, postmodern critics see women's subjective construction of themselves as culturally specific, and they therefore deny any universality in the experience of gender inequalities (for discussion see Jackson, 1997; Baden and Goetz, 1998). This line of thinking is not, however, pursued here.

While gender seems to have been comprehensively taken on board by agencies involved in development policy and practice, the manner in which this has occurred deserves careful scrutiny. In particular, the development profession has found it much easier to assimilate gender through its links to other development objectives than to challenge directly the social and institutional mechanisms by which gender inequalities are perpetuated over time. Thus support to women is often legitimised indirectly by arguing that it will reduce poverty, or increase economic efficiency, or improve environmental management, or lower population growth. In other words, gender as a policy criterion is interpreted as an *instrument* for achieving poverty, efficiency, environment or population goals; and by adopting this approach gender equality is seldom placed up front as the leading goal in its own right. In this sense, the integration of gender into the procedures of aid donors, NGOs, and government agencies responsible for devising and implementing development policies and projects is a lot less threatening to prevailing social conventions and institutional rigidities than appearances may at times suggest.

This distinction between gender as an approach to promoting greater equality between men and women, and support for women as a means to achieving other goals, is an important one for rural livelihoods because interventions directed at improving the welfare of rural women often have unintended side-effects due to neglect of the impact on project success of prevailing unequal gender relations. A by now classic case-study illustrating this was the attempt in The Gambia in the 1980s to raise women's incomes by promoting irrigated, high yielding varieties of rice, traditionally regarded in that country as a crop under female control. Not only did the rice projects result in loss of control over rice production to males, but in the ensuring struggle between men and women over labour inputs and crop rights, the ownership of rice-growing lands passed from women to men. This case-study is cited a lot because it was extensively written up for publication by a number of researchers (e.g. J. A. Carney, 1988; Webb, 1991). However, it is only one of numerous instances in which the supposed gains of women-centred development initiatives are captured by men, through the unmodified operation of prevailing gender relations.

A focus on gender means differentiating the livelihoods of women compared to men, which has not been done in any systematic way so far in this book. The household as a construct, no matter how flexibly defined with respect to its residential and spatial composition (see Chapter 1), represents a problem in this regard because it has proved exceedingly difficult at both theoretical and empirical levels to capture at one and the same time both the separate and the joint nature of resources, distribution and consumption within households. Economists have made some progress in moving away from the unitary concept of the household, to bargaining models and to collective approaches that infer intra-household sharing rules from empirical evidence rather than according to deductive logic. However, these economic models remain analytically static in nature, and they are unable to capture the renegotiation and adaptation of gender roles that occur in practice when households are caught up in changing circumstances that threaten the viability of their existing livelihoods (Hart, 1995; 1997).

This chapter explores gender and rural livelihoods, first, through examining in greater depth the gender dimension of the three aspects of the livelihoods approach and of diversification as a strategy treated in the preceding three chapters, that is, poverty, agriculture and the environment. Gender makes its appearance in all three of these development policy areas in the guise of an instrumental role for women being discovered that is thought to further goals specific to each area on its own, that is, reducing poverty, raising farm efficiency, and improving natural resource management. Second, the chapter considers the gender differentiated operation of labour markets as a cause of the different livelihood diversification options experienced by men and women. Third, the chapter discusses the asset basis of livelihoods from a gender perspective, emphasising especially unequal ownership and rights to land between men and women. The final section of the chapter draws these various threads together to reach some preliminary conclusions concerning gender and livelihood diversification.

Gender and poverty

Several key issues concerning the livelihood relationships between rural women and men arise in the context of poverty and its incidence in the rural economy (Kabeer, 1997a). One proposition is that rural women are poorer, on average, than rural men, and this itself has two different strands. A first strand is that female-headed households are poorer, for a variety of reasons, than male-headed households. A second strand is that inequality in the distribution of consumption within the household makes women, in general, poorer than men irrespective of the headship of the household. A second proposition is that additional cash income obtained by the household has quite different effects on the welfare of women and children, depending on whether the recipient of that income is male or female.

These propositions are important for the understanding of rural livelihoods, both analytically and for policy purposes. If it is true that women are already, or are becoming, impoverished compared to men, then the reasons for this need to be well understood in order to discover the policy levers by which the even worse poverty of women can be reversed. Aside from intra-household distributional factors, these reasons must lie in the construction of women's livelihoods compared to those of men, even allowing for the livelihood overlaps that occur within the household. This means, within the livelihoods framework, that women are disadvantaged with respect to either assets or activities, or some combination of both, linked to inequalities of access to resources and income generating opportunities. Gender inequalities with respect to assets and labour markets are examined in later sections of this chapter. Here, the focus is initially on whether the greater poverty of women compared to men is adequately substantiated, and on intra-household distributional issues.

It is relevant at this point to recall from Chapter 4 that poverty is typically measured by economists from household level income and expenditure data, with adult equivalent average per capita expenditure being the preferred measure of material well-being. It follows from this that most poverty data is only able to distinguish the welfare levels of women separately from those of men by using the sex of the household head as a proxy variable for well-being comparisons between men and women. It is not feasible from household level data to distinguish welfare by sex for individuals, because household-level consumption is averaged across individuals.

According to various influential documents (e.g. World Bank, 1989; Jazairy, 1992), female-headed households are found to be poorer than male-headed households, and indeed the people within such households were for some time dubbed the 'poorest of the poor' (Tinker, 1990). The policy inference follows that assisting female-headed rural households to raise their standard of living will have the dual beneficial effects both of reducing gender inequalities in incomes, and of reducing poverty overall. Thus measures that increase the incomes of rural women are justified by reference not to gender inequality, but to their role in contributing to rural poverty reduction. Moreover, this conclusion is reinforced by empirical observation of a rising trend in female-headed households due both to an increased incidence of marital breakdown and to the long-term migration of males to urban areas in pursuit of non-farm wage incomes (Buvinic and Gupta, 1997).

A number of livelihood considerations can be invoked in support of the idea that female-headed households could be an especially disadvantaged social category. Such households are typically found to be smaller than male-headed households. They therefore contain less available labour for farm work and other income generating activities. The crop area that can be cultivated and managed by them is correspondingly reduced. The woman who is also a household head is likely to be highly time constrained by domestic responsibilities and unable, therefore, to do much farm work or to participate in off-farm and non-farm labour markets. Women may end up worse off than men from marital disintegration due to the unequal division of assets on family break-up (Bruce, 1989). They may, also, lose social status in their communities, and the reciprocal contributions to family resources that go with that status.

However, neither the evidence nor the logic of the association between poverty and female headship is uncontroversial (Kabeer, 1997b; Chant, 1997; Jackson, 1998a; 1998b; see also the case-study given in Box 7.1). The tendency to equate uncritically extreme poverty and social disadvantage with women has been termed the 'feminisation of poverty'. There is, in fact, conflicting evidence concerning the relative poverty of female-headed households, with a number of individual case-studies providing contrary evidence (Agarwal, 1986; Kennedy and Peters, 1992; Lloyd and Gage-Brandon, 1993). In addition, several difficulties surround the definition of female and male household headship, as these are defined in sample surveys. These include (1) the automatic assumption that a household is headed by the most senior male present, even though women can quite often head households containing senior males; (2) the confusion that arises between *de jure* and *de facto* female-headed households; (3) biases in the assignment of household heads in cultural contexts where headship is meaningless or where households have multiple heads.

These complications reduce confidence in the robustness of the statistical exercises that appear to demonstrate the relative poverty of female-headed households. In addition, there are important counter arguments to those advanced to explain the disadvantages of female headship. Many of these centre on inequalities of resource distribution within the household in contrast to inequalities of income across households, which is the basis of the female-headed household argument. Specifically, if membership of a male-headed household results in high inequality of consumption between females and males, then females may, in fact, be better off as independent household heads despite other disadvantages that accrue to that status. This proposition is difficult to substantiate empirically because very few studies have been done that accurately separate female from male consumption within households. Nevertheless, a lot of indirect evidence exists, especially in South Asia, for the relative deprivation of women and girl children within male-headed households.

It is widely agreed that existing methods for measuring or assessing poverty are inadequate for discovering gender inequalities of consumption within households. An outcome of this is that the depth of poverty is underestimated in conventional poverty studies (Kabeer, 1996). Nor do participatory methods necessarily overcome this problem, because most participatory methods do not allow the experience of women individually to emerge from group discussions, for a variety of different reasons (Kabeer, 1996; Jackson, 1998a). However, fragmentary evidence does seem to suggest that intra-household inequality of consumption between men and women is a more important source of gender inequality than the differences in average consumption between male- and female-headed households. But, in addition, there are highly variable cross-cultural differences in the incidence of intra-household inequality between men and women.

Linking this discussion to livelihood diversification, it is apparent that control over income streams coming into the household may make significant differences to the consumption patterns of men, women and children. This, again, is clearly an important gender relations issue, since the differential access of men and women to independent sources of cash income will depend on who in the household is able to diversify, and the control that is then achieved over income streams. The general hypothesis is that women are more likely than men to spend cash resources under their jurisdiction on basic household needs (Dwyer and Bruce, 1988; Alderman *et al.*, 1995; Kabeer, 1998). Another well-documented dynamic is that when women diversify and create new streams of income, men can interpret this as an opportunity to reduce or withdraw their financial contributions to the domestic budget.

This hypothesis is difficult to test, due to the sensitivity and complexity of its implied data requirements, but it receives support from some case-studies. For example, Mencher (1988) finds for sample households in South India that women spend cash income that comes into their hands wholly on family needs,

Box 7.1. Gender of household head, income and nutrition in Kenya and Malawi

A study undertaken at selected sites in Kenya and Malawi in the early 1990s demonstrated that the relationship between the gender of the household head, the level of income, and the nutritional status of the family is more complicated than the simple equating of female-headed households to greater poverty. Specifically, the food security and child nutrition status of the household depends not just on income level, but also on the uses to which income is put. If female headship of a household results in more income being spent on food and other essentials for family health, then it is possible that the food security and nutritional status of the household may exceed that of male-headed households despite overall income being lower.

Sample surveys were undertaken in rural locations in Kenya and Malawi. The Kenya research site was characterised by high-quality land, low population density, and a maize-sugarcane production mix. The Malawi research site was characterised by land scarcity and the dominance of maize and tobacco in farm output. Households in the sample surveys at both sites were distinguished between their male or female headship. Female headship was further distinguished between *de jure* female heads (legally or customarily recognised headship), and *de facto* female heads (households where the male was absent for more than 50 per cent of the time). In Malawi, this latter category was subdivided again between households with males working as migrants in South Africa and those with males absent within Malawi itself.

Table 7.1. Household characteristics by gender of head, Kenya and Malawi

	Kenya		Malawi	
	Male	Female	Male	Female
Household size	9.55	9.10	6.26	5.64
Adult males	2.00	1.43	1.29	0.40
Adult females	2.28	2.46	1.46	1.64
Children	5.28	5.22	3.51	3.60
Dependency ratio	1.23	1.34	1.28	1.76
Expenditures				
per capita	2,854.00	2,561.00	81.07	71.66
% food	76.00	80.00	62.00	66.00

Note: Expenditures are in KShs per annum for Kenya data and in Kwacha (for 10 months) for Malawi data. *Source*: Kennedy and Peters (1992: 1078).

Table 7.1 displays summary data derived from the sample surveys, simplified just to show the differences between male- and female-headed households. Some of the key results recorded in the table or arising from the further differentiation of female-headed households were as follows:

1. Male-headed households are larger than female-headed households, and, as expected, male-headed households have significantly more adult male members than female-headed households.
2. Differences between household size and composition between Kenya and Malawi reflect the prevalence of polygamy in the Kenya sample.
3. In both countries, male-headed households have more potential income earners than do female-headed households, and this is reflected in the differences in levels of the dependency ratio (the number of children per adult) between groups.
4. Given these differences in household composition, it is not surprising that male-headed households earn higher incomes than female-headed households, where expenditure is taken as a proxy for income.
5. However, when the data is disaggregated, not all female-headed households are poorer than male ones; in Malawi, for example, the highest per capita expenditure levels are among the female-headed, 'migrant' households, reflecting remittance income from males working in South Africa.
6. In both countries, the poorest households are the *de facto* female-headed households, excluding the migrant households mentioned above.
7. In both countries, female-headed households allocate a higher proportion of expenditures to food than male-headed households; and *de facto* female-headed households allocate the largest share of available income on food.
8. In both countries, children in *de facto* female headed households receive a higher proportion of total available household calories than children in other household groups.

These results demonstrate that household food security and child nutrition are not a simple function of total household income. The gender of the household decision maker makes a difference to the allocation of available income between different expenditures. In addition, female-headed households are not a homogeneous group. Different circumstances and behaviour were observed between *de jure*, *de facto*, and 'migrant' female-headed households in this study. The findings suggest that gender influences the quality of diets within households via the degree of control that women can exercise over income flows.

Source: Kennedy and Peters (1992).

while men, by contrast, tend to retain a significant proportion for personal consumption. Kennedy and Peters (1992) find in a Kenya sample that the share of total household income controlled by women has a positive and significant influence on the calory consumption of the household (Box 7.1). A similar finding is reported by D. Thomas (1990) for a sample of households in Brazil, where unearned income (e.g. remittances) in the hands of mothers, has a greater positive effect on family health indicators than the same income in the hands of fathers. The direction of these findings is also corroborated by Côte d'Ivoire data analysed by Hoddinott and Haddad (1995). While not contradicting these results, Hopkins et al. (1994) point to important seasonal aspects of income flows and their expenditure differentiated between men and women.

It has to be recognised, however, that the available evidence in this area is fragmented and its accuracy compromised by the typical inadequacy of the data that is collected at this level of detail, and the assumptions that are built into the statistical models from which results are derived. Harriss-White (1997) highlights this problem by referring to the different findings and policy conclusions regarding the different food consumption patterns of males and females (including children of both sexes) that have been derived by different researchers utilising the same dataset, collected by the International Crop Research Institute for the Semi-Arid Tropics (ICRISAT) in South India in the late 1970s. Five different researchers with access to this data set came up with five distinct, and sometimes opposing, sets of findings and conclusions.

In summary, considerations of gender deepen and extend the poverty dimension of the rural livelihoods approach. In particular, they point to inequalities between men and women in the experience of poverty, that is, within the rural population that is identified as falling below the poverty line measured according to conventional criteria. This inequality has tended to be statistically associated with the difference in income levels between female- and male-headed poor households, leading to the identification of female-headed households as a constituency meriting special attention for raising income levels. However, there are important flaws in the sequence of steps by which this policy conclusion is deduced. Many researchers consider that intra-household inequality of consumption between men and women is likely to be of greater significance than inter-household inequality based on the sex of the household head. In addition, it is possible that the intra-household distribution of money income between women and men makes a significant difference to patterns of household expenditure, with cash income in the hands of women being utilised primarily for family welfare purposes, while cash income in the hands of men is often retained for personal consumption expenditures.

Gender and agriculture

The significance of women's participation in agricultural production in developing countries has been appreciated ever since the publication of the classic contribution in this area by Ester Boserup (Boserup, 1970). Boserup put forward a simple threefold classification of farming systems according to the varying degrees of women's engagement in farm work. This classification comprised, first, high female participation combined with low technology in sub-Saharan Africa; second, low female participation associated with animal draft technology, hired labour, and cultural proscriptions on women's work outside the home; and, third, sharing of farm work between women and men associated with intensive cultivation, land scarcity and small farm size.

Women's roles in agriculture are of course much more heterogeneous than is suggested by this classification; they vary between different types of farming system, between ethnic groups that may be located adjacently to each other but have different gender divisions of labour, and between different levels of income and wealth within the same cultural systems. They also change over time, according to new pressures and opportunities, and the way gender relations adapt to these. Some of the earlier evidence regarding divisions of farm work between men and women is summarised in Ellis (1993: 179). This reveals the wide variations that can be observed in different contexts, as exemplified by a study in Bangladesh that exhibited a ratio of men's time in farming to women's time of 8 to 1 (Cain et al., 1979), compared to a study in Uganda where the reverse ratio of women's farm work time to men's was 1.23 to 1 (Hanger, 1973).

Gender inequalities make their mark in agriculture as they do in other facets of rural livelihoods. For example, women's pre-eminence in cultivation and harvesting in sub-Saharan Africa is not complemented by ownership of resources, by control over resource use, or by decision-making capabilities, all of which tend to remain firmly within the male sphere. In the following paragraphs, three agricultural aspects of gender are examined briefly in turn. The first concerns farm productivity and the adoption of new technology. The second considers the scope for women who are engaged in agriculture to undertake off-farm or non-farm income earning activities. The third considers the impact on women and on agriculture of patterns of migration by male members of farm households.

The common practice in sub-Saharan Africa is for women and men to have separate spheres of competence where agriculture is concerned. This often involves a division of cultivated plots, with women contributing labour time to crops that are grown on male-designated fields, but also being permitted to cultivate their own crops on fields that are assigned for this purpose. Of course there are many variations around this approximate theme. Labour time committed to women's plots tends to be gender specific, that is, the entire cycle of land clearing, sowing, weeding, and harvesting is undertaken by women, and in some instances, post-harvest sales and the income thus obtained also remain under women's control. By contrast, labour time deployed on male crops will tend to be gender-sequential, involving a division of labour for the different tasks in the agricultural calendar. Gender-sequential divisions of labour also tend to characterise women's engagement in agricultural production in regions other than sub-Saharan Africa. The distinction between gender-specific and gender-sequential farm work is attributable to Whitehead (1985).

The ability of women to respond to improved cultivation practices or new technology is limited by gender asymmetries in the sub-Saharan Africa case (Dey Abbas, 1997). First, women obtain their rights to cultivate fields almost exclusively through men. Women's independent ownership (or inalienable customary allocation) of land is negligible in sub-Saharan Africa, as elsewhere, a factor that is taken up again below. Second, it is usual for women's obligations to provide labour for male or homestead-designated fields to take precedence over their rights to engage in own-account farming or other income-generating activities. Third, income obtained by women from own-account activities could rarely, if ever, be utilised to purchase farm inputs or equipment since the cultural expectation in most cases is for that income to be used for family consumption needs.

These and many related factors mean that targeting women to achieve increases in farm output is a lot more complicated than simply directing advice and agricultural service facilities to women rather than men. Again here we have the distinction between tackling gender inequality directly and utilising a surrogate approach, which is to target women while having another end in view. In this instance, the end is to achieve rising efficiency in agricultural production, and support to women engaged in farming is adopted as the means for achieving this goal, at the same time, therefore, being able to point to the gender relevance of the policy being pursued. However, projects that have sought to achieve this dual purpose have run into all sorts of difficulties deriving from gender relations themselves (Dey Abbas, 1997: 250–258). These have included struggles between men and women over control of women's labour time, resulting in failures of projects to achieve their objectives, and loss by women of assets previously under their control.

Comparisons of productivity between men and women farmers in the sub-Saharan African context evidently have little meaning given the distinct circumstances under which each operates. The most productive fields tend to be allocated to joint household or male-specific outputs. Men are able to mobilise labour, including the women of the household, and have decision-making capabilities over inputs and investments. Men often produce high value crops for sale rather than staple food crops for home consumption. Plots wholly under the control of women are likely to differ with respect to most of these attributes, and in a simple comparison of yields or gross margins per hectare may exhibit apparently lower efficiency than joint or male fields. However, it would be quite erroneous to infer from this that women were less competent farmers than men, or that agricultural efficiency in general would be best served by targeting improvements on women's fields while neglecting gender relations.

It is often pointed out that women's obligations in the domestic sphere, and, in sub-Saharan Africa, in farming, leave little scope for diversification into non-farm activities. This arises in the context of the scope that exists for targeting women with new and innovative means of securing independent income sources from men. There are evidently wide variations of experience with respect to this consideration. Where it is permissible and commonplace for women to engage in agricultural marketing, then scope may exist for strengthening women's income-generating capabilities in food marketing and processing activities. In many African countries, beer brewing is a significant sideline activity for women. More generally, non-farm activities are more likely to be accessible to women where such activities are complementary to daily and seasonal obligations in the home and in agriculture rather than in conflict with them.

A significant feature of household income diversification in sub-Saharan Africa has been the so-called 'feminisation of agriculture', caused by predominantly male involvement in long distance migration to cities, mines and plantations (Low, 1986; Berry, 1989; Hart, 1994). This factor has already been considered in Chapter 5 above in terms of its purportedly negative effects on farm performance. These negative effects result from the withdrawal of able-bodied labour, the heavy domestic obligations of the women left behind, the lack of innovation and farm investment due to the absence of those who hold the decision-making roles on such matters, and the logical use of remittance income to purchase food shortfalls (Low, 1986). The predominance of males, and often younger males, in many different types of seasonal and circular migration is noted by many researchers (Agarwal, 1990; Bigsten, 1996; Breman, 1996).

The topic of male out-migration is continued below under the heading of labour markets. In the meantime, it is undoubtedly true that the options of women left behind on the farm are curtailed, irrespective of purported impacts on agricultural efficiency, new technology and growth. At one level, this is just a matter of absolute time constraints, when the women left behind have to undertake male as well as female farm activities and continue with the full range of domestic obligations. At another level, it is to do with the continued pervasive influence of male decision-making prerogatives, even when the men are not there to oversee the implementation of their decisions. Field studies, including surveys of women on farms and PRA exercises, frequently reaffirm the retention of the resource allocation role by absent male household heads (e.g. David *et al.*, 1995).

Gender and environment

As with poverty and agriculture, a strong strand of thinking has been to view women as having an instrumental role with respect to the conservation of the environment; in other words, information, training and empowerment directed to rural women will result in improved management of environmental resources. This thinking results from variants of the notion that women are the natural custodians of the environment or, put another way, 'women's pivotal role in natural resources management' (Flint, 1991: 57). There are plenty of reasons, located in gender relations as properly understood, to be somewhat sceptical of this linear association between women and beneficial environmental impacts (Joekes *et al.* 1995; Green *et al.*, 1998). From a livelihoods framework perspective, what is interesting is a gender differentiated view of the issues raised in Chapter 6 above, namely poverty-environment interactions, sustainability, and resource management institutions.

Three different perspectives on gender and the environment come together to result in the idea that there may be a 'synergistic' relationship between women and the good husbandry of environmental resources (Jackson, 1993a; Leach *et al.*, 1995). A first perspective refers descriptively to the widespread involvement of women rather than men in utilising and interacting with environmental resources, for example, collecting water and firewood, growing food crops, collecting wild plants for nutritional and medicinal purposes, and so on. A second theorises that women are closer to nature at a conceptual level than men, and therefore that women intuitively understand the sustainable level of utilisation of natural resources, and the need to conserve diversity. This is the 'ecofeminist' perspective (Shiva, 1988; Mies and Shiva, 1993), the arguments of which are examined critically by Jackson (1993b). This perspective comes perilously close to suggesting a biological rather than social determination of women's purportedly more positive attitude to environmental conservation than that of men.

A third perspective emphasises women's proactive role in carrying out conservation technologies such as building terraces, planting trees, and safeguarding diversity, often in opposition to the wishes of men. The Chipko movement that arose in the 1970s in a rural area of Uttar Pradesh in India and involved women hugging trees to prevent their felling by logging companies, is often cited as enshrining this view. However, the Chipko movement, like other examples of rural protest, had historical antecedents which were little to do with the ecological conservation motivations ascribed to it (Jackson, 1993b).

It is a small step from these perspectives to draw the policy conclusion that women can beneficially be co-opted into policies and projects designed to reverse land degradation, carry out resource conservation activities, and become the guardians of adjacent ecosystems and natural habitats (World Bank, 1992). Mobilising rural women is seen as involving a coincidence of interest between women themselves and the larger environmental concerns of the international community. Jackson (1993a: 660) is dubious of the credentials of this approach for the pursuit of greater gender equality: 'empowerment [for women] is called for when it is expected that women's choices, rather than men's, will be preferable to policy-makers'. A practically certain consequence of the approach is that women are expected to take on more tasks, for example, in conservation or participating in community forestry initiatives over and above those they are already expected to do in food production and the domestic sphere (Jackson, 1993b). Men, meanwhile, remain in a position to capture the benefits of improved environmental practices, when it becomes interesting for them to do so.

The flaws in the 'women as good custodians of the environment' approach become evident when it is considered that women's access to, and ability to influence the quality of, natural resources occurs through gender relations in which men typically possess the socially accepted control over resources and a considerable amount of decision-making power concerning the use to which those resources are put. Tree planting is a good case in point. There are many African societies in which the ownership of trees by women is culturally not permissible, but women are allowed to utilise the products of trees that are owned by men. This in practice causes complex problems of contestation, negotiation, and strategising between men and women when agroforestry and similar donor or NGO projects arrive in villages with tree planting as the goal in mind, and women as the means to achieve the goal.

In reality, the relationship between men, women and natural resource management is complex, diverse, and changes according to pressures on livelihoods, and opportunities in the wider economy. A complementarity between women's interests and environmental conservation certainly cannot just be assumed. A critical issue to which this chapter returns later, is that of men and women's different position with respect to rights and control over assets, especially land (e.g. Jackson, 1993a: 657–658). Women often have insecure land rights that diminish their incentive for conservation. They may also be so constrained by labour shortage, due, for example, to male out-migration, that conservation activities are just not possible to carry out. Rather differently, women are often placed under social pressure by men to comply with cultural expectations concerning their provisioning role within the family. With respect to domestic needs such as firewood for cooking, it will often be the case that compliance with role imperatives supersedes resource conservation criteria in the formation of women's daily priorities.

Similarly to previous discussions in this book about stereotypes of the poor and the environment (Chapter 6), stereotypical representations of women and the environment are not very helpful either for advancing women's interests or for ameliorating environmental change of a type that may prove detrimental in the future to human livelihoods. The point made in Chapter 6 about large events often being more decisive than small events in determining the pace and direction of environmental change holds true also for relations between women and the environment, as a case-study in Malaysia of the impact of logging on livelihoods described by Heyzer (1995) illustrates rather dramatically.

Meanwhile, the integration of gender into the concept of sustainable rural livelihoods is likely to prove quite a challenge. The sustainability of women's and men's rural livelihoods are inextricably woven together in prevailing gender relations, and these relations involve divisions of labour that evolve as circumstances change. Livelihood diversification, as manifested, for example, by male out-migration from the rural economy, may make livelihoods more secure (David *et al.*, 1995), but at the same time this may neither improve the well-being and capabilities of women, nor assist with the conservation of the rural environment.

Labour markets, migration and gender

In some ways examining gender through the way that labour markets work is easier than examining it in the household because jobs involve individuals, not households, and gender inequalities are out in the open and plain to see. So far this chapter has focused on various dimensions of gender inequality that arise mainly in the context of the household as the site in which the socially defined roles and constraints on women and men are played out. A labour market perspective leads out of the household and into the economy at large. It provides a national, and even, in some instances, international stage upon which different income earning opportunities for women compared to men present themselves.

Two features of labour markets have tended to preoccupy writers concerned with income earning inequalities between men and women. One is occupational segregation, and the other is wage differentials. These two facets overlap to some extent because wage differentials by sex tend to persist even within single occupations where men and women undertake the same work. The existence of legislation in industrialised countries intended to minimise this type of gender discrimination is not a good indicator of the position in developing countries where such differentials tend to be widespread and persistent.

Occupational segregation refers to some types of formal sector job being regarded as male, while other types are regarded as female. Women tend be employed mainly, for example, in service industries, caring professions, secretarial and clerical occupations, and domestic service. Men tend to be employed in manufacturing, construction, skilled labour, senior management, and self-employment. Surveys of the gender composition of economic sectors and subsectors demonstrate that male-dominated occupations comprise by far the largest proportion of formal sector jobs in developing countries, ranging up to 85 per cent in some countries, while female-dominated occupations may constitute as little as five per cent.

The emergence of new industries that provide manual work for women, viz. electronics and textiles factories can help to improve these ratios, but notions of job segregation along gender lines remain deeply entrenched in social norms and expectations. 'Female' jobs are often related to perceived female characteristics such as dexterity ('nimble fingers'), docility, patience, caring, ability to cook, and so on (Pearson, 1998). Similar stereotypes apply also to men. Because of gender segregation, women have a narrower range of occupational choices compared to men over a wide range of labour market circumstances (Baden and Milward, 1995).

Many studies have demonstrated that women in developing countries, as also in industrialised countries, earn less than men in formal labour markets (see, for example, the data compiled in Baden and Milward (1995: 27). In most countries, women's wage levels are around three-quarters of male wages, although some countries display considerably lower ratios than this. These wage differentials are partly a function of women being engaged in lower wage occupations than men, and partly a function of wage discrimination within the same occupations. A more recent trend has been for women to gain access to more formal sector work, but for this to be in low-paid jobs, offering minimum job security, and offering none of the fringe benefits such as social security or pensions that in the past have been associated with formal sector jobs. This is a worldwide phenomenon occurring as much in the industrialised countries as elsewhere (Standing, 1989). It invokes yet another feminisation expression, this time the 'feminisation of the labour force'.

The development of highly segregated labour markets impacts on household strategic options, foreclosing some options while making others more available. For example, new branches of employment created in the service and information technology sectors often require an obedient workforce working long hours at anti-social times. For these reasons, young women are often targeted to comprise the labour force, and this curtails opportunities for women with children, older women, and men. At the same time, the jobs thus created are impermanent for the individuals who participate in them, not necessarily leading to skills that can be used to sustain income-earning capabilities in the future.

Notwithstanding such trends, in most poor developing countries, rural women's access to formal jobs of any kind is simply very limited. This points to the informal sector as the place where women may be able to establish non-farm sources of income in the face of failures in farm-based livelihoods. Studies concerning gender aspects of the informal sector come up with mixed findings. While the participation rate of women in informal sector activities can be fairly high it never approaches parity with that of men. As in the formal sector, women tend to specialise in different branches of activity in the informal sector from men, for example, dressmaking and food preparation vs. carpentry and vehicle repair. The informal sector has been found to be highly differentiated by gender, by incomes, and by size of enterprise (e.g. Tripp, 1992).

This brief review of labour markets reinforces the rather limited options that rural women in practice face for diversifying their independent sources of income. The constraints are both household ones, deriving from prior obligations in domestic tasks and farming, and labour market ones deriving from occupational segregation and wage differentials between men and women. It is for these reasons that the potential for participation by women in small-scale, non-farm activities, preferably located in rural areas for reasons of complementarity and access, is advocated so strongly in the microcredit literature, and is also acted on as a policy goal by many rural NGOs.

In cultures that practice the seclusion of women, or *purdah*, the capability of women to engage in income-earning activities outside the home is typically curtailed (Hart, 1994; Kabeer, 1998). This does not mean, however, that women are entirely excluded from separate income generation (Cain *et al.*, 1979). Rather, income-earning activities must take forms that comply with seclusion, and are therefore likely to comprise activities that can be carried out within the home. It has been observed that the strictness of compliance with seclusion tends to rise with income, because it is a manifestation of male success and social status to have achieved sufficient income for women not to engage in work outside the home. Paradoxically, therefore, women from poorer households may be able to exercise wider choices of non-farm income generation than women from richer households. However, in the state of West Bengal in India seclusion excludes women from even poor households from employment opportunities in agricultural labour markets (Rogaly, 1997). In South Asia, caste is also a critical factor determining the flexibility with which seclusion is interpreted, and the ability of women to engage in labour markets.

The differential access to labour markets of men and women is revealed in some ways at its most evident when comparing patterns of migration by gender. Migration as a livelihood option is pursued mainly by men, whether by reference to long-term urban migration, variable-term circular migration, or short-term seasonal migration. There are, of course, exceptions to this generalisation, such as, for example, the migration of women from South Asia to the Middle East to take up placements in domestic service. The dominance of men in migration may also be partly generational; in some countries a rising cohort of young, better educated, rural women are less likely than their forebears to accept a lifetime of drudgery on the farm as their lot. However, this sort of social change in slow and uneven across cultural contexts. In sub-Saharan Africa, especially southern Africa, male migration is a long-established social norm, and despite its apparent disadvantages for family cohesion, as well as the advent of less buoyant formal labour markets now than in the past, it appears set to continue to be a strong characteristic of rural livelihood strategies in that region.

Various propositions about gender, poverty, farm productivity and the environment have been linked to the prevalence of men in migration patterns in low-income countries. For example, male migration leads to *de facto* female-

Box 7.2. Male migration, agriculture and the environment
in the Sahel

A comparative study of male out-migration in several locations in the Sahel examined patterns of male migration and their social and environmental effects (David *et al.*, 1995). The study was undertaken at four sites, one each in Senegal, Burkina Faso, Mali and the Sudan. It sought particularly to address conflicting views about migration with respect to agriculture and the environment, that is, whether male out-migration is detrimental or beneficial for environmental management and agricultural productivity. However, in the process of investigating this central issue, the study also collected and processed quantitative and qualitative data on a wide variety of social, economic and natural resource aspects of the household and village impacts of migration. The conclusions of the study are reproduced here, since they provide informative insights into the complexity of effects that surround male migration as one particular manifestation of livelihood diversification. The following points all refer to features or effects of male out-migration in the Sahel (David *et al.*, 1995: 11 18):

- migration has highly variable forms, e.g. seasonal vs long term migration, and diverse effects—diversity of experience across families and locations is a principal finding of the study;
- migration does not create female headed households—men remain household heads, except in those rare instances of total abandonment where the migrant male disappears and never comes back;
- a good deal of inter-household reciprocity between women generally ensures the continued well-being of women left behind;
- women become decisively the higher proportion of the stable working population in the rural areas from which migration takes place;
- migration has no effect on patriarchal patterns of decision-making, nor on the normative gender divisions of labour at household and village level;
- few generalisations can be made about the effects of male out migration on labour availability for agriculture in rural areas; in some instances adequate labour continues to be available from household or reciprocal community sources, in other instances men reappear to participate in seasonal peaks in the labour requirements of agriculture;
- the effects of migration on women's natural resource management capabilities are diverse and not generalisable; they depend on the prevailing division of labour, land tenure, and the workloads of women;
- remittances by migrants are rarely invested in agriculture, they are typically used to improve food security via food purchases or to secure other basic needs;

- pressure on off-farm renewable natural resources, such as firewood, charcoal, etc., is not affected markedly either way by male migration;
- migration does not lead to freeing-up of land in rural areas, since even permanent migrants continue to exert their customary rights over land that is regarded as belonging to them.

As a general observation, the study concludes that male out-migration does contribute to the viability and sustainability of rural livelihoods. This is so because remittances ensure the food security of those left behind in rural areas, and the patterns and duration of migration are adapted to changes in seasonal and annual shortfalls in food and basic needs. Therefore within the prevailing gender relations of those rural societies, migration plays a valuable role in livelihood sustainability.

headed households with consequent associations to poverty (see earlier this chapter); it is also held to lead to less innovation in agriculture (Chapter 5 above), and to less conservation of natural resources (Chapter 6 above). However, a detailed study of male migration and its effects undertaken in selected Sahelian countries (David *et al.*, 1995; see Box 7.2) reveals that experience in all these regards is heterogeneous, and does not lead to useful generalisation. The one feature of migration that is found to apply widely is the significance of remittance income for ensuring the seasonal food security of the resident rural family.

Assets and gender

Assets were identified at a very early stage of this book as a defining attribute of livelihoods. The livelihoods approach emphasises that the options open to individuals and households are determined in large measure by their asset status, that is, with respect to land, physical assets, education, social networks, and financial capital. Recent writing on both urban and rural livelihoods converges on the nature and use of assets as the key to determining constraints and choices for raising living standards or just surviving (Guyer, 1997; Moser, 1998). Differences between men and women in ownership and control over assets have been shown in several instances already in this book to be a critical attribute of their separate livelihood capabilities.

In a rural and agricultural context, land is the fundamental asset. In all societies worldwide, women's ownership or access rights to land is rarely as firmly designated as that of men (Dwyer and Bruce, 1988), and, indeed it is becoming even less so over time as previous matrilineal rules of inheritance are replaced by patrilineal ones, and the registration of land converted from customary to private tenure tends to happen almost exclusively under male title holders. Land has properties that are quite distinct from other resources and types of capital. Ownership of it is a measure of social status, it represents a store of wealth, its value as an asset in a market economy rises continuously as its use becomes more intense and its scarcity increases, and it provides collateral against loans that can be used to improve future income streams.

The exclusion of women from land ownership can be regarded as one of the most pernicious of all gender inequalities, and, therefore, also one that most urgently requires commitment to change (Agarwal, 1994a; 1994b). Tackling inequality of land ownership means tackling directly a key institutional mechanism by which gender inequalities are reproduced from one generation to the next. In this sense, as a gender strategy in the policy arena it differs greatly from the poverty, efficiency and environment gender strategies described earlier in this chapter. Many countries have discriminatory laws with respect to inheritance, ownership and control over property. These laws may prohibit outright the independent ownership of land or other property by women, or they may be phrased in such a way that the acquisition of property by women is a most unlikely occurrence, giving precedence for the transfer of land to remote male members of families above immediate female kin. Where such laws are open to contest and interpretation, past legal decisions will almost always have favoured male above female claimants, so that legal precedence ensures the persistence of women's exclusion from land ownership.

It is not difficult to perceive how lack of land ownership reinforces women's dependence on men and curtails their capability to make independent livelihood choices. In respect of engagement in agricultural activities it means, as we have already seen, that women's access to land occurs through men and is therefore dependent on the maintenance of the goodwill of those same men for its continuity across seasons, and for investment in its improvement. This also means that projects aimed to improve the productivity of land worked by women end up by benefiting the men who own the land anyway, or who have prior claims on the output from the land. Since land ownership is one of the most powerful means of raising funds for everything from education to physical capital and to starting an own business, women's exclusion on these counts can also quite often be traced to their lack of rights in land.

Gender inequalities and gender differences also occur with respect to assets other than land. In the past this certainly applied to access to capital in conventional credit schemes since women were even less able than poor men to supply the collateral against which loans were disbursed. This may have been redressed by group lending approaches that have been directed specifically to women. However, prevailing gender relations can sabotage even these schemes, so that although loans are ostensibly to women in microcredit groups, the funds are utilised by male members of the household for their own projects. In effect women become the loan repayment guarantors of men (Anker, 1993; Goetz and Sen Gupta, 1996).

Discrimination against girls in education results in women having overall education levels lower than those of men, representing gender inequality in human capital. The outcomes of this are that women are less able to engage in labour markets that require prior educational qualifications, and are proportionately more likely to end up in unskilled labour markets offering low wages and little job security. It follows in part from educational inequalities, but also from other socioeconomic differences between themselves and men, that rural women seek to gain income, or the use of assets, through familial relationships rather than market relations (Lockwood, 1997). Whereas men rely more on markets, for crop sales, for wage labour, and so on, women rely more on social networks and on setting up and maintaining non-market reciprocal exchanges to ensure survival and improve livelihood security (Berry, 1989; Vaa *et al.*, 1989; Dennis, 1991). In this sense, women rely on, and create, more of a particular form of social capital than men, where this social capital is taken to refer to informal networks rather than to formal associations or organisations.

Summary

Drawing the threads of the argument together, this chapter sets out to identify some of the key gender dimensions of rural livelihoods. It approaches this in two main ways. The first is by elaborating the gender dimension of poverty, agriculture and the environment as topics in the study of rural livelihood strategies. The second is by examining gender inequalities in asset ownership and labour markets, corresponding to the assets and activities components of the livelihoods framework set out in Chapter 2.

Gender inequality is a pervasive feature of rural livelihoods. Women have unequal ownership or access rights to land, their access to productive resources occurs through the mediation of men, their decision-making capabilities concerning resource use and output choices are often severely restricted. Moreover, women confront narrower labour markets than men and unequal earnings prospects in such labour markets as are open to them. Their lower education, resulting from discriminatory access as children, means that when they do engage in labour markets it is likely to be in low wage work with little job security.

These factors add up to male rather than female engagement in livelihood diversification, as the typical occurrence. A lot of the previous arguments about diversification, for example, its role in reducing risk, smoothing consumption, overcoming credit constraints, need to be interpreted in this light. Diversification certainly fulfils these functions, but it may do so in ways that reinforce rather than reduce prevailing gender inequalities. Diversification may have the effect of trapping women in customary roles, while permitting men to enjoy new freedoms and expanded choices in how they compose their own and their families' livelihoods.

The foregoing interpretation does, however, overstate its case since it is couched in terms that give women no agency over the conduct of their own lives. Of course women find many ways to exercise their individual capabilities in pursuit of rural livelihoods. These often, perforce, take non-market forms, and the degree to which women build up and participate in reciprocal support arrangements with other women is documented in many studies. In addition, women do discover 'niches' in the market economy that enable them to engage in activities that men do not find so threatening as to take them over or to foreclose them. This may be in crop marketing and food processing where these enterprises have traditionally allowed female participation, or they may be in new crops, such as fruit and vegetables, that have not formerly been part of traditional farming systems.

The various arguments and findings discussed in this chapter do suggest that institutional reform is a priority agenda if the aim is to reduce gender inequalities. In particular, the exclusion of women from land inheritance and property ownership is a great reinforcer of existing rural gender relations in a wide variety of circumstances. Livelihood diversification, even when diversification options are directed to women, does little to erode the institutional mechanisms that reproduce gender inequality over time; and the predominance of men in diverse livelihood activities outside the home effectively reinforces rather than diminishes such institutions. For similar reasons, it is sometimes asserted that women carry a disproportionate burden of the adjustments to livelihoods provoked by macro reform policies, the topic to which this book turns in the next chapter.

— CHAPTER 8 —
Macro Policies and Reform Agendas

In this chapter we move from micro level aspects of rural livelihoods to the aggregate, national-level, economic and policy context that contributes to shaping over time livelihood options and decisions. As we shall see, this is not just a one-way process; just as macro level trends and events alter the viability of distinct patterns of livelihood, so also livelihood strategies and patterns influence the effectiveness of macro policies in achieving their stated goals. In particular, livelihood strategies that involve diverse activities across sectors make it more difficult to predict the income distribution effects of policies that alter relative returns to different activities, than if individuals or households were engaged in single occupations (Jamal, 1995).

Macro policies are policies that seek to influence variables that have an economy-wide impact on the pace and direction of economic and social change. In the purely economic sphere, this means variables such as the exchange rate of the country, its level of interest rates, its rate and pattern of taxation, the government budget, and the size of the country's debt burden. In the social and political sphere, although also with economic consequences, it means factors such as the division of economic activities between the state and private agencies, the role of markets, the degree of centralisation of state power, the accountability of state agencies, and adherence to the rule of law.

Macro policies contrast with micro policies (see Chapter 2) that seek to affect the operating environment of productive enterprises and the income of individuals or households at sectoral or local levels. Examples of micro policies are a fertiliser subsidy aimed to encourage maize farmers to increase yields, or micro credit made available to women processors of palm oil in order to raise the income-generating capacity of rural women in a particular location.

In practice, it is the livelihood strategies of individuals and households that connect macro and micro policy levels. When macro policies are inimical to rural livelihoods, then poverty and inequality grow, farm families may retreat into subsistence (e.g. Bevan *et al.*, 1989; Tschirley and Weber, 1994), risk increases, and the vulnerability of rural families to stress and disaster rises. Conversely, macro policies may provide an encouraging environment for rural livelihoods, lowering risk, stimulating flexibility, widening options, and reducing vulnerability. Much of the debate of the past fifteen years regarding macro policies (e.g.

Cornia and Helleiner, 1994; van der Geest, 1994; Engberg-Pedersen *et al.*, 1996) is about whether the conventional macro policies advocated by the IMF and the World Bank are inimical or encouraging to livelihoods in these ways. Macro policies impact on rural livelihoods in many different direct and indirect ways (Streeten, 1989; Addison and Demery, 1989). Some of these are: their influence on the rate of inflation; rates of return to assets such as labour and land; employment options in different branches of activity; and human capital formation in the shape of access to adequate nutrition, health and education services.

The next section of this chapter sketches out the main components and sequences of macro policies as these have evolved in developing countries since the early 1980s, leading to an overview of the state of thinking about them at the time of writing. Readers familiar with the general arguments about adjustment and reform programmes can skip this section without losing the thread of the book as far as livelihoods and diversification are concerned.

The chapter continues with a section that traces the principle links between macro policies and micro level outcomes, with particular regard to the predicted outcomes for rural individuals and households, and the way those outcomes are modified by ongoing processes of rural livelihood adaptation. The chapter concludes by taking a tentatively upbeat view of the impact of reform on rural livelihoods, based on the notion that critics of reform tend to underplay just how bad things were, and how much worse they were becoming, in many countries, before reform processes were initiated.

Macro policies and reform

The evolving terminology surrounding macro policies coincides more or less with both the focus of different components of policy, and with the sequence in which these components have attained authenticity over time. Macro policies encompass the elements of stabilisation, adjustment, and reform (see Figure 8.1). Stabilisation means taking action to reduce a balance of payments deficit, reduce the government budget deficit, and reduce the rate of inflation. It is concerned primarily with the short-term management of the demand side of the economy, and typically involves periodic squeezes on purchasing power in order to control the rate of inflation. Adjustment means adopting policies to improve resource allocation, increase economic efficiency, expand growth potential, and enhance the resilience of the economy to shocks (World Bank, 1990a, 23). It is concerned primarily with the longer term supply-side of the economy, and involves institutional change (e.g. privatisation of state enterprises), as well as price liberalisation and infrastructural investment. Reform means addressing wider organisational, administrative and political issues, such as the effectiveness and size of the civil service, the public accountability of state agencies, tax reform, and political pluralism.

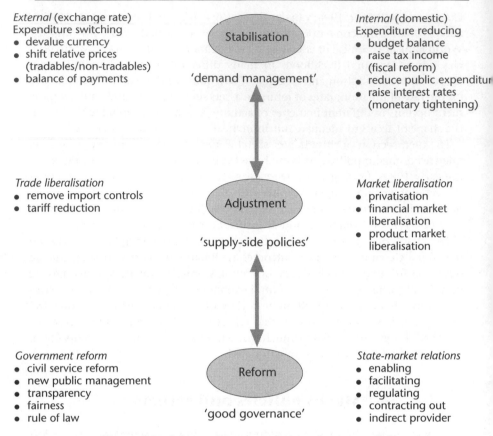

External (exchange rate)
Expenditure switching
• devalue currency
• shift relative prices
  (tradables/non-tradables)
• balance of payments

Stabilisation

'demand management'

Internal (domestic)
Expenditure reducing
• budget balance
• raise tax income
  (fiscal reform)
• reduce public expenditur
• raise interest rates
  (monetary tightening)

Trade liberalisation
• remove import controls
• tariff reduction

Adjustment

'supply-side policies'

Market liberalisation
• privatisation
• financial market
  liberalisation
• product market
  liberalisation

Government reform
• civil service reform
• new public management
• transparency
• fairness
• rule of law

Reform

'good governance'

State-market relations
• enabling
• facilitating
• regulating
• contracting out
• indirect provider

Figure 8.1. Schematic representation of macro policies

The preference increasingly is to refer to all these components jointly as 're-form', whereas formerly debates centred on 'structural adjustment policies' comprising mainly the economic elements of stabilisation and adjustment (Helleiner, 1994). The evolution of ideas around reform has been partly sequential, in that reform agendas have expanded in scope, and have been modified by debate as time has gone on since their inception in the early 1980s. However, all three components as described above also apply simultaneously, so that the later preoccupations, say, with political plurality are not seen as making it any less necessary to ensure macroeconomic stability. It is also notable that the shift in scope over time has been from the narrow economic to the broader economic and to the institutional, social and political.

Early phases of reform were driven predominantly by the international financial institutions, viz. the IMF and the World Bank, in the context of conditionality. The origins of reform and its major features during the 1980s are described in many sources (e.g. Demery, 1994; Please, 1994). In essence, they involved the provision of balance of payments support to countries on the brink of bankruptcy in their external accounts, in exchange for compliance with a string of conditions related to macroeconomic management and policy change, some of which are described in more detail below. At the time, this also involved a shift from project finance by donors to so-called programme finance; in other words, from loans or grants for individual development projects to quick-disbursing finance in support of imports. The conditionality aspect of reforms raises problems concerning their ownership and compliance with conditionality clauses, and these remain ongoing sources of conflict between donor and recipient governments (Engberg-Pedersen *et al.*, 1996).

The short and medium term goals of reform are implicit in the foregoing description of its phases and components. They are to do with stability, efficiency, infrastructural provision, and social services. There are, however, two overarching considerations that subsume these and other proximate goals. The first of these is to do with the flexibility and adaptability of national economies. The second is to do with the role and nature of the state as an agent purportedly acting on behalf of the well-being of its citizens.

It is observed by Killick (1993: ix) that 'all economies at all times need to adjust or adapt to changing circumstances in order to achieve a reasonable pace of development.' In other words, the world does not stand still. The more rigid are the economic processes and structures of a country, the less they are able to cope with change. Therefore a primary objective of reform is to strengthen the ability of the economy to recover from stress and shocks (Streeten, 1989). There is an evident parallel between the discussion of secure and resilient livelihoods that feature in earlier chapters of this book and the notion of the flexible economy advanced in a macroeconomic context (Killick, 1993; 1995). In both cases, the emphasis is on making the system 'less vulnerable to future shocks' (Streeten, 1989: 4).

Many writers consider that a market economy, however imperfect in its functioning, offers a higher degree of flexibility and adaptability than an economy in which the state is heavily involved in day-to-day economic decision-making. This is because the market economy has a built in responsiveness by private producers to the short and long run price changes they experience, whereas state agencies tend to be much less responsive in that way, for all sorts of reasons. It is thus that the goal of making an economy better able to cope with change and shocks, merges into, and provides an important rationale for, the separate goal of reducing the role of the state in the economy. This second objective is also justified by reference to other arguments. Whereas the state was previously regarded as independent, overseeing and benevolent, more recently it has come to be thought of as an actor, like any other, safeguarding its own interests. Moreover, serious doubts surround the mode of operation of the unreformed state; the prevalence within it of corruption, patronage, rent-seeking, waste, and inefficiency.

The components and phases of reform, and the mechanism by which reform processes are meant to work, are examined in more detail at this point, although without getting into too much economic technicality. Figure 8.1 may continue to be helpful in this regard.

Stabilisation

Stabilisation is concerned partly with balancing the books on the external account (balance of payments) and on the internal account (government budget), and partly with reducing or keeping control over the domestic rate of inflation. These elements are all interrelated since running persistent external account and budgetary deficits tends to stoke up the rate of inflation, amongst other adverse effects. The chief instruments of stabilisation are the exchange rate of the country, its fiscal policy (tax revenue and public spending), and its monetary policy (principally, interest rate levels).

External imbalance is corrected by currency devaluation, which makes imports more expensive in local currency terms, and raises the local currency price of exports, thus inhibiting demand for the former and encouraging more supply of the latter. The government budget imbalance is corrected by increasing taxes, or reducing public expenditure, or a combination of both. The rate of inflation is brought under control by raising interest rates, and utilising other devices within the banking system to reduce the growth of the money supply in circulation and squeeze the volume of credit in the economy.

We shall return to potential conflicts and sequencing problems with these instruments shortly. In the meantime, these mechanisms for stabilising the macro economy are often grouped together under the headings of expenditure-reducing policies and expenditure-switching policies. The expenditure-reducing policies are those that involve a contractionary monetary and fiscal stance in the domestic market. The expenditure-switching policies, of which the exchange rate depreciation is the principal one, are designed to switch expenditure from foreign to domestic sources, thus stimulating domestic production rather than imports.

Adjustment

As defined earlier, adjustment is concerned more with the longer-term supply side of the economy, its capability for efficient resource allocation, and its competitiveness in world markets. The term 'structural' in structural adjustment policies simply refers to the structure of the economy, i.e. the composition of GDP and its pattern of growth, not to any subtle theory about the organisational model of society.

Adjustment involves many different elements that are regarded as improving the competitiveness and efficiency of the economy. These include trade liberalisation (reducing import and export taxes, dismantling import quotas); foreign exchange liberalisation (dismantling exchange controls, allowing free convertibility of the domestic currency in both directions); domestic market liberalisation (dismantling price controls, reducing subsidies, e.g. on food or fertiliser, eliminating commodity-specific taxes); financial market liberalisation (removing credit subsidies, and eliminating interest rate ceilings); and privatisation (divesting parastatal agencies in the productive and service sectors either wholly or partially to private investors). Adjustment is also typically taken to include attention to infrastructure, both economic infrastructure (roads, railways, telecommunications, energy supplies) and social infrastructure (health and education services).

Reform

Reform has followed on from stabilisation and adjustment and is now regarded as an integral part of the whole process of making governments and economies more responsive, flexible, efficient, and effective. Reform refers in part to overhauling different parts of the machinery of government, for example, civil service reform (reducing the size of the civil service, and improving its effectiveness in the roles it discharges), and tax collection reform (improving tax recovery, closing avoidance loopholes, eliminating the scope for tax revenues to 'disappear' on their way to the treasury).

Reform also encompasses what has come to be referred to as 'good governance': the public accountability of government agencies, the transparency of their decision-making, the fairness of their decisions, and the even-handed application of the rule of law. Taking an even wider ambit, some advocates would include factors such as multi-party democracy, political and social plurality, decentralisation of decision-making, and freedom of the press in the reform process. This is all very well, but it should not be forgotten that many of these factors are deeply political processes, that cannot just be enacted as technocratic solutions like a change in the level of interest rates (Mkandawire, 1994a; Engberg-Pedersen et al., 1996).

Sequencing

For many low-income developing countries, actual sequences of reform have followed this process of widening out the reform agenda; however, as already stated, the taking on of new dimensions of reform does not mean that the earlier dimensions go away; so, for example, fiscal rectitude remains a component of reform just as strongly under the much wider current scope of reform as it did in the era when stabilisation was virtually the sole focus.

Sequencing has been an important issue at the level of technical detail within and between the broad components of reform (Mosley et al., 1991). For example, across-the-board reductions in import tariffs (trade liberalisation) are not helpful either to fiscal balance (when tax revenues are predominantly composed of such tariffs) or to rehabilitating domestic production capacity when this immediately has to face competition from liberalised imports. Likewise, liberalising trade before exports start to grow is potentially destabilising since the impact of the initial currency devaluation may be partially or wholly negated (imports grow while exports still stagnate), resulting in the need for more devaluation, greater inflationary pressure, and even more of a squeeze on domestic economic activity, perhaps ending in severe recession.

Ownership

Many debates surround the ownership of reform, and the driving force behind it in the form of the IMF, World Bank, and other aid donors. Conditionality implies the imposition of ways of doing things on national governments by outside agencies, seen as representing international capital and Western systems of values. This is captured by the phrase 'external intrusion into domestic policy formation' (Helleiner, 1994: 10). Its credibility becomes self-evidently more debatable as the reform agenda widens to include broad domestic political considerations such as multi-party democracy or decentralisation of government.

However, there are many different strands and counterposing views on the ownership issue. Some would argue that conditionality is entirely reasonable for the advance year-after-year of large quantities of cash from the international community. In similar vein, others would point to the lack of representativeness and poor conduct of many low-income country governments, for example, abuses of office, rampant corruption, erratic and inefficient provision of public services, even in countries regarded as having the 'best' states in these regards (Mkandawire, 1994a).

Another strand of thinking is that conditionality tends to minimise local involvement in the formulation and implementation of the reform agenda. Negotiations between the donors and national governments, especially in sub-Saharan Africa, tend to involve just a few, very senior, and often unelected, government functionaries. Lack of involvement and a sense of ownership by the officials and politicians who are supposed to implement decisions results in a great deal of evasion and thwarting of reform. Technical assistance provided by the World Bank to push forward particular goals such as tax reform or improvements in government accounting procedures result in little spread of commitment or skills, and are not sustained once the technical assistance personnel have gone home.

It is evident that questions about the ownership and driving force of reform are not resolved by facile partisanship in one direction or the other. Coming at this from a different direction, the increasing consensus that development should involve empowerment and participation at grassroots level, including pluralistic means of engaging in local level decision-making, is not at odds, in a broad sense, with demands made by donors concerning the 'good governance' conduct of governments and their agencies. Indeed, where administrative and political aspects of reform are concerned the public at large in low-income countries may have rather similar views of the defects of their states to those of the international agencies (Mkandawire, 1994a).

On the other hand, this does not make it politically palatable to be subjected to continuous and overt outsider interference. A dimension in which external agencies are inevitably on weak ground is the local political process, and this limits in practice their ability to impose blueprint solutions on diverse sociopolitical contexts.

Outcomes

Analyses and interpretations of the experience of reform, its relative success or failure in achieving stated objectives, yield an uneven and, in many aspects, inconclusive picture. There are severe methodological problems in interpreting events and trends, either sequentially within a single country, or by making comparisons across countries. Before and after comparisons are hampered by the counter-factual case, that is, what would have happened had the reform not been implemented? With and without comparisons for a single country are simply not feasible, and when done across countries they confront the difficulty of separating differences arising from factors unique to each country from those arising due to reform processes.

Social dimensions of reform were flagged at an early stage in the process (Cornia and Jolly, 1987), and subsequent reform packages contained components designed to protect those most vulnerable to its detrimental effects. The key fear was that reductions in public expenditure necessitated in order to achieve fiscal balance would result in severe declines in social spending on health and education, to the detriment of the entire population, and of the poor especially. A counter-argument in this area was that since most social spending took place in urban areas and was accessed predominantly by the rich and middle classes, the impact on the rural poor was in reality rather small. Some research suggests that public spending on social services, was, in most countries, maintained or even increased in real terms after the mid-1980s (Sahn *et al.*, 1996).

Evaluations of the economic impacts of reform get mixed up with sequencing and avoidance issues. One cross-country comparison of experience in the 1980s concluded that reform achieved its goal of switching resources into export growth, but that its impact on net investment was negative, and its effect on economic growth overall was insignificant (Mosley *et al.*, 1991). Avoidance factors that arise in this context include, for example, nominal devaluations that are not always sustained as real devaluations, and continued adherence to administered prices in key sectors that dilute the impact of relative price shifts (Commander, 1989).

In an early 1990s review of reform experiences, the World Bank concluded that reform worked best in those countries that followed the conditionality prescriptions most closely (World Bank, 1994; Husain and Faruqee, 1994). Likewise, Duncan and Howell (1992) concluded from a descriptive comparison of case-study countries in sub-Saharan Africa that where adjustment measures were significantly implemented, their impact on the real incomes of most groups of rural small farmers was positive. Taking a rather different tack, Stewart (1994a; 1994b) set up a shopping list of structural changes that could be regarded as beneficial outcomes of reform, only to find that actual reform rarely measured up to these desired results.

Difficulties have certainly occurred with reforms in relation to public administration and the role of the state. Demery (1994) puts the viewpoint that little progress has actually been made in redefining the role of the state as a facilitator and enabler of private sector activities. Similarly, 'African governments are not yet much better at managing market economies than they were at managing economies through heavy intervention' (Husain and Faruqee, 1994: 427). In its own review, the World Bank (1994) identified privatisation, fiscal reform, civil service reform, and financial services reform as areas in which little real progress had been made. This can be attributed in part to evasion of those conditionality clauses that governments or officials do not wish to follow (Gibbon, 1992).

Privatisation, in particular, turns out to reveal deeper weaknesses in the logic of reform (Mkandawire, 1994b; Gibbon, 1996). In sub-Saharan African countries, the comparative absence of a class of domestic risk-taking entrepreneurs has resulted in difficulty in finding purchasers for state-owned medium and large-scale industry. The most viable concerns are 'cherry-picked' either by foreign companies or by a narrow group of domestic elites so that ownership becomes highly concentrated in a few hands and competition is stifled. Meanwhile, some privatised concerns subsequently collapse due to the inadvisable continuation of management styles carried over from state ownership (Cook and Kirkpatrick, 1995).

A primary goal of civil service reform has been to reduce the aggregate number of civil servants in low-income countries. In the early 1980s, for example, civil service employment in Africa corresponded to 54 per cent of the non-agricultural labour-force, as compared to 24 per cent in the industrialised countries (Nafziger, 1997: 575). Efforts by the World Bank to secure reductions in civil service numbers have been particularly prone to evasion by implementing agencies. Targets for retrenchment are seldom adhered to, are difficult to monitor due to inaccurate data, and re-hiring elsewhere in the system is rife (Engberg-Pedersen *et al.*, 1996: 48–52). At the same time, civil service salaries have undergone steep declines in real terms throughout the reform period, causing demotivation, moonlighting, absenteeism, and corruption, all of which act in ways contrary to the intended spirit of the reform process.

At the time of writing, the World Bank's view of reform has moved on again, with a particular emphasis on the role of the state in creating markets where these do not just spring into being of their own volition (World Bank, 1997). A growing body of literature addresses the problem of trust in transactions (e.g. Platteau, 1994a; 1994b), without which market development is fragile and feeble, and individuals depend more on personal contacts and networks for undertaking exchanges than on prices determined in reasonably complete or competitive markets. The free market position of many liberalisers in the 1980s is rejected as underestimating the weakness or absence of resource and output markets, especially in sub-Saharan Africa. Instead, government and markets are seen as complements rather than substitutes, with the government helping to create markets where they are missing, and providing the regulation without which markets cannot function properly (Stiglitz, 1998).

Macro-micro links and rural livelihoods

Macro policies link to micro level outcomes via the effects they have in various markets, and on the provision of public goods and social services. The principal markets in this respect are output markets, labour markets, financial markets, and input markets (World Bank, 1990a; Duncan and Howell, 1992). It is appropriate that the preceding section should end on a note of caution about markets; if markets do not work well, then the switching of incentives that macro policies attempt to achieve may not occur, or other factors may swamp their effects. At the household level, it is not just changing relative prices that provoke livelihood responses but also the social relations of the household (Chapter 7 above) and the access of individuals to assets that enable them to participate in or to create new patterns of economic activity for themselves.

Stabilisation has a particular set of predicted impacts on output markets that follow from the idea of expenditure switching described above, and that provide the best starting point for tracing the potential rural livelihood implications of macro policies. The effect of a real devaluation of the domestic currency is to raise the price in domestic currency of tradable branches of output relative to non-tradable branches. Tradable outputs refer to exports, import substitutes (e.g. home production of substitutes for imported consumer goods), and outputs that may be able to switch into either of these roles due to the change in relative prices. Non-tradable outputs comprise products and services that cannot be traded internationally, or that are naturally protected from foreign competition by reason of location. They include the construction industry, wholesaling, retailing, and many urban informal sector services and activities.

In economies where the principal tradable outputs are agricultural in origin, and where domestic industry has hitherto been heavily protected to secure its economic viability, the chief outcome of stabilisation should be to favour the agricultural sector, thus causing a switch in resources from urban and industrial activities to agricultural ones. This direction of change is thought to be reinforced by market liberalisation. Trade liberalisation reduces the viability of uncompetitive domestic industries, and also allows competitive farm inputs to enter the domestic market. Reductions in export taxation directly raise returns to export commodity producers. Internal market liberalisation lifts administrative price controls on food commodities. The sequence of events thus set in motion should involve higher returns to labour in agriculture, and the creation of new jobs in agricultural linkage industries such as input supply and export processing. In short, the virtuous role of agriculture envisaged in the growth linkage model (Chapter 5) should come into play. The implication for rural livelihoods is that they should improve relative to urban livelihoods, and that diversification options will emerge in agriculture-related industries or in consumer goods sectors supplying farmers.

A number of practical factors serve to modify this idealised version of events. One consideration is that switches of resources between sectors are only likely to occur if resources are mobile and markets exist for them. In Africa, for example, rural labour markets are poorly developed and for practical purposes in some places non-existent. There are also historical and gender aspects to this. Men have historically participated in non-rural labour markets, while women do not participate much in labour markets at all, due to prior commitments in domestic work and food crop production (Chapter 7). Similarly, credit markets hardly exist in rural sub-Saharan Africa, and the immediate impact of financial liberalisation is to make the likelihood of their coming into being even lower, since it is common for interest rates to rise to prohibitive levels in order to control inflation during the reform process. Finally, farm input markets may be damaged by liberalisation, at least in its early phases. The elimination of fertiliser and other subsidies acts as a direct disincentive to the continued use of purchased inputs. At the same time, the dismantling of state delivery agencies prior to the emergence of a domestic private capacity results in patchy geographical availability, especially in remote locations.

It seems from various studies that small-farm export crop producers did, in general, gain at first from adjustment. However, these initial gains were subsequently eroded by a persistent fall in world commodity prices during the 1990s, prompting greater emphasis to be placed in later policy documents on export diversification. The prices of tradable foods rise like those of export crops following a devaluation; however, in countries previously characterised by the monopoly purchase of food by state agencies, it is probable that parallel market prices had already risen in line with the degree of exchange rate overvaluation, before devaluation occurred (Sahn, 1994). At household level, the impact of food price changes on incomes depends on factors that vary across households, such as (1) the proportion of supply that is retained for subsistence rather than sold, (2) whether the household is in food surplus or in food deficit overall, (3) whether the household purchases traded or non-traded foods, and (4) the substitutability between foods in the consumption pattern of the household.

There are also, of course, gender differences in the impacts of changing prices and labour markets that occur during reform (Horton et al., 1994; Haddad et al., 1995). The argument can be constructed, although it is difficult to substantiate in practice, that it is rural women who carry a disproportionate share of the negative consequences of reform, that is, the welfare of rural women declines relative to that of men. Components of this scenario include (1) women having to work longer hours in export crop production, the returns to which accrue to men, (2) the non-tradable food crops that women specialise in (e.g. cassava, yams, millets, sorghum) experiencing a decline in relative prices, (3) women having to take on more arduous caring roles due to the decline in social services caused by cuts in public expenditure. On the other hand, there are reasons to be wary of arguments that persistently see women as helpless victims of changing events (Jackson, 1998a). It is equally possible that social and economic change opens up new opportunities for women, and enables them to renegotiate the social norms of their relations with men.

Reform and livelihood diversification

Most attempts to analyse the complex micro impacts of macro policies have very little to say about diversification as a livelihood strategy. This is because most such analyses persist in seeing the economy as composed of neatly defined sectors or sub-sectors, with employment patterns corresponding to these sectoral divisions. There are some exceptions to this orthodoxy, for example Sahn and Sarris (1991: 259) note that 'the diversity of income sources implies that the implications of movements in relative prices on smallholder welfare are indeed complex'.

Jamal (1995) likewise takes a different view. He notes that the ostensible impact of reform is to shift relative prices away from industry and towards agriculture, and that labour should move also from the declining to the growing sectors. This should be reinforced by the sharply deteriorating trend in real urban wages, the shedding of employees by industries forced into rationalisation by competition or privatisation, and the retrenchment of civil servants in later stages of reform (Jamal and Weeks, 1988; 1993). However, in reality rural–urban migration has continued to take place apace in all sub-Saharan African economies. Instead of movements of labour into full-time occupations, both rural and urban families have diversified their income sources by straddling the rural–urban divide. The outcome is that in many African countries 'the whole wage-earning class has disappeared as a distinct entity, mutating into a wage earning-cum-informal sector-cum-farming conglomerate' (Jamal, 1995: 2).

The interpretation given by Jamal is summarised in Box 8.1 and Figure 8.2. The adoption of cross-sectoral diversification strategies (called, rather obscurely, 'fusions' by Jamal) by both rural and urban families is argued to have important implications for the efficacy of macro policies. Essentially, it means that changing relative prices across sectors are internalised within households rather than acting as an external stimulus to the free movement of resources, including labour, between sectors. This blunts macro policy instruments and makes their outcomes unpredictable for resource allocation as well as for welfare.

Box 8.1. Livelihood strategies and macro reform policies

A collection of papers edited by Jamal (1995) represents one of the few attempts to recognise that employment patterns in low-income countries do not correspond to the neat divisions between economic sectors and sub-sectors upon which much macroeconomic analysis is predicated. For Jamal, post-reform labour markets in sub-Saharan Africa appear to work as illustrated by Figure 8.2. Both rural and urban families pursue diverse cross-sectoral livelihood strategies in which, amongst other features, remittances are transferred from urban to rural families and food is transferred from rural to urban families.

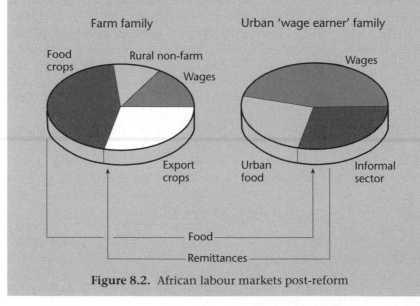

Figure 8.2. African labour markets post-reform

It is worth citing in full Jamal's (1995: 21–22) endeavour to capture authentically the livelihood strategies that have accompanied reform in sub-Saharan African countries:

> The fusions [i.e. cross-sectoral diversification strategies] help to explain the present-day workings of African economies and in particular why 'adjustment' does not proceed as anticipated: why no major shifts occur in labour allocation between urban and rural areas despite massive changes in factor prices, or between food crops and export crops, again despite significant shifts in relative prices. Wage earners—by resorting to growing their own food or collecting it from their rural-based relatives and by participating in petty trade—have effectively ceased to be just wage earners and have become at the same time part-time subsistence farmers and informal sector operators, and like them have acquired some immunity from market prices. Similarly the fact that rural families operate as farmers as well as wage earners and business people gives them immunity from shifts in relative factor prices. Rural-urban linkages intensify these tendencies. This explains the dramatic changes in the rural-urban terms of trade witnessed recently, of which the decline in urban wages is one side. Were rural and urban families distinct entities, and within the urban areas were wage earners distinct from informal sector traders, such massive changes in relative prices simply could not happen since they imply huge shifts in income, in most cases from the poorer to the richer groups, enough if true to engender social unrest. What has happened in African countries is that terms of trade and their implicit income distributions have become 'internalised' within the extended family straddling the rural-urban and formal-informal divides. In this way most of the tension has vanished from relative price changes. Prices, we can bear being reminded, are incomes to producers and costs to consumers, but if both producers and consumers exist within the same family—in the extreme if one and the same person is both producer and a consumer (e.g. of urban grown food crops)—then prices lose most of their bite as mechanisms for distribution. While this simplifies the task of advocates of 'structural adjustment programmes' in demanding massive turnarounds in prices, it also explains why no genuine 'structural adjustment'—i.e. a shift of labour back to rural areas—happens. Effectively by increasing their production of food and collection of provisions from rural relatives, urban families *have* adjusted structurally; that they would do this by actually going back to the rural areas remains a forlorn hope.

It is not necessary to agree with all the propositions contained in this passage to see that this is a valuable insight that shifts the focus of discussion concerning the impacts of reform from an abstract sectoral level exercise to one that tries to place actual micro-level human survival strategies at the forefront of its implications. This approach is important also in another way. It

draws attention to the two-way interactions of livelihoods and macro policies. Instead of the typical method, which is to attempt to measure and to explain the one-way impacts of reform on a set of economic variables (prices,
resource flows, outputs, incomes), this approach allows people's micro-level
responses to impact back on the macro policies, and thence to modify or
even negate their efficacy.

The interactive approach to livelihoods and macro policies suggested by
Jamal would be difficult to model in a formal sense, and even more difficult
to test due to the broad range of data that would be required to do so. For this
reason, it is unlikely to enter the mainstream of economic debate on reform
policies, although no doubt some efforts will be made at some stage, by someone, to capture some of this two-way complexity in more formal terms. There
remains plenty of scope, however, to improve our descriptive understanding
of the broader economic policy implications of diverse livelihood strategies
by rural and urban families.

The potential upside of reform for rural livelihoods

The reform process in low-income countries has been unusually prone to snap
judgements about its efficacy, lacking in historical perspective, and steeped in
prejudices either in favour or against the international financial institutions that
have been, and still are, its prime movers. Both proponents and detractors of reform felt impelled to rush into assessments of its benefits or disbenefits in the
late 1980s or early 1990s (many such reviews are cited earlier in this chapter),
often within just three or four years of the accedence to reform programmes by
a large number of sub-Saharan African countries. These assessments lack credibility, at least in the prematurity of their conclusions about success or failure, if
not in their contributions to ideas for modifying the reform process over time.

No one would pretend that the reform process has produced unqualified
benefits for rural livelihoods. The social impact on the most vulnerable groups
in rural society of contractions in public social services, the problems of sequencing of economic policy reversals, the indiscriminate axing of good as well
as defective government agencies undertaking service functions in rural development—these and other downsides have been emphasised in the critical literature. Nevertheless, they are not the whole picture, and the intention here is to
indicate, using some illustrative examples, some of the ways that rural livelihoods may have gained from reform.

One factor that tends to be underestimated by critics of reform is how bad
things were before reform was instigated. In different ways, Ghana and Tanzania

are two sub-Saharan African countries that were sliding into an abyss of macro crisis and declining living standards up to the point when reform programmes were adopted by their governments in the 1980s. It has been said of pre-reform Ghana, for example, that 'while other African countries have also declined since independence, the Ghanaian experience stands out for the comprehensiveness with which successive governments pursued economic destruction.' (Herbst, 1993: 17) By the end of the 1970s, real per capita income in Ghana was below two-thirds of its level at independence in 1957, and 'hardly any area influenced by public policy was not in distress' (Cassen, 1994: 7).

Ghana initiated a macroeconomic reform process in 1983, and during the following decade real per capita income is estimated to have risen by 1.4 per cent per annum, despite an average population growth rate of 2.8 per cent. Living standards surveys suggest that the incidence of poverty in Ghana may have declined between the mid-1980s and the early 1990s, falling from 37 per cent to 32 per cent for the population as a whole, and from 42 per cent to 33 per cent for the rural population (World Bank, 1995). Given that the share of agriculture in GDP appears to have declined in this period, a possible explanation of rising rural living standards is that they have depended on improving access to non-farm sources of rural household income. Some suggestive evidence on this is provided by living standards surveys, for example the 1988/89 Ghana Living Standards Survey (GLSS) found that on average nearly 40 per cent of rural household income was attributable to wage, non-farm self-employment and remittance income (Ghana, 1993; see also Table 9.1 in the next chapter).

Tanzania was another sub-Saharan African country in serious economic difficulties at the start of the 1980s. A decline of 10 per cent in GDP per capita is thought to have occurred in the relatively short interval between 1979 and 1982 (World Bank, 1984). The government of Tanzania agreed somewhat reluctantly to the country's first structural adjustment programme in 1986. Prior to that the government had made several attempts to reverse the deteriorating macroeconomic situation on its own, through internally-devised economic recovery programmes.

Macroeconomic data for Tanzania is difficult to interpret. It is acknowledged in official documents that many of the statistics underlying the compilation of macroeconomic aggregates in the 1980s and 1990s bore little relation to actual trends. For this reason, the national accounts were revised in the mid-1990s, based partly on a household income and expenditure survey conducted in 1991. This newer data displays different patterns of macroeconomic change from the older data (Tanzania, 1997).

According to the revisions, real GDP grew by 3.7 per cent per year between 1985 and 1995. This implies slow positive growth in per capita income post-reform, of the order of 0.7 per cent per year over that ten-year period. However, the revised GDP per capita series is about 20 per cent above the old series, reflecting a decision to incorporate previously unmeasured informal sector activity into the national accounts (Bagachwa and Naho, 1995). The result is that Tanzania's estimated per capita GDP in 1996 was US$206, whereas it would have been US$171 under the previous series.

Previous data suggested that agriculture was a growing share of GDP from the mid-1980s to the mid-1990s. This allowed one World Bank report (World Bank, 1994) to praise the virtues of the SAP in terms of agricultural growth, which was reported as having achieved a 5 per cent a year rise from 1984 to 1992, raising the share of agriculture in GDP from 44 per cent in the mid-1970s to 60 per cent in the early 1990s. The revised GDP data displays no such trend. Instead it suggests that agriculture was a steadily declining contributor to GDP from the mid-1980s to the mid-1990s, falling from around 52 per cent to 46 per cent in that period.

In view of these ambiguities in macroeconomic aggregates, it is difficult to identify firmly the trends in the national economy that constitute the opportunity context within which rural livelihoods were evolving. There is no doubt that considerable liberalisation took place in the 1990s, including abolition of controls on agricultural input and output prices, reform and divestiture of parastatals, liberalisation of import regimes, and the move to market exchange rates (World Bank, 1996d). The reforms occurred against a background of extensive state controls in Tanzania over the preceding thirty years; at the time of the first SAP in the mid-1980s, almost all production and exchange in Tanzania, even down to village shops, was conducted by parastatals, and virtually all agricultural output was supposed to be delivered through parastatal marketing channels (Ellis, 1982; 1988).

There is a widely accepted view that rural livelihoods were compromised by the immediately pre-reform Tanzanian state. Local officials had become increasingly capricious in their insistence that farmers grew designated crops, often burning or uprooting food crops in fields that infringed by-laws enforcing minimum cultivated areas of export crops like cotton or coffee. Unpredictable behaviour by parastatal crop authorities meant that designated crops did not get collected from village stores, or farmers did not get paid for their crop sales, sometimes for months, sometimes not at all. The lack of consumer goods reduced motivation to produce for the market and pushed many farm families back into subsistence (Bevan *et al.*, 1988). Prohibitions on private engagement in self-employment activities gave little scope for members of farm families to pursue or to develop alternative income-generating activities.

Several researchers in the 1980s pointed to the lack of ability of households to diversify income sources that accompanied the former broad scope of state involvement in the economy (Collier *et al.*, 1986; Bevan *et al.*, 1988). An increase in diversity might therefore occur as an outcome of liberalisation. This seems to be confirmed by studies of the size and diversity of the urban and rural informal economies in the 1990s (Maliyamkono and Bagachwa, 1993; Bagachwa and Naho, 1995; Bagachwa, 1997). An agricultural diversification and intensification study (Tanzania, 1994; 1995) found that 87 per cent of rural households obtained cash income from trade, wages, or self-employment. The same study also collected evidence suggesting that non-farm income sources might have an equalising effect on rural incomes since they would help to overcome the lack of access to land as an asset which was found to be the basic cause of poverty in some rural communities.

From the viewpoint of post-reform rural livelihoods, one of the most interesting 1990s studies of rural livelihoods in Tanzania was a participatory survey of twelve villages, utilising focus group techniques, undertaken under SIDA auspices in 1992 (Booth *et al.*, 1993). This study found that liberalisation had brought benefits to the poor as well as to the better off. It had achieved this by permitting economic activity in villages to diversify away from crop production, and by increasing the availability of consumer goods which acted as a stimulus to income generation for poor and rich alike. Household level income diversification was considered a positive development by women and young people in villages, because aside from providing new sources of cash income, it also enabled them to renegotiate social relations with males and elders in the village social context.

It is just possible, then, that irrespective of uneven results in terms of macroeconomic performance, the reform process in countries like Ghana and Tanzania has had a beneficial impact on rural livelihoods. It has done so by reducing high rates of inflation, diminishing the exposure of individuals and households to the capriciousness of local officialdom, dismantling controls over crop sales through official channels, lessening previous prohibitions on the free movement of goods and people, and permitting economic diversity to spring up where previously monolithic agencies of the state predominated. This last point is important and should not be underestimated. In many countries market liberalisation has reduced the profile in the economy of state and parastatal agencies that formerly curtailed diversity and constrained opportunities and outcomes.

On a rather different tack, it is not entirely coincidental that the macro reform process in low-income countries occurred in the same period as widespread changes in the methods and processes of local-level development initiatives. The retreat of the state from rural projects and services has been accompanied by the rapid rise of NGOs to take over some of the same, and some different, roles. This process is encouraged by donor agencies that redirect some proportion of grants and loans that would previously have been allocated to government bodies to NGOs instead. The rise of participatory approaches to rural development also parallels this process, and while it arises from different intellectual origins, the rapidity of its uptake in the 1990s was facilitated by the decline in the legitimacy of state power at local levels propelled by the widening ripples of reform. Critics of adjustment who are also champions of local-level participation may tend to underestimate the interdependence that in practice characterised these two apparently distinct processes of policy change occurring during the last fifteen years of the twentieth century.

Summary

This chapter examines the macroeconomic context of diverse rural livelihoods, placing emphasis on macro reform processes and their potential effects on the options and strategies available to rural households. In terms of the livelihoods framework (Chapter 2), macro policy constitutes a most important part of the opportunity context of rural livelihoods. However, further than this, it is the livelihood strategies of individuals and households that connect macro and micro policy levels. When macro policies are inimical to rural livelihoods, then there is little that micro level initiatives can do to achieve sustainable improvements in people's lives. Conversely, macro policies may provide an encouraging environment for rural livelihoods, lowering risk, stimulating flexibility, widening options and reducing vulnerability; and this context also gives micro policies leverage to achieve real gains in improving the capabilities and well-being of individuals and households.

The principle components and historical sequence of the macro reform process is traced, from its origins in economic stabilisation, through adjustment, and to the larger social and political concerns of reform. The reform process constitutes an ever widening agenda, rather than a sequence in which earlier preoccupations are dropped in favour of later substitutions. In its more recent manifestations, reform accepts the complementarity of government and markets, and is increasingly concerned with issues of good governance involving attributes of accountability, transparency, fairness and rule of law. Aspects of reform that have been identified as detrimental include declining social provision, poor sequencing, lack of ownership, evasion of conditionality, weak privatisation, and the inflexible imposition of a blueprint approach on widely varying individual country circumstances.

The macro–micro links between reform and rural livelihoods are traced, beginning with the changes in relative prices that occur with real devaluations of the exchange rate. These should result in higher returns to the production of tradable commodities, and to agricultural outputs in particular; however, considerations such as poorly working factor markets and the elimination of input subsidies may substantively lessen the force of these effects. The cross-sectoral diversification strategies of rural and urban households also modify the impact of economic signals produced by reform policies because intra-household adaptations are substituted for resource mobility involving independent economic agents across sectors.

The chapter concludes with a tentatively upbeat view of the long-run impact of reform on rural livelihoods. This view does not seek to side-step a number of justifiable criticisms that have been levelled at reform, but it does draw attention to beneficial impacts of reform for rural individuals and families, including the reversal of headlong trajectories of economic decline, the dismantling of bureaucratic controls over the free movement of commodities and people, and the reduction in the profile of state and parastatal agencies that formerly curtailed diversity and constrained opportunities and outcomes. Reform is an unfinished agenda. Rural livelihoods remain constrained in many instances by an inimical rather than facilitating or enabling context of local administration, and the governance dimension of the reform agenda is likely to remain at the forefront of progress in rural poverty reduction for some time to come.

PART III

Investigating Livelihoods for Policy Purposes

— CHAPTER 9 —

Methods and Livelihoods

This and the next chapter are concerned with appropriate methods for investigating livelihoods, in the context of applying the livelihoods approach to rural projects and policies. First, in this chapter, a general discussion of alternative methods for discovering important attributes of livelihoods is provided, focusing in particular on the activity and income dimension of livelihoods in accordance with the diversity theme of the book as a whole. Second, in the next chapter, a case-study of implementing a combined participatory and small sample survey approach to discovering livelihood attributes in three villages in Tanzania is presented.

These chapters do not pretend to be innovative in terms of methods. The view is taken that there are plenty of field methods around on which to draw in order to put together combinations that can capture the livelihood strategies and constraints of the poor as a prerequisite to good policy or project design. Also relevant in this context is the distinction between elicitive and empowering uses of participatory research methods, and this is taken up later in this chapter.

Previous chapters, especially Chapter 2 in which the livelihoods framework is set out, have raised in a general way the difficulty of putting boundaries around information gathering on rural livelihoods, so that data is pertinent to the task in hand, minimises disruption to the daily routines of respondents or participants, and is timely and cost effective in its collection and analysis. If achieved successfully, these precepts comply with the criterion known as 'optimal ignorance' (McCracken et al., 1988: 12), meaning that researchers consciously avoid collecting information that is superfluous to the needs of the project or policy being contemplated or implemented.

Livelihoods represent particular challenges for limiting the scope of empirical enquiry in this way. This is due to the complex interrelationships between assets, access and activities, making it difficult to decide what factors to include or exclude from investigation. Intertemporal social processes, such as kinship networks and reciprocal obligations, are particularly difficult to research. However, even the apparently straightforward economic category of income causes multiple problems when incomes are diverse, are derived from spatially dispersed sources, and involve self-employment activities in which personal income and business cash flow are inextricably woven together.

Arguments found elsewhere in this book suggest that knowledge about liveli-hood strategies is relevant to policy, whether that policy is macro or micro in scale. For example, it is important to know the actual rather than hypothesised activity portfolios of poor rural people, and how these are changing over time, so that support can be provided that facilitates and strengthens emerging, rather than declining, patterns of activity. It is also relevant for poverty reduction pur-poses in a particular location to know how poor people's livelihood strategies differ from those of the better off. Finally, the consequences of macro policies cannot be traced without a more accurate picture of how people respond and adapt to those policies. There is woeful ignorance in this area, and macro poli-cies in general proceed with little knowledge or feedback as to the changes in livelihood strategies they provoke at local levels in rural areas.

The field methods best suited to investigate rural poverty and to facilitate poverty reduction policies have been characterised in recent history by a widen-ing divergence between formal sample survey methods and participatory methods. On the one hand, the search for objective, quantifiable, measures of poverty led, in the 1990s, to formal sample surveys of ever increasing size and complexity. On the other hand, beginning in the 1980s, the rise of Rapid Rural Appraisal (RRA), evolving into Participatory Rural Appraisal (PRA), signalled the rejection of formal sample surveys as the most appropriate approach to achiev-ing a better understanding of rural livelihoods. Moreover, PRA casts doubt on the validity of fieldwork undertaken primarily as an extractive exercise, in which outsiders obtain data for use disconnected from the communities visited during the data collection exercise.

This chapter proceeds by elaborating this contrast between formal sample sur-veys and participatory methods, beginning with rural household surveys. In doing so it also reveals the perils of attempting to utilise secondary data from such surveys as a means of gaining an accurate picture of the composition of household incomes as an indicator of rural livelihood strategies.

Secondary income data and formal sample surveys

Secondary data available on rural income portfolios result from large- and small-scale sample surveys. Large-scale, formal, sample surveys undertaken by central statistical offices in developing countries are primarily conducted for macroeco-nomic or poverty estimation purposes; they constitute the basis of calculating cost-of-living indices, as well as contributing to the estimation of national ac-counts data. In most low-income countries, such surveys are conducted inter-mittently, sampling procedures change between surveys, they rely on one-visit questionnaires for data collection, and their focus is more on household expen-diture than on income. As is illustrated in due course, such surveys yield dubious results concerning the level and composition of household incomes, and much caution is required in making comparisons over time or between countries from data derived from them.

The position is not much better with respect to micro level household income studies. There can be found, of course, in most low-income countries an abundance of small-scale, location specific, sample survey data sets on rural incomes collected by various agencies for numerous different purposes. But inspection of such studies often reveal intractable problems of coverage and relevance. Supposedly total income turns out to be just farm income, or just cash income, or includes non-farm business income but neglects remittances, or neglects non-farm income earned by household members other than the household head, or turns out to have been based on a one visit survey relying on one person's recall of events over the previous year. For making comparisons across surveys, there is the added problem of lack of compatibility concerning the definitional categories of income components, so that individual income streams may be assigned to different sub-categories in the data analysis of different surveys.

Both large- and small-scale sample surveys are seen to share some similar problems with the collection of income data, and these are summarised as follows:

1. the timing of one visit surveys, e.g. middle of the dry season, during the crop growing period, just after harvest, one month after harvest etc., can make enormous differences in reported income;

2. many surveys collect data only from the household head, thus the cash earnings of other members of the households are inaccurately estimated or neglected;

3. some surveys report farm net income as if it corresponds to total household incomes, thus perpetuating the idea that small farmers depend just on farming for their livelihoods;

4. many surveys fail to enquire whether there are absent household members who normally contribute income to the household;

5. non-farm self-employment poses particular difficulties for its contribution to net income because data is required on both revenues and costs, and confusion arises between the personal and business attribution of 'net profits'.

Mainly, but not exclusively spear-headed by the World Bank, large-scale sample surveys administered in developing countries grew in frequency, size and complexity during the 1990s. The principal reasons cited for this were, to obtain better and more consistent estimates of poverty across the developing countries, to facilitate spatial and temporal comparisons of living standards, and to provide the benchmark data against which the success or failure of poverty reduction policies could be compared (e.g Ravallion, 1992).

A lot of the earlier work on such surveys was undertaken within the framework of the World Bank's Living Standards Measurement Survey (LSMS) programme (Glewwe and van der Gaag, 1988); however, as implemented in different countries, large-scale household budget surveys have had many different names such as the Living Standards Surveys (Ghana), Human Resource Development Survey (Tanzania), and Welfare Monitoring Surveys (Kenya). These surveys are typically conducted by central statistical offices, sometimes with help from local universities, and have depended a lot on technical assistance inputs by outside experts.

Living standards measurement surveys tend to have several important characteristics in common (Deaton, 1997). First, they are supposedly representative, not just of the country as a whole, but of the various provinces and districts within the country. This means that they comply with random sampling procedures within a national sampling frame which is thought to approximate closely underlying total population characteristics. Second, they are large, typically 3,000 households or more, perhaps equivalent to 0.2 per cent or so of the entire population. Third, they are complex, collecting data on demography, expenditure, incomes, assets, education and health, including the height and weight of members of respondent's households. Fourth, they generally rely on one visit answers to survey questions, although the size of the questionnaires may mean that survey completion has to be spread over more than one session with individual respondents.

These exercises have some important downsides. They are expensive to set up and to carry out, with a high level, perhaps even total, reliance on external funds for their execution. In this sense, they are unsustainable without outside assistance, and it is doubtful that any low-income country would conduct them in the absence of such assistance. They are extractive, in the sense that only data entry and, perhaps, relatively simple statistical compilations are undertaken locally, while most of the advanced analysis goes on elsewhere. They are prone to a wide variety of inaccuracies of recording and measurement due to the necessity of having a lot of pre-coded categories and questions, and to problems of recall across many different types of question.

Nevertheless, such surveys have generated a good deal of living standards data, and they form the quantitative basis of the poverty assessments that the World Bank undertook in many low-income countries in the 1990s, as well as intending to provide greater accuracy of worldwide estimates of the incidence of poverty according to the per capita consumption criterion.

As already indicated, amongst the least accurate data to emerge from these large-scale sample surveys is that on income portfolios due to factors such as inaccurate recall, incomplete listing of income sources, and absent household members. For these reasons, mean per capita income as calculated from such surveys are typically lower than mean per capita expenditure recorded, sometimes by a wide margin. As discussed in Chapter 4 above both theoretical and practical objections to income as a measure of household welfare can be made (Glewwe and van der Gaag, 1988). The theoretical objection is that income fluctuates month by month and year by year, so that income measurement at a point in time could be anywhere within a wide band of the average income obtained by the household. The practical objection is the point made above about the complexity of measuring the net income contribution of self-employment activities. To this must be added an understandably higher degree of suspicion on the part of respondents surrounding detailed questions about income than occurs with questions about consumption. Deaton (1997: 30) concludes that the 'practical and conceptual difficulties of collecting good income data are severe enough to raise doubts about the value of trying; the costs are large and the data may not always be of great value once collected.'

The outcome of these considerations is that economists researching poverty are much more comfortable working with expenditure than with income data. However, this also has the curious implication that the more that is known about poverty, its incidence, depth, severity and spatial occurrence, as found by these surveys, the less is known about the livelihood strategies of the poor, the way they adapt to adverse trends and events, and the evolving income sources that enable them to survive less or more precariously over time. Large-scale surveys, by the consensus of many leading thinkers in this area, are unable to help very much with the income side of livelihoods.

Case-studies of large-scale household budget surveys in selected sub-Saharan African countries illustrate many of the foregoing points, and individually demonstrate additional reasons why expensive living standards measurement studies perform poorly as a means of monitoring the impact of macro policy changes on the livelihood strategies of the rural poor. The case-studies here are taken from Ghana, Kenya and Tanzania. Each of these countries has received budgetary and technical assistance in order to undertake country-wide income and expenditure surveys. The purpose of these surveys is to monitor household welfare under conditions of economic policy change, especially in order to ensure that poverty impacts are well understood and safety-nets are put in place for those adversely affected by processes of change. Data from such surveys is also used by economic research organisations to undertake economic policy analysis, on all kinds of topics ranging from the sophisticated analysis of poverty and its attributes to economic relations of gender within the household.

Ghana is particularly bountiful as a source of externally-funded, large-scale household surveys. This may reflect the perception by the international donor community of Ghana as one of the success stories of structural adjustment in the 1980s and early 1990s. The surveys are entitled the Ghana Living Standards Surveys, and three rounds of such surveys (GLSS1, GLSS2 and GLSS3) were undertaken in 1987/88, 1988/89 and 1991/92 respectively. A fourth survey (GLSS4) was planned to take place in the late 1990s. The income portfolio data discussed here is derived from GLSS1 and GLSS2. Data on household income and expenditure was collected from 3,172 households in 1987/88 and 3,434 households in 1988/89, using the same questionnaire for both surveys, and in each case the surveys were carried out between the fourth quarter of the first year and the third quarter of the second year. Income portfolios compiled from these two surveys are shown in Table 9.1.

Table 9.1. Ghana: rural household income portfolios, 1987/88 and 1988/89

	GLSS 1		GLSS 2	
	Cedis	%	Cedis	%
Income sources				
Wages	14,724	6.3	20,553	9.1
Farm income	169,374	72.5	130,903	58.2
Non-farm self	37,225	15.9	55,049	24.5
Rental income[a]	2,767	1.2	3,687	1.6
Remittances	7,231	3.1	11,996	5.3
Other income	2,241	1.0	2,704	1.2
Total income	233,562	100.0	224,892	100.0
Total expenditure	282,080		307,831	

[a] Imputed rental income mainly comprises owner-occupied housing.
Source: Ghana (1993: 23).

These figures demonstrate many of the difficulties concerning data accuracy, and the use of such data for livelihood monitoring purposes on the income side, that characterise this type of large-scale sample survey. It is worth noting, first, that the income figures collected underestimated household standards of living, as indicated by the shortfall between average household income and average household expenditure. This is a common occurrence in surveys of this type, but these shortfalls are quite large, income is underestimated by 20 per cent in the first survey and by 37 per cent in the second. This is assuming of course, that expenditure estimates are reasonably robust, which may itself be an heroic assumption.

Second, while these two surveys took place just twelve months from each other, and used an identical sampling frame and questionnaire, the income proportions they exhibit change dramatically over this time interval. The contribution of own-account farming to household income appears to fall from over 73 to 58 per cent, and the corresponding share of non-farm income sources rises from 27 to 42 per cent. Non-farm self-employment demonstrates a particularly spectacular rise from 16 to 25 per cent of household income in this interval.

Now there may be valid explanations for these somewhat implausible changes in household income sources in rural Ghana over an interval of one year. For example, the figures in Table 9.1 have not been adjusted for inflation, and although this is less important when comparing percentages than when comparing absolute values, it cannot be assumed that prices have risen uniformly, and that therefore proportions were unaffected by price changes occurring unevenly between resources, sectors, and outputs. Also, the shortfalls in the income data as compared to the expenditure data are not necessarily distributed evenly across income sources, and the pattern of understatement may differ in the two surveys. However, when all is said and done, the principal conclusion that must be derived from the mismatch between these two surveys is that they are fundamentally flawed for work on rural livelihood strategies and the income portfolios with which they are associated.

A second case-study is provided by Kenya, a country that is acknowledged to have had a good statistical service in the past, although difficulties in managing routine data collection and processing emerged there during the 1990s (World Bank, 1995b). The Kenya statistical service has undertaken several large-scale household surveys at intervals over the years, however, the single one considered here is the second Welfare Monitoring Survey (WMS2), carried out in 1994 by the Central Bureau of Statistics with assistance from the World Bank (Kenya, 1996). The main purpose of this and a preceding survey (WMS1) was to monitor poverty trends, particularly the effects of Kenya's structural adjustment programme. Over 10,000 households were drawn from a sample frame based on the 1989 population census and included both urban and rural households. The results of this survey for rural income portfolios by province are summarised in Table 9.2.

The Kenya WMS2 was a single visit survey, and the timing of the survey is thought to have had an important effect on these results. For example, for the country as a whole, subsistence consumption appears to be only 10 per cent of rural household income. However, the survey was conducted mainly in the preharvest season when many households could have been buying in food crops, particularly maize, in order to tide them over until the first food harvests were realised.

As is expected, given differences in agroecology, infrastructure, economic activities, and proximity to urban centres, income portfolios in Kenya vary across provinces, as also between individual districts within provinces. However, many of the results displayed in Table 9.2 run counter to common sense and reveal significant data quality problems. For example, North-Eastern Province is justifiably regarded as one of the poorest provinces in Kenya (Narayan and Nyamwaya, 1995). It is remote from markets and services, and the principal livelihood there is nomadic pastoralism. Yet in Table 9.2 it appears as the second richest province, after Rift Valley which is at the heart of Kenya's most productive commercial agriculture. Then, again, it hardly seems likely that Coast Province, most of which is agriculturally marginal, should display a higher proportion of income from crop sales than Central Province which produces export and commercial food crops in substantial quantities.

Table 9.2. Kenya: composition of rural incomes by province, 1994

	Central	Coast	Eastern	North-Eastern	Nyanza	Rift Valley	Western	Total
Agricultural income (%)	*30.0*	*38.6*	*37.7*	*59.9*	*35.1*	*51.6*	*43.8*	*42.2*
Subsistence consumption	10.1	5.9	13.8	12.0	11.9	8.8	11.6	10.5
Livestock sales	7.6	6.9	13.8	47.2	12.2	17.0	13.3	14.0
Crop sales	11.9	25.7	9.4	0.5	10.6	25.2	18.4	17.2
Other agricultural income	0.4	0.1	0.7	0.2	0.4	0.6	0.5	0.5
Non-farm income (%)	*70.0*	*61.4*	*62.3*	*40.1*	*64.9*	*48.4*	*56.2*	*57.9*
Wages/salaries/profits	48.5	45.5	44.9	28.4	41.6	37.5	38.1	41.3
Other non-agricultural	21.5	15.9	17.4	11.7	23.3	10.9	18.1	16.5
Total income (KShs)	6,839	7,400	6,133	7,601	5,882	10,028	6,431	7,305

Source: Kenya (1996b).

No doubt if traced in detail, reasons can be found for the inaccuracies in these income portfolios across provinces. However, what the Kenya example illustrates in common with the Ghana experience is that these very expensive exercises in large-scale household data collection are for practical purposes not very helpful as a guide to the livelihood strategies of rural households under economic policy change.

The final example given here covers a series of large-scale sample surveys undertaken in Tanzania between 1969 and 1991 (Table 9.3). These surveys vary in their size and in the methods by which samples were selected in order to achieve representativeness across the country, with the 1976/77 Household Budget Survey generally being acknowledged as complying most completely with the requisite statistical criteria (Sarris and van den Brink, 1993). As must be expected, cautionary remarks are required regarding the comparability of these data sets. Different surveys treat different income categories in different ways. In compiling Table 9.3, the category designated farm cash income includes crop and livestock cash income only. Other natural resource based income sources are included in business income, that is, non-farm self-employment. Remittances, where applicable, include other transfer payments such as pensions. Wages include off-farm agricultural wages as well as non-farm wage incomes.

Table 9.3. Tanzania: rural income portfolios from large-scale surveys

	Sample characteristics				
Year of survey	1969	1976/77	1980	1983	1991
No. of rural hh	n.a.	3,247	600	498	477
Mean hh size	4.61	5.80	5.30	6.89	6.22
Total income per hh					
(TShs)	1,750	5,583	3,892	70,514	225,569
Income per capita					
(TShs)	380	930	734	1,549	36,252
	Percentage composition of rural household incomes (%)				
Subsistence	43.9	49.2	49.0	44.9	35.2
Farm cash	24.3	18.8	27.5	17.6	54.0
Crops	17.3	16.8	14.1	10.3	50.5
Livestock	7.0	2.0	13.4	7.2	3.5
Non-farm cash	31.8	32.0	23.5	37.5	10.8
Wages	12.7	7.5	n.a.	6.4	5.5
Business	16.9	22.2	19.5	26.3	4.2
Remittances	2.3	2.4	4.0	4.8	1.1
Total income	100.0	100.0	100.0	100.0	100.0

Sources: Tanzania (1969; 1977), Collier *et al.* (1986), Bevan *et al.* (1988), Sarris and van den Brink (1993), World Bank (1993), Ferreira (1993), Sarris and Tinios (1995).

The question arises as to whether these surveys yield any useful insights into evolving rural livelihoods in Tanzania over the more than two decades that they span. The answer is probably not very many. The firmest figures in the table are the share of subsistence income in total income, which tends to be reported clearly in all sources, followed by the totals for farm cash income and non-farm cash income. Income shares have moved erratically with no clear trends and some very odd results indeed emerge from the 1991 survey, locally referred to as the Cornell-ERB Survey, the expenditure side of which provided the statistical basis for the World Bank poverty report on Tanzania (Ferreira, 1994; World Bank, 1993a). Income data from that survey purport to show that farm income (including subsistence) was 89.2 per cent of total income, implying that only 10.8 per cent of rural household incomes in 1991 came from non-farm sources. The majority of quantitative and qualitative data on Tanzanian rural livelihoods in the 1990s (see also discussion in Chapter 8 above) makes this a most unlikely representation of the actual situation in rural Tanzania in that period.

Some broad observations concerning rural livelihoods in Tanzania can, perhaps, be deduced from the figures shown in Table 9.3, especially if the dubious 1991 data is excluded from such an overview. First, there is the significance of the non-monetary contribution to overall income portfolios through the 1970s and 1980s. Second, wages do not appear to have been a very significant source of rural incomes in Tanzania over that historical period, indicating the absence and little development of rural labour markets whether in agriculture itself or in rural non-farm enterprises. Third, some evidence of growth in non-farm self-employment (business) incomes and in remittances seems apparent in all but the last survey (Sarris and van den Brink, 1993).

Essentially, however, the Tanzania examples, like those of Ghana and Kenya, reveal far more about the defects of large-scale household surveys for generating policy-relevant data on rural livelihoods than about the useful outputs of such surveys. Indeed, the income data from such surveys is so parlous that the detached observer may be forgiven for becoming sceptical also about the expenditure data deriving from them, upon which such great edifices of poverty analysis are built. This is notwithstanding the accepted wisdom that expenditure data is sufficiently more accurate than income data to have confidence in its accuracy for describing the incidence of poverty, and other facets of material living standards in rural and urban populations in low income countries (Deaton, 1997).

Participatory methods

While poverty analysis by economists has proceeded in one direction—the devising and implementing of ever more comprehensive questionnaire surveys—practical poverty reduction activities undertaken at local levels by NGOs and aid agencies have been proceeding in an entirely different direction, utilising a family of approaches collectively known as Participatory Rural Appraisal (PRA). The origins and strands of PRA are described in Chambers (1994a; 1994b; 1994c). An important antecedent, which in practical terms still continues to characterise quite a lot of policy research in rural communities is Rapid Rural Appraisal (RRA) (e.g. Chambers, 1981; McCracken *et al.*, 1988). RRA sought to achieve a quicker, more accurate, and less expensive means of gathering relevant local information for project purposes than formal sample surveys. It also sought to correct perceived anti-poverty biases in fieldwork with spatial, project, personal, seasonal and diplomatic dimensions (Chambers, 1994a: 956).

After gathering momentum for a decade or so, RRA, by then merging into PRA, had assembled and widely tested a rich and diverse set of field methods, both for eliciting information in rural communities, and for involving members of communities themselves in setting priorities for projects and policies. These methods include group discussions, drawing maps, transect walks, time lines and trend analysis, seasonal calendars, wealth ranking, matrix scoring and ranking, and many others. The emphasis of these methods is on active involvement by respondents, the outsider as learner rather than teacher, and qualitative prioritising or ordinal ranking of variables and options, instead of the quantitative measurement of them.

While all such methods tend nowadays to be referred to as participatory, Chambers (1994a) rightly suggests that a distinction still needs to be made between extractive or elicitive exercises, where outsiders obtain information which is then analysed and acted on outside its site of origin, and facilitating or participatory exercises, where the entire cycle of information gathering, establishing priorities, deciding on action, and implementing decisions is conducted jointly and interactively with those whose lives are affected by the decisions taken. In this sense, quite a lot of elicitive work by donor agencies, like, for example, the Participatory Poverty Assessments (PPAs) financed by the World Bank and other donors are more RRA than PRA in character.

PRA has been defined as 'a family of approaches that enable people to express and analyse the realities of their lives and conditions, to plan themselves what action to take, and to monitor and evaluate the results' (Chambers and Blackburn, 1996: 1). In this interpretation PRA becomes a vehicle for empowering people to take control of their own lives, and, ideally, many of its key components become institutionalised as ongoing processes of plural and democratic decision-making in rural communities. The primary role of the outsider in 'true' PRA is as facilitator and equal sharer of ideas and information; it is not information acquisition, and it is not arriving with pre-packaged technical solutions to local problems.

In evolving from RRA to PRA, participatory methods have certainly lost their sense of urgency. Whereas a prime motive for RRA, as a substitute for formal sample surveys, was to speed up data gathering and analysis so that it could be acted on quickly in the solution of problems or in the setting up of projects, a prime motive of PRA is to facilitate people to take charge of their own agendas for change, which is a gradual and continuing process. Whereas RRA could be interpreted as a means to achieve various desirable ends, for example, more rapid identification of successful from unsuccessful crop hybrids tested in poor farmers' fields, PRA is to an important degree an end itself.

In keeping with most contemporary usage, the ensuing discussion uses PRA as a shorthand for approaches based on participatory methods, irrespective of whether they are primarily elicitive or empowering in character. RRA seems to have virtually disappeared from the vocabulary of participatory field methods; meanwhile the specifically 'rural' character of PRA is becoming redundant as the same methods are used in urban areas, and its use spreads elsewhere, for example, as a means of improving participation in organisations. The term Participatory Learning and Action (PLA) has been proposed as a more appropriate description of these approaches (e.g. Pretty *et al.*, 1995).

The argument of this book suggests that knowledge of livelihoods, and especially of the diversification strategies of the poor requires rather more precision than just remarking that it occurs, in a vague way. It is useful for policy and projects to make links between livelihood strategies and standards of living, to distinguish beneficial types of diversity from detrimental types, to capture the spatially dispersed character of livelihoods, and to make connections between macroeconomic policies and micro level livelihood adaptations. For these reasons, it is the elicitive rather than empowering strengths of PRA which are of chief interest in the current context, without in any way inferring that the latter should not have priority over the former in other contexts.

PRA provides many useful tools for discovering, quite quickly, the mediating processes within which livelihood strategies are adopted, that is, those related to social relations (e.g. customary divisions of labour), institutions (e.g. rules governing access to land and mediation of land disputes), and organisations (e.g. village committees, credit groups, women's groups, health centres). Key informants, semi-structured interviews, informal group discussions, focus group discussions, Venn diagrams and so on can all contribute in this regard. PRA methods are also excellent for discovering the current and past contextual circumstances governing livelihood decisions, for example, emerging environmental problems (water sources, firewood), changing patterns of activity as perceived for the village as a whole, key current constraints and problems.

It is, perhaps, worth making the distinction between diagrammatic PRA techniques (see Table 9.4 below) as output and as an information collection method. A calendar which plots price fluctuations for an essential commodity through the year, for example, is useful as a graphic output if it assists interpretation of the context of livelihood vulnerability; and this would be true whether the calendar arose from a participatory exercise, or whether it was constructed by a researcher or project planner from structured questionnaire data. However, many practitioners consider that these techniques possess separate merit as a means of communication, since they 'allow information to be set out visually. This has many advantages over purely verbal description in improving clarity. It also generates a new focus of discussion, in which questions can be addressed to the diagram rather than direct to the interviewee' (Woodhouse, 1998: 141–142). On the other hand, Mohan (1998), warns that doctrinaire use of such techniques can alienate respondents, citing a case in which participants had considered these visual methods to be patronising.

Wealth and income issues are addressed in PRA by using ranking methods. There are many different variants of these, for example, selected informants, group discussion or self-ranking, and these may yield differing results for grouping households into wealth or income categories. A common approach is to seek a small number of informants who are themselves diverse by reference to their position in village society, and ask them to assign households into categories, as well as to state the reasons for their assignment. Households are then scored according to their position in each individual ranking, and these scores are summed across rankings to obtain a combined wealth ranking.

This exercise is useful at local levels of interactive decision-making for identifying the poorest households in village communities. It may also yield quite a lot of descriptive information on the livelihoods pursued by households assigned to different wealth groups, for example, commonly, wealthy households are characterised by access to, or ownership of, far more non-farm assets and activities than poor households. Nevertheless, the method yields information that remains at a broad brush level of description; the definition of relative wealth is likely to remain fuzzy around the edges after discussion; income sources are descriptive (e.g. that a household mainly grows coffee for a living) rather than conveying accurate information on significance (the household may indeed be seen by other villagers as primarily growing coffee, but may, in fact, depend more for its standard of living on remittances from a relative working in the capital city).

PRA methods possess their own risks of inaccuracy when they are utilised for elicitive purposes. The following problems have been noted with respect to focus group discussions and village meetings as data collection exercises:

1. group meetings can project a preferred image of the community, village or group that may not correspond to the underlying reality of people's lives (Mosse, 1994; Pottier and Orone, 1995);
2. local power structures and social conventions can influence the progress and outcomes of such meetings (Woodhouse, 1998: 143–145);
3. they place considerable demands on time and this has the effect of selecting those who can afford the time to attend the meetings (Leurs, 1996: 70);
4. there is a danger that key informants self-select for a particular social group, and do not include the richest or the poorest in the community (Johnson and Mayoux, 1998: 155);
5. the group level aggregate picture that emerges from such meetings may mask local differentiation (Woodhouse, 1998); and, arising from all these points,

Table 9.4. Typical characteristics of different field methods

	Approach			
	Large-scale sample survey	Small-scale sample survey	Semi-structured or participatory enquiry	Case-study
Techniques	Interviews to complete predetermined questionnaires	Interviews to complete predetermined questionnaires	Secondary data and aerial photography review; direct observation; semi-structured interviews; ranking; stories and portraits; maps and transects; seasonal calendars; time lines; trend analysis; ethno-biographies; flow diagrams; decision trees; Venn diagrams; matrices; workshops	Multiple methods
Informants	Household members (esp. head)	Household members (esp. head)	Community groups; sub-groups; key informants; households; individuals	

Informant selection basis	Probability sampling at regional or national level	Probability sampling of specific, localised population	Probability sampling of specific, localised population	As necessary to develop theoretical model as enquiry proceeds
Content selection	Predetermined by researcher/planner	Predetermined by researcher/planner	Developed by participants and researcher/facilitator as enquiry proceeds	Developed by researcher/planner as enquiry proceeds
Typical unit of measurement	Household; individual	Household; individual	Community/village; household; individual	Household; individual
Rigour/validity	Adherence to probability sampling (interpretation validity requires supplementary information)	Adherence to probability sampling (interpretation validity requires supplementary information)	Triangulation and documentation: cross-checking with secondary data	Triangulation: record keeping; adoption of contrastive approach
Generalisation	Statistical inferences	Statistical inferences	Extrapolation unsafe	Theoretical or analytic generalizations

Sources: Abbot and Guijt (1997), Chambers (1992), McCracken *et al.* (1988), Robson (1993), Thomas (1998), Woodhouse (1998).

6. there is a need to triangulate findings that derive from more than one set of field methods.

These concerns arise in part because PRA has 'increasingly been seen as a "new orthodoxy"' (Farrington 1998: 2), raising doubts about its uncritical adoption as a comprehensive 'package', without due assessment of the validity and appropriateness of specific methods to the particular context in which they are to be used (Biggs and Smith, 1998; Gueye, 1995).

Combining methods

It is apparent from the foregoing discussion that neither sample surveys nor participatory methods provide, as separate packages, a complete approach to investigating livelihood diversity for policy purposes. A combination of the two approaches is required, each serving different but complementary roles within an overall research design. Examples of such a complementary approach can be found in a number of different investigative contexts (e.g. Moser, 1996; Woodhouse, 1998); in some cases, it has been found that a follow-up, semi-structured group enquiry can give clearer insights into the results of a pre-planned sample survey; in others, an exploratory rapid appraisal has been found to offer the best method to ensure appropriateness in the design of a sample survey.

In the present context of seeking to achieve an adequate understanding of livelihood strategies, participatory investigations have two main roles: the first is to discover the evolving livelihood context, the changing access, activities, constraints, and key problems as identified for the community as a whole; the second is to stratify the community between wealth or income groups. Sample survey methods come into their own to discover reasonably accurate asset and activity profiles and resulting income portfolios. Samples are small and are focused on eliciting only that information that the broader participatory exercise is unable to uncover.

The collection of income data is a sensitive matter that therefore requires the building of trust between researchers and the households that are chosen for sample survey work. Preceding formal data collection by a PRA exercise is one way of achieving this. Identifying a research co-ordinator who is resident in the village and already held in trust by village members is another. While not always possible for reason of resources and time pressures, accurate livelihood research should involve repeat visits to the same households at different points across the calendar year, both to verify recall data collected previously, and to gain an insight into the seasonality characteristics of livelihood strategies. Even with one-visit surveys, provision for several repeat visits spread over several days to follow up on matters of detail with different household members is likely to result in much better research results than can be obtained from a single visit.

Summary

In summary, a variety of field methods are available for the type of initial investigation of rural livelihoods that is being considered in this and the next chapter. The more prominent of these methods are listed in Table 9.4 above, as are the characteristics of the broad approaches with which they are typically associated. These approaches and methods, however, are not seen here as being mutually exclusive, rather they can be seen as a portfolio from which a hybrid approach can be developed which utilises the strengths of particular methods that are appropriate to a particular investigation, whilst avoiding attendant weaknesses.

The principal strength of the sample survey is its capacity to yield detailed information at a household or individual level about a population, whilst minimising investigative resource demand by gathering this information from a small sample. Moreover, the ease with which a sample survey can be standardised increases the capacity of this method to produce information that is readily comparable between investigations. The definition of the population that a sample can represent can be localised, such as a single village, or can refer to a much wider population at regional or national level, with a resultant effect on the scale of the survey itself. In the case of national surveys, the large scale necessary to achieve representativeness has been seen to be a serious weakness of that approach, since it results in surveys that are expensive to set up and to carry out, typically inefficient in use of resources, with a high level, perhaps even total, reliance on external funds for their execution, and yielding results which appear to be of little utility for monitoring the impacts of policy on livelihood strategies.

CHAPTER 10

A Case-Study in Rural Tanzania

The purpose of this chapter is to review, critically, the procedure and outcomes of a combined participatory and small-scale survey approach to investigating rural livelihoods, conducted in three villages in northern Tanzania in 1997. The site of the fieldwork was three villages in the highland zone of Hai District, in Kilimanjaro Region (see Map 10.1), a location typically thought of as a small-farm coffee production area, where coffee might be expected to dominate household income portfolios.

This was an experimental exercise guided especially by considerations of cost-effectiveness and timeliness in obtaining policy useful research results. It had a small budget and comprised three main components:

1. Semi-structured focus group discussions designed to be written up in a single, one-page, spreadsheet table per village;
2. A participatory wealth ranking exercise;
3. A sample survey which consisted of four one-page forms, dealing with:
   (*a*) demographic data, absent family members and remittance income;
   (*b*) land as an asset and farm income data;
   (*c*) non-farm income sources;
   (*d*) household assets, including production as well as consumption assets.

The three villages were selected purposively to represent three differing degrees of remoteness from public infrastructure and services, so that effects of location on income portfolios could be highlighted. Within each village, thirty households were interviewed, these being stratified between three income-wealth categories identified using the wealth ranking exercise, so that there were ten households in each category.

In terms of the assets-access-activities framework, these research components were anticipated to fulfil different roles. It was intended that the focus group discussions would provide a broad brush background on all three dimensions of the framework, as seen from a community perspective, and would be especially helpful concerning perceptions of change and access. The wealth ranking was intended to permit the assets and activities of the poorest households in each of these villages to be distinguished from those of better-off households. The sample survey was intended to provide quantitative data in support of the latter objective.

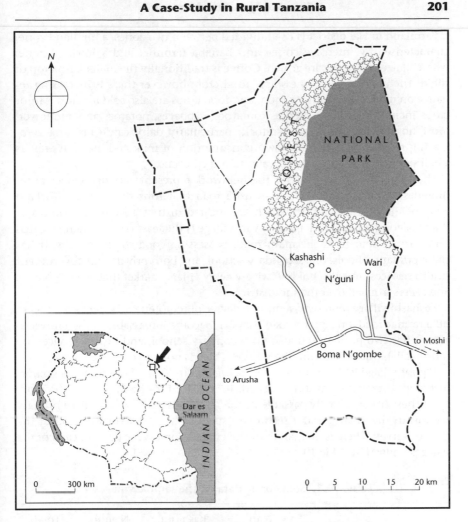

Map 10.1. Hai district, Kilimanjaro region, Tanzania

The study area and villages

The Hai district of Kilimanjaro Region in Tanzania is located on the slopes of Mount Kilimanjaro, and covers an area of 2,160 km^2. The district had a population in 1988 of around 200,000 corresponding to some 38,000 households. The highland zone of the district had a population density of around 200 persons per km^2 in 1988, compared to 30 persons per km^2 for Tanzania as a whole. Land in Hai district is divided between areas designated as national park and forest, and land used for farming (Map 10.1).

Farmland in Hai district is itself divided between two zones, a highland zone, characterised by intensive coffee and banana farming, and a lowland zone, where maize and beans are grown. Coffee is traditionally the major cash crop of the district, and bananas the staple food crop; however there is increasing reliance on maize and beans for food, and food crops are also sold for cash. Minor crops include vegetables such as tomatoes, cabbages, potatoes and sunflower. Most households also keep livestock, particularly dairy cattle utilising zero-grazing regimes, for sales and own consumption of milk and meat, as well as small stock such as goats, sheep, rabbits and chickens.

The three villages selected for the fieldwork represent varying degrees of remoteness from the main Moshi–Arusha road that runs through the lowland zone of the district, and on which are located district government offices at Boma N'gombe (Map 10.1 again). Wari village is the least remote, being located on a tarmac spur from the main road, possessing good social services. It has three primary schools, one secondary school, and both private and government health services, and also holds a twice-weekly village market that attracts buyers and sellers from all over the sub-district.

Kashashi village represents a middle degree of remoteness, being located 5 km off a tarmac road, on a gravel road that can become impassable in the rainy season. It has two primary schools, no secondary school, and health services are only available at 10 km from the village. There is no market in the village.

N'guni village is the most remote, being about 40 km from Boma N'gombe. Although three different dirt roads connect N'guni to the Moshi–Arusha road, all of these become barely passable in the rainy season. There are three primary schools in the village, and a secondary school was under construction at the time of survey. There is no market in the village. Some basic data on each of the villages is given in Table 10.1.

Table 10.1. Some basic data on the sample villages

	Wari	Kashashi	N'guni	Total
No. of households	1,007	456	502	1,965
Total population	6,888	3,600	2,850	13,338
Distance to district HQ (km)	25	20	40	—

The focus group discussions

The semi-structured group discussions focused on changes and trends over the preceding decade in five main areas of livelihoods: changes in main income sources; the emergence of new activities; agricultural production and marketing problems; access to natural resources; and ways in which life was perceived to have improved or worsened over the past ten years. Participants in group discussions were asked to compare the situation now with that obtaining five and ten years ago.

For each of the above topics, discussions were summarised as a list of events, activities, income sources etc., that had been identified (for example, a list of aspects of people's lives that had improved over the last decade), qualified by a brief account of comments that had arisen. Whilst the subsequent sample survey was expected to provide a detailed account of current income sources, the information gained in the group discussions gave an overall picture of change in these aspects of people's lives, and it was able to capture asset issues such as overall land availability which could not be picked up in a survey that investigated land holding in terms of current area owned by households.

In summarising the findings of the group discussions, by village, and subsequently in comparison between villages, the 'vulnerability context' (D. Carney, 1998) predominated due to the focus of the discussions on changes and trends. For example, for the most remote village selected for investigation, N'guni, it was possible to summarise the findings of the group discussions as set out in Box 10.1.

In addition to the lists of factors summarised in Box 10.1, arising from the questions used as a basis for the group discussions, the wider debate that ensued gave insights into the processes that linked these components. The complexity of tracing these feedback relationships represents a challenge for livelihoods work. To take agricultural intensification and diversification in response to the changes in the fortunes of coffee as an example, across the villages people turned to increased dairying, french beans, potatoes, sunflowers, beekeeping and aquaculture. Some of these new enterprises were successful, others not. An attempt to include all these links on a single diagram was found to confuse the picture, but by focusing on the most prominent change, strength or emerging trend that the discussions revealed—in this case, the increasing importance of dairy production—it was found that the factors that participants in the discussion identified as influential could be linked across the components, and tied in with related responses in other villages. Again utilising the remote N'guni village as an example, this descriptive linking exercise is shown in Box 10.2.

In summary of the main features that were discovered from the group discussions across all three villages, coffee was stated to have been the main income source ten years previously, but had declined drastically in importance as a result of the low prices for coffee compared with the cost of inputs, the high incidence of coffee berry disease, and ageing coffee trees. It is interesting to note as an aside that the devaluations of the exchange rate that had accompanied economic reform, which might have been expected to increase the prices farmers received for coffee in local currency, did not seem to have reversed the slide in the fortunes of coffee. Farmers had diversified from coffee into dairying during

Box 10.1. Livelihood features emerging from group discussions, N'guni village, Hai district

Vulnerability context	*Shocks*
	High incidence of coffee berry disease
	Trends
	Rising costs of pesticides
	Ageing coffee trees
	Declining coffee prices
	Rising costs and diminishing availability of veterinary services
	Rising costs and diminishing availability of concentrates
	Diminishing rainfall
	Deterioration in public health services
	Improved transport services
	Improved availability of consumer goods
	Improved market access for milk (via women's association)
	Land fragmentation due to population pressure
	Forest encroachment
	Damage to water courses by bankside cultivation
Transforming structures and processes	Introduction of improved dairy cattle
Livelihood strategies	Intensification and diversification of agricultural production:
	■ dairying replaced coffee as leading income generating activity, although coffee still important
	■ French beans
	■ potatoes; switch from subsistence to commercial production
	■ aquaculture
Livelihood assets	*Natural capital*
	Land scarcity
	Scarcity of forest products
	Physical capital
	Poor access during rains
	Water shortages

Box 10.2. Influences on the changing importance of dairy production, N'guni village, Hai district

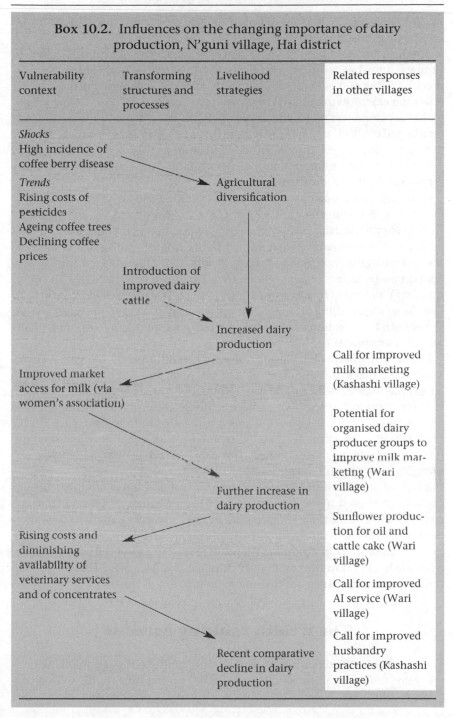

Vulnerability context	Transforming structures and processes	Livelihood strategies	Related responses in other villages
Shocks High incidence of coffee berry disease			
Trends Rising costs of pesticides Ageing coffee trees Declining coffee prices		Agricultural diversification	
	Introduction of improved dairy cattle	Increased dairy production	
Improved market access for milk (via women's association)			Call for improved milk marketing (Kashashi village)
		Further increase in dairy production	Potential for organised dairy producer groups to improve milk marketing (Wari village)
Rising costs and diminishing availability of veterinary services and of concentrates			Sunflower production for oil and cattle cake (Wari village)
			Call for improved AI service (Wari village)
		Recent comparative decline in dairy production	Call for improved husbandry practices (Kashashi village)

the previous decade, and the strength of this switch was associated with increased investment in improved breeds of dairy cattle.

Attempts had also been made to diversify into other agricultural activities. Farmers in the two more remote villages had tried french beans about five years previously, but this activity lost popularity and was abandoned because of disease problems. Potatoes were now grown on a commercial basis in one village, and aquaculture was increasing in popularity in two villages. In Wari, the least remote village, the only new activity mentioned apart from dairying was the growing of sunflowers, utilised for oil extraction as well as for supplementary feed for dairy cattle. Interestingly, new non-farm opportunities were scarcely mentioned in the group discussions.

Emerging environmental constraints were identified in all villages. The supply of new land for cultivation in the highland zone was exhausted, and farm sizes were becoming smaller as they were subdivided between children. Land was available in the lowlands, but at some distance from the villages, and this land was not suitable for coffee and banana production. Most villagers were dependent on on-farm trees (mainly species *Grevillea* grown as a shade tree for coffee) for timber and wood fuel, but tree planting to replace trees felled was said to be rare. Some illegal felling of trees for timber was said to occur in the forest reserve. Water both for irrigation and for drinking purposes was identified as potentially an increasing problem.

Despite the insights into livelihood strategies afforded by the group discussions, they shed little light on those who adopted, and those who were able to adopt, the strategy of increasing dairy production. Such identification was difficult from the group discussions alone, oriented as they were to describing trends and changes at the village level. It was not possible to infer from such discussions whether, for example, dairying represented an equal potential opportunity for everybody in the village, nor who would benefit if dairying was identified for policy intervention.

It is possible that a different organisation and subdivision of group discussions could have elicited more in these areas. However, where livelihood strategies across all income strata are characterised by their diversity and variability, there is quite a high risk that focus group discussions are unable to capture with sufficient accuracy for policy purposes the assets and strategies of the poor as distinct from the better off in the community. It remains to be assessed below whether the sample survey turned out to be more helpful in this respect.

The wealth ranking exercise

The criteria identified during the participatory household wealth ranking exercise were similar in all three villages. Middle income households were distinguished from the poorest by the size of their coffee/banana plots, their ownership of one or two improved dairy cattle and their possession of brick or concrete iron-roofed houses, rather than mud and thatch houses. The wealthiest households owned at least two improved cattle, a large coffee/banana plot, a business such as a shop or a grain mill, and an expensive asset, such as a motor-cycle. Using these criteria, all households in each village were designated as low, middle or high income. The percentages falling into each group in the three vil-lages are shown in Table 10.2.

Table 10.2. Relative size of village income groups as defined by wealth ranking (%)

Village	Low-income	Middle-income	High-income	Total
Wari	37	34	29	100
Kashashi	49	31	20	100
N'guni	34	40	26	100

According to the wealth ranking exercise, the medium-remote village of Kashashi was the poorest, with almost half of its households falling into the low-income category and only a fifth into the high-income category. The least-remote village of Wari had the highest proportion of high-income households, and the remote village of N'guni was characterised by the predominance of middle-income households.

Sample survey results

The purpose of the sample survey was to elicit more accurate and policy-relevant information on the two critical dimensions of livelihoods—assets and activities. A total of 90 households were interviewed, i.e. 30 in each village, and these were distributed equally across the three income classes identified in the wealth rank-ing exercise. Since the consequent sub-samples of 10 households were not pro-portional to the relative size of the income classes in the total populations of the survey villages, the ensuing statistical analysis applied weights to correct for this occurrence. The year of the survey, 1997, was identified by villagers as a particu-larly bad year for coffee due to drought and disease problems. While this may therefore have caused atypical findings, it will have permitted some insight into the adaptation of livelihoods to the unanticipated decline of a principal income source.

In the statistical work that follows, two households from the least remote Wari village were omitted from the analysis because they represented extreme outliers in the data set. One of these households owned two shops, two cars, and had an annual income four times the next highest in thc sample. The other, although being placed by villagers in the middle wealth category, was recorded as farming 84 acres, whereas the next largest area farmed by a single household was 17 acres. From a viewpoint of appreciating the variation that can occur in livelihood circumstances, these were interesting examples. Nevertheless, their presence in the sample was judged to distort unduly sample means and measures of dispersion, and for these reasons they were excluded.

Incomes and assets by village and income group

Some basic features of livelihoods in Hai District as revealed by the sample survey are summarised in Tables 10.3 and 10.4, at this stage using unweighted data. The three village samples differed in their average income levels and asset profiles. Average total household income was highest in the least-remote Wari village (Tshs 1,044,864), followed by N'guni (Tshs 972,970) and then Kashashi (TShs 809,065). The relative poverty of Kashashi, compared to the other two villages, is confirmed by asset indicators in Table 10.3, for example, less than 50 per cent of households in Kashashi were found to own houses constructed of brick or cement, compared with 73 per cent in N'guni and 90 per cent in Wari, and only a small minority of households had electricity, against 75 per cent of households in Wari.

Table 10.4 summarises the same basic sample characteristics, only this time across villages by income-wealth group as identified in the wealth ranking exer-

Table 10.3. Household characteristics by village

Household characteristics (mean values for sample)	Wari (n = 28)	Kashashi (n = 30)	N'guni (n = 30)	All cases (n = 88)
Household income (TShs)	1,044,864	809,065	972,370	939,763
Per capita income (TShs)	207,778	110,337	146,102	153,533
Household size (no.)	5.2	6.0	5.9	5.7
Age of household head (yrs)	64.9	58.0	58.3	60.3
Land owned (ha)	2.8	5.3	5.2	4.5
Area farmed (ha)	3.1	5.8	5.7	4.9
Cattle owned (no.)	2.2	2.9	3.3	2.8
Goats/sheep owned (no.)	0.8	2.1	2.1	1.7
Households with:				
Electricity (%)	75.0	3.3	50.0	42.0
Piped water (%)	75.0	63.3	46.7	61.4
Brick or concrete houses (%)	92.9	46.7	73.3	70.5

Note: The exchange rate at time of survey in mid-1997 was TShs 600 = US$1.00.

Table 10.4. Household characteristics by income-wealth group

Household characteristics (mean values from sample)	Low-income (n = 30)	Medium-income (n = 29)	High-income (n = 29)
Household income (TShs)	455,261	894,130	1,486,606
Income per capita (TShs)	70,652	98,161	294,645
Household size (no.)	5.1	6.9	5.2
Age of household head (yrs)	59.9	58.1	62.9
Education levels (household heads)			
No formal education (%)	13.3	0.0	0.0
1–4 years education (%)	53.3	24.1	31.0
5–8 years education (%)	30.0	62.1	58.6
> 8 years education (%)	3.3	13.8	10.3
Land owned (ha)	2.9	4.3	6.2
Area farmed (ha)	3.1	5.0	6.7
Cattle owned (no.)	1.5	3.0	3.9
Goats/sheep owned (no.)	1.0	2.6	1.4
Households with:			
Electricity (%)	20.0	44.8	62.1
Piped water (%)	33.3	62.1	89.7
Brick or concrete houses (%)	46.7	69.0	96.6

Note: The exchange rate at time of survey in mid-1997 was TShs 600 = US$1.00.

cise. The latter is shown to have identified the three income-wealth groups with a reasonable degree of accuracy. Mean annual household income in the richest households was approximately four times that for the poorest group, and twice that of the middle group. For both total and per capita incomes the means for the income-wealth groups turned out to be statistically different from each other at the 0.95 confidence level. Nevertheless, these groups do overlap, containing households at each end of their distributions that fall into the income interval described by the adjacent income wealth class.

As might be expected, given the villagers' own criteria for distinguishing wealth groups, significant differences between the income-wealth groups also occur with respect to assets. In particular, the low-income group is marked by lower educational attainment, land ownership, area farmed, cattle owned, access to electricity, piped water, and house construction by comparison to the other two income-wealth groups.

Household incomes and strategies

In the analysis that follows, the activity dimension of livelihoods is examined first, followed by a consideration of assets. There are several potential ways that the activities profile of villages and income-wealth groups can be captured statistically given the quantitative data that was collected in the sample surveys. The methods used here comprise analysis of income portfolios, use of diversity indices, and construction of typologies of livelihood strategy, across villages, and across income-wealth groups.

Income portfolios were constructed for each household, and the proportions were summarised as village means and as income-wealth group means, and displayed as tables (Tables 10.5 and 10.6 below) and as pie charts. Figure 10.1 provides an example of the latter, done for the sample as a whole.

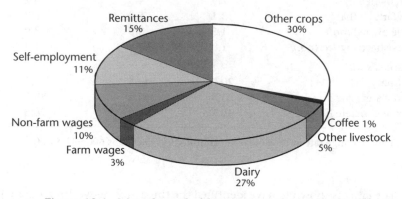

Figure 10.1. Mean household income portfolio, all villages

This exercise revealed strengths and flaws in the income portfolio approach. While apparently giving quite a concise and accessible picture of livelihood strategies, the size of the standard deviations around mean income shares reveals the heterogeneity of household income strategies across villages and groups, such that the existence of distinct strategies cannot be inferred from the data. In the case of the low-income group, for example, while livestock income—principally dairy—constitutes more than a quarter of mean total income for this group, roughly 20 per cent of low-income households have no livestock income at all.

It is probable that income portfolios are more useful for describing broad village or multi-village activity profiles than they are for distinguishing the livelihood strategies of sub-groups within larger populations. Thus the mean portfolio across villages (Table 10.5 and Figure 10.1) describes, to the extent that the sampling procedure adequately represents the villages as a whole, the overall significance of those different income sources for that population. For the three Hai villages, the critical feature is the remarkably low contribution of coffee to total village income, in a district where coffee is thought of as the principal agricultural activity. Indeed, coffee, was recorded by many households as yielding a negative net income since they had incurred outlays on production that were not recouped through the final value of coffee sales. This explains the negative value attached to the mean share of coffee in Wari village, as shown in Table 10.5.

Table 10.5. Mean household income portfolios, by village (proportion of net total income)

Income source	N'guni (n = 30)		Kashashi (n = 30)		Wari (n = 28)		All villages (n = 88)	
	Mean	s.d.	Mean	s.d.	Mean	s.d.	Mean	s.d.
Crops	0.33	0.29	0.35	0.26	0.27	0.23	0.31	0.25
of which coffee	0.05	0.14	0.05	0.20	0.04	0.11	0.01	0.15
Livestock	0.40	0.31	0.34	0.28	0.25	0.28	0.31	0.29
of which dairy	0.37	0.31	0.25	0.25	0.22	0.27	0.26	0.28
Total farm	0.73	0.28	0.69	0.33	0.53	0.32	0.62	0.32
Farm wages	0.04	0.14	0.06	0.21	0.00	0.00	0.03	0.13
Non-farm employment	0.09	0.19	0.05	0.21	0.12	0.28	0.10	0.25
Self-employment	0.03	0.10	0.10	0.18	0.16	0.26	0.11	0.22
Remittances and transfers	0.10	0.21	0.10	0.16	0.19	0.26	0.15	0.23
Total non-farm	0.27	0.28	0.31	0.33	0.47	0.32	0.38	0.32

These tables confirm the descriptive findings of the focus group discussions, but strengthens the confidence with which policy decisions might be based on such findings. Even considering that the survey year was a bad one for coffee, the results do seem to suggest that efforts to facilitate livelihoods in these villages would do well to look more closely at the alternatives to coffee, and especially at dairying, which was the biggest single income source in the remoter villages.

Despite the problem of high variation around sample means, broad differences in the farm–non-farm income share across villages are notable, and those between Wari and each of the other two villages were statistically significant. As might be expected, remoteness is associated with higher reliance on farming, and the proportion of income obtained from agriculture descends from 73 per cent for the remote village of N'guni to 69 per cent for the medium-remote village of Kashashi, and to 53 per cent for the least-remote village of Wari.

Proximity to roads and services appears to have a particularly notable impact on the significance of non-farm self-employment and remittance income in village income portfolios.

With regard to comparisons across income groups, variations around sample means make it difficult to draw firm conclusions with any degree of confidence. Nevertheless some features revealed in Table 10.6 are worth noting. Crop income seems to be less important for the high-income-wealth group than for the other groups (on average only 23 per cent of their income portfolio); while non-farm employment and self-employment, taken together, are more important for the better-off income groups (over a quarter of total income) than for the poor group (only 10 per cent of total income). Overall, the poor are distinguished by their reliance on crop income, and their relative lack of access or low returns to other income sources, although the significance of remittances for them is proportionately just as high, in this case-study, as for rich households.

Table 10.6. Mean household income portfolios, by income group (proportion of net total income)

Income source	Low-income		Middle-income		High-income	
	Mean	s.d.	Mean	s.d.	Mean	s.d.
Crops	0.36	0.29	0.30	0.21	0.23	0.25
of which coffee	*0.00*	*0.15*	*0.01*	*0.16*	*0.00*	*0.15*
Livestock	0.27	0.29	0.35	0.30	0.33	0.28
of which dairy	*0.21*	*0.27*	*0.30*	*0.28*	*0.29*	*0.28*
Total farm	0.62	0.34	0.65	0.28	0.55	0.35
Farm wages	0.06	0.20	0.00	0.00	0.00	0.00
Non-farm employment	0.04	0.17	0.13	0.26	0.16	0.31
Self-employment	0.07	0.17	0.16	0.26	0.12	0.21
Remittances	0.21	0.26	0.06	0.11	0.18	0.27
Total non-farm	0.38	0.34	0.35	0.28	0.45	0.35

Diversity indices

It is apparent from the foregoing discussion that utilising income portfolios in order to evaluate the livelihood strategies of poor rural families is compromised by the twin factors of, first, high variability around sample means, and, second, inability to capture the relative level of participation in each activity (e.g. what proportion of low income households engage in non-farm self-employment).

One possible way of getting round these problems is to find a summary statistic that captures both income shares and participation shares in a single figure that can be compared across sample groups. An index of diversity, as commonly used in studies of biodiversity and also found in portfolio analysis in financial economics, promises to be useful in this regard.

A number of different diversity indices were tried out, initially on a set of hypothetical data. Of these, it was considered after experimentation that a measure proposed by Chang (1997) described diversity best in terms of both the number of activities and the distribution of total income between them. In addition this index has the appeal that it is relatively simple to calculate, the formula for doing so being:

$$\frac{1}{\text{Sum of squares of proportional contributions to total income}}.$$

Furthermore, the logic of the formula suits the application being addressed since the index is the inverse of a market concentration index known as the Herfindahl-Hirschman Index. The maximum index value possible is equal to the number of income sources, and this would be attained if total income was equally distributed between each source. Table 10.7 provides an example.

Table 10.7. Inverse Herfindahl-Hirschman Index values

Proportional contribution to total income of each hypothetical income source				Index value
Source 1	Source 2	Source 3	Source 4	
1.0				1.00
0.9	0.1			1.22
0.5	0.5			2.00
0.8	0.1	0.1		1.52
0.5	0.3	0.2		2.63
0.33	0.33	0.33		3.00
0.7	0.1	0.1	0.1	1.92
0.4	0.2	0.2	0.2	3.57
0.25	0.25	0.25	0.25	4.00

The livelihood diversity index value was calculated for each household in the sample, using the entire range of income sources (i.e. bananas, maize, chickens, pigs etc.) rather than the grouped income sources utilised for the income portfolios. Means were calculated for each village and for each income group, with the results shown in Table 10.8.

Table 10.8. Mean diversity indices, by village and income group

	By village		
	N'guni (n = 30)	Kashashi (n = 30)	Wari (n = 28)
Mean index value	2.54	2.82	2.23
Std. deviation	1.12	1.12	0.83
	By income group		
	Low-income (n = 30)	Middle-income (n = 29)	High-income (n = 29)
Mean index value	2.39	2.56	2.37
Std. deviation	0.88	1.09	1.08

These results are not, in practice, found to be any more illuminating about the relationship between activity composition and poverty than the income portfolio analysis already conducted. The comparison across villages comes up with the unexpected finding that livelihood strategies in the least-remote village, Wari, are less diverse than in the two more remote villages, and this result is significant ($p = 0.03$, 2-tailed) for the difference between Wari and Kashashi. However, no significant differences in degrees of diversity are found between different income groups, thus the utility of diversity indices for providing a single indicator of livelihood strategy differences between rich and poor is thrown into some doubt.

Indeed, even though the diversity index combines information on both the number of income sources and the distribution of total income between them, it turns out to provide surprisingly little insight into the livelihood strategies of sub-groups defined by location or income-wealth category. A regression analysis indicated that only 22 per cent of variation in the diversity indices of the sample households was attributable to the number of income sources ($p = 0.01$, 2-tailed), emphasising that diversity indices add little to the information obtained from the breakdown of total income that income portfolios offer.

Typologies of livelihood strategies

The problems identified with income portfolios and diversity indices may possibly be overcome by regrouping the data into more homogeneous groups, and compiling mean portfolios that describe observable group strategies. This approach classifies each household according to a typology of livelihood strategies, and replaces mean income portfolios with a proportional measure of the distribution of households between different types. Rather than attempting to identify the typical household strategy within a village or income group, this method illustrates which type of strategies are being followed by most people in each group, and as such has the potential to offer better guidance for the type of support for the poorest households that the livelihoods framework seeks to address.

The difficulty with classifying strategies into types is, of course, the compromise that has to be found between specificity and practicability. A simple typology based on diversity might classify households according to the proportion of total household income that is derived from one specific source, that is, from milk, or bananas, or salaries for example. Following from this starting point, households in the survey were classified according to whether they obtained more than half, more than two-thirds, or more than three-quarters of their total income from a single source. The proportions of households in each income-wealth group that fell into each of these three types turned out as shown in Table 10.9.

Table 10.9. Percentage of households by typology of specialisation and by income group

Type	Specialisation category	Low-income	Middle-income	High-income
I	>50% of total household income from single specific source	69	64	68
II	>66% of total household income from single specific source	25	33	43
III	>75% of total household income from single specific source	15	17	32

Clearly the same procedure can be done across villages as well as across the income-wealth groups as displayed in Table 10.9. This appears to give a more accurate picture of degrees of specialisation than the mean diversity indices shown above, with results that can be generalised to a wider population, using appropriate statistical tests. In Table 10.9, comparisons between income-wealth groups indicate that:

1. roughly two-thirds of the households in each income group receive more than half their total income from a single specific source (Type I);
2. more households in the high-income group than in the other two income groups have specialisation rather than diversification strategies;
3. examination of the village data shows that this specialisation is predominantly in dairying in the two more-remote villages (N'guni and Kashashi)

and in varying non-dairy activities (crops, wages, trading etc.) in the less-re-mote Wari village.

The possibly surprising result that a large proportion of the households in the study follow livelihood strategies in which income is relatively concentrated emphasises the value of uncovering the proportion of total income derived from each source. One household, for example, had ten different income sources, and might have been described as following a diverse strategy on this basis. However, that household's total income was strongly concentrated in only two of them: 46 per cent from milk and 24 per cent from bananas.

The idea of specialisation threshold levels lends itself to further elaboration, by constructing livelihood types that represent different combinations along a specialisation-diversification continuum. The purpose of this is to reveal within which category of activities (e.g. crops, livestock, non-farm etc) specialisation occurs, and to explore the combinations of activities that feature for the roughly one-third of each income-wealth group that do not display these degrees of specialisation (see Table 10.9 again).

The typologies constructed here were guided in principle by a farm classification system used in the UK by the Ministry of Agriculture, Fisheries and Food (MAFF), in which 'robust types' of farm are identified by the proportional contribution of each enterprise to the total farm budget. On inspection of the Hai villages income data, it was decided that the principal types of activity could be broadly described as crop production, livestock production (including dairying), and non-farm income (taken in the sense of all non-own-account farming income). Two typologies were constructed, the first, following the MAFF example, was based on a 'break point' of income sources that comprised two-thirds of total income, resulting in six classes of livelihood strategy as shown in Table 10.10.

A second typology was constructed similarly, but pushed the 'break-point' to three-quarters of total income. This exercise, the categories of which are not reproduced in full here, resulted in seven categories rather than the six described in Table 10.10, including a 'mixed category', giving it greater potential to capture the more diverse livelihood strategies in the sample of households.

Sample households were classified according to these typologies, and the results for income-wealth groups and the 'Type 66' and 'Type 75' threshold levels are summarised in Tables 10.11 and 10.12. Some interesting insights into livelihood strategies can be observed from these tables. Poor households are more likely to specialise in crop production than either middle- or high-income households, and this is accentuated with the higher specialisation threshold in the Type 75 classification. High-income households are more likely to specialise in non-farm activities, or to follow a mixed crop-livestock agricultural strategy, and again this is revealed more robustly by the 'Type 75' classification where more than 60 per cent of high-income households follow one or other of these

Table 10.10. 'Type 66' livelihood strategy categories

Strategy ID	Category shares in total income	Strategy type
I	Crop income ≥ 66%	Principally crops
II	Livestock income ≥ 66%	Principally livestock
III	Non-farm income ≥ 66%	Principally non-farm
IV	Crop income and livestock income together ≥ 66%	
	Crop income < 66%, but > non-farm income	Crop/livestock
	Livestock income < 66%, but > non-farm income	
V	Livestock income and non-farm income together ≥ 66%	
	Livestock income < 66%, but > crop income	Livestock/non-farm
	Non-farm income < 66%, but > crop income	
VI	Crop income and non-farm income together ≥ 66%	
	Crop income < 66%, but > livestock income	Crop/non-farm
	Non-farm income < 66%, but > livestock income	

two strategies. The threshold level chosen is seen to make big differences to strategy patterns in some instances. For example, using the 75 per cent threshold, relatively few high-income households follow the combined crop-non-farm strategy, however, the comparison in this respect with the other income groups is much less distinct using the 66 per cent threshold.

These strategy comparisons can be presented in a variety of different ways in order to clarify patterns that may prove useful for policy purposes. For example, strategy types can be ranked by the percentage of households in each group that falls within it, and this facilitates comparisons of the predominant strategy types

Table 10.11. 'Type 66' distribution of households, by income group (%)

Type	Income-wealth group		
	Low-income (n = 30)	Middle-income (n = 29)	High-income (n = 29)
Principally crops	17.4	8.5	6.3
Principally livestock	10.0	15.6	12.9
Principally non-farm	27.8	14.0	33.3
Crop/livestock	24.6	28.2	25.3
Livestock/non-farm	7.4	10.6	8.9
Crop/non-farm	12.9	23.2	13.2
Total	100.0	100.0	100.0

Table 10.12. 'Type 75' distribution of households, by income group (%)

Type	Income-wealth group		
	Low-income (n = 30)	Middle-income (n = 29)	High-income (n = 29)
Principally crops	12.5	2.9	5.7
Principally livestock	10.0	12.9	6.9
Principally non-farm	18.0	7.9	30.2
Crop/livestock	21.7	31.2	30.8
Livestock/non-farm	7.4	10.0	13.9
Crop/non-farm	27.5	32.1	7.5
Mixed	2.9	2.9	5.1
Total	100.0	100.0	100.0

in each income-wealth group, as shown for the 'Type 66' classification in Table 10.13. Alternatively, the same information can be conveyed visually utilising radial graphs, as shown for the 'Type 66' and 'Type 75' threshold levels in Figures 10.2 and 10.3 respectively.

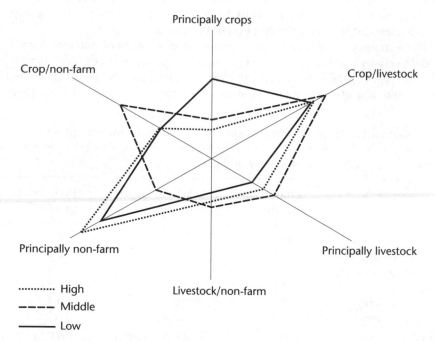

Figure 10.2. 'Type 66' distribution of households, by income group

Table 1C.13. Type 66' ranked typology, by income group (%)

Low income group (n = 30)		Middle income group (n = 29)		High income group (n = 29)	
Principally non-farm	27.8	Crop/livestock	28.2	Principally non-farm	33.3
Crop/livestock	24.6	Crop/non-farm	23.2	Crop/livestock	25.3
Principally crops	17.4	Principally livestock	15.6	Crop/non-farm	13.2
Crop/non-farm	12.9	Principally non-farm	14.0	Principally livestock	12.9
Principally livestock	10.0	Livestock/non-farm	11.6	Livestock/non-farm	8.9
Livestock/ non-farm	7.4	Principally crops	3.5	Principally crops	6.3
Total	100.0	Total	100.0	Total	100.0

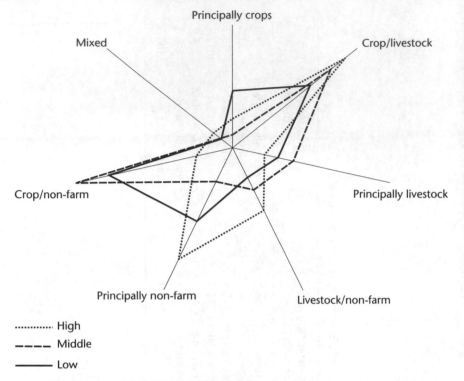

Figure 10.3. 'Type 75' distribution of households, by income group

The combined use of radial graphs and detailed tables appears to offer a valuable means of interpreting income data from a sample of rural households, distinguished by income-wealth groups or by village. The graphs offer an immediate visual reference to 'group profiles' within the limitations of the typology, revealing variations within and between groups. Since the axes have true scales, quantitative comparisons are being made, and these are supported by the details found in the tables. While the Hai district results display a great amount of heterogeneity of strategies across all income-wealth groups, clearer differences are evident in the village comparisons not reproduced here, and in other study sites this approach could prove invaluable as a guide to distinguishing the livelihood strategies of the poor from the better off in rural communities.

Some cautionary remarks are nevertheless required regarding this type of analysis. The first of these is a loss in the capacity of the analysis to capture livelihood diversity that results from constructing 'typical strategies'. For example, under the 'Type 75' classification of strategies (Table 10.12 above), it appears that 40 per cent of low-income households follow specialisation strategies in crop production, or in livestock keeping, or in non-farm activities. However, in the earlier Table 10.9, based on individual rather than grouped income sources, it was observed that only 15 per cent of low-income households obtained more than 75 per cent of their income from single *specific* income sources. There is clearly a trade-off between specificity and typology of income sources, and the main casualty of this trade-off is the ability to convey diversity of income sources when similar sources are grouped together in order to construct typologies.

Second, the difference in 'group profiles' between the radial graphs for the 'Type 66' and 'Type 75' typologies indicates the need for careful consideration of the threshold level as a workable definition of alternative strategy types. The 'Type 66' classification has an interpretative advantage when displayed as a radial graph since the strategy types follow a readily understandable sequence, and the smaller number of them aids visual clarity. The difference in the threshold level manifests itself in changes in group profiles observable across Figures 10.2 and 10.3, illustrated in particular by the axis designated 'principally non-farm' between the two graphs.

Finally, there is the issue of the underlying variation within and between groups, implying that only very large differences between group means turn out to possess statistical significance. In some instances, significant differences be tween groups are indeed observed, and subsequent discussion can proceed with some degree of confidence that a distinguishing feature of the livelihoods of the poor has been discovered. However, this is the exception rather than the rule, and practitioners using this type of data but lacking either the time or the expertise to undertake the requisite statistical tests should be aware that high variability round sample means warrants caution in jumping to conclusions about differences in livelihood strategies across different social groups.

However, even given these caveats, it is apparent that the 'typology' approach to household income data takes us rather further than either simple income portfolios or diversity indices for describing livelihood strategies across villages or income-wealth groups. For example, in the foregoing analysis it emerges that quite a large proportion of households in both high- and low-income groups depend principally on non-farm income sources, yet they are in separate income-wealth classes, and have quite different material standards of living. This observation is consistent with the proposition that the poor diversify in less remunerative labour markets than the better off, reflecting especially human capital constraints.

Subsistence consumption in household strategies

The data collected on incomes in the Hai district villages included the value of food produced and directly consumed by each household, in addition to the various cash income streams. The subsistence share of total income is one of the more straightforward pieces of information to obtain from this type of data, and may on its own provide valuable insights into differences in circumstances across villages or income-wealth groups. This is especially so in an export crop production zone, like Hai district, where the ability of the household to buffer its food security through self-consumption is often thought to be compromised by the land and labour requirements of the cash crop.

The subsistence share of total incomes is compared across villages and across income-wealth groups in Table 10.14. This displays mean shares for the sub-groups, as well as the standard deviations associated with those mean shares. Across villages, the subsistence share varies between 26 per cent (Wari) and 31 per cent (N'guni), thus following, as might be predicted, relative remoteness from markets and cash earning opportunities. The differences between Wari and the two more-remote villages are statistically significant at the 95 per cent confidence level. Across income-wealth groups, the high-income group is distinguished by its substantially lower reliance on subsistence consumption than the lower income groups, and, not surprisingly, this is also statistically significant.

Table 10.14. Mean subsistence shares, by village and income group

	N'guni (n = 30)	Kashashi (n = 30)	Wari (n = 28)
Mean subsistence share	0.31	0.32	0.26
Std. deviation	0.15	0.22	0.18
	Low-income	Middle-income	High-income
Mean subsistence share	0.35	0.29	0.17
Std. deviation	0.22	0.14	0.14

It is possible to undertake more detailed analysis of the subsistence share. For example, the share itself can be divided into ranges, and the proportion of total households falling into each range can be examined to see whether any policy-relevant patterns emerge from this exercise. As shown in Table 10.15, this gives some additional insights especially into patterns of reliance on subsistence contrasted between poor and high income-wealth households. Whereas nearly half of high-income households rely on subsistence for less than 10 per cent of their total income, by contrast more than half of low-income households rely on subsistence sources for more than a third of their total income. While these figures at one level merely correspond to commonsense, nevertheless the particular values obtained could strengthen arguments for instituting food security measures in projects when it is apparent that the poor would benefit disproportionately by attention being paid to the subsistence component of their livelihoods.

Table 10.15. Distribution of households by subsistence intervals (%)

Subsistence intervals	Low-income (n = 30)	Middle-income (n = 29)	High-income (n = 29)
< 0.10	9.3	2.9	46.0
0.10–0.20	18.7	25.8	13.1
0.20–0.30	15.5	34.6	21.6
0.30–0.40	22.2	10.6	11.4
0.40–0.50	9.3	18.5	4.3
> 0.50	24.9	7.6	3.5
Total	100.0	100.0	100.0

Household assets

The sample survey contained a number of questions about household assets, including the educational level of household members, land ownership, dairy cattle owned, herd and flock sizes for goats, sheep and hens, housing quality, access to electricity and piped water, and count data for a variety of domestic assets including tools, utensils, forms of transport and consumer goods. The livelihoods approach (Chapter 2 above; D. Carney, 1998; Bebbington, 1999) places a lot of emphasis on assets, especially on the identification of those assets possessed by the rural poor that can be utilised or built upon to increase the resilience and security of their livelihoods.

Asset data may be handled in a variety of different ways. One is to tabulate the levels of key assets by sub-groups of the target population, with a view to gaining a quick impression of relative differences between groups. This has already been done in a preliminary way in Tables 10.3 and 10.4 above, however, the impressions provided there can be refined by grouping assets according to the asset classification of the livelihood framework, and by converting some collections of assets into single indices for comparative purposes across groups. This is done in Table 10.16, which makes some adjustments to the raw data collected on various assets.

The main finding of Table 10.16 is the relative deficit across the range of assets of the low income-wealth group compared to the other two groups. Whereas differences between the high- and middle-income group are in general not statistically significant due to within group variation, the low-income group, by contrast, differs significantly in most asset attributes. In particular education, land access, livestock, housing, transport and service access indicators are low for this group.

Any number of these assets, or asset categories, can be plotted on a radial graph in order to provide a visual impression of key differences between social groups defined according to wealth ranking or other criteria. This is the equivalent of plotting asset pentagons (D. Carney, 1998: 6–7); however, with sample survey data it is unnecessary to regard these as merely an illustrative device plotted on the back-of-an-envelope from qualitative impressions. Instead, it is quite simple, with a spreadsheet, to plot assets using measured quantities, and more sophisticated analysis can group assets utilising indices, and standardise the axes so that different assets are more easily compared with each other.

Table 10.16. Household assets, by income-wealth group

Asset	Statistic	Low-income (n = 30)	Middle-income (n = 29)	High-income (n = 29)
Human capital				
Total household size	Mean no. in AEUs	6.82	7.88	7.68
Education of household head	% > Std VI	0.34	0.76	0.60
Education of household	Mean no. > Std VI	4.80	7.22	7.06
Drinkable water	% with	0.65	0.82	0.98
Natural capital				
Total area cultivated	Mean area in acres	2.90	4.58	5.74
Total area owned	Mean area in acres	2.66	3.83	6.62
Milk cattle owned	Mean no.	0.78	1.37	1.51
Financial capital				
Livestock holding	Mean no. in CEUs	1.67	3.12	3.42
Physical capital				
Housing	% with concrete/brick	0.56	0.77	0.98
Piped water	% with	0.38	0.66	0.92
Mains electricity	% with	0.29	0.57	0.75
Transport	% with any type	0.05	0.17	0.15
Tools of the trade	Mean no.	9.02	12.46	12.97

Note: AEU = adult equivalent units; CEU = cattle equivalent units.

Probably the simplest type of asset plot to construct is one that ignores the asset categories of the livelihoods framework, and just selects five or six key measurable assets for the population under study. This is done in Figure 10.4 below, where household size, education level of the household head, land owned, dairy cattle owned, and access to electricity are plotted for the three income-wealth groups using unweighted data from the sample survey. This shows in a visually rather striking way the big differences for education, cattle and electricity between the low income and the other two groups. Of course in different settings, the five or six assets utilised for this exercise would vary according to local cir-

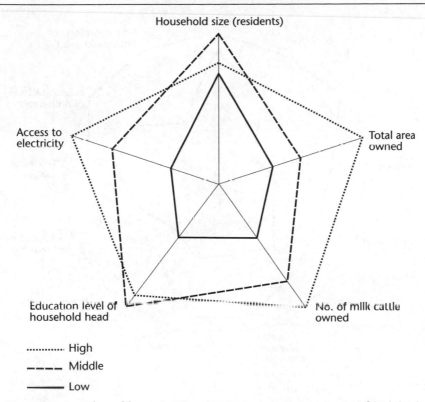

Figure 10.4. Selected household assets, by income group (unweighted data)

cumstances; for example, in fishing villages, ownership of boats and nets would be key assets.

Alternatively, quite complicated work can be done with asset data. Figure 10.5 takes the asset levels provided in Table 10.16 above, and standardises the scales for each asset so that they are all measured out of 10. This involves, for each asset variable, finding the maximum value of that variable, dividing the maximum value by 10 to give an appropriate standardising factor, then multiplying each value of the variable by this factor. Doing this assists the visual interpretation of a graph that measures thirteen categories of asset for each of three income groups. In contrast to Figure 10.4, each of these asset variables has also been weighted properly according to sample proportions, and some of them represent indices combining groups of unlike items.

Whether Figure 10.5 is worth the additional time and effort compared to Figure 10.4 is a point worth considering. Again, education level, land owned, and electricity access are shown to be critical assets distinguishing the poor from the better-off members of these rural communities. To these must be added transport,

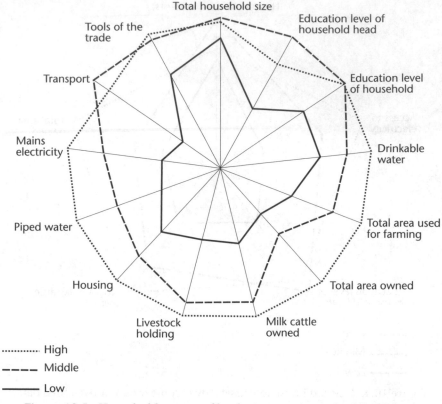

.... High

— — — Middle

———— Low

Figure 10.5. Household asset profiles, by income group (weighted data)

since the poor do not even own bicycles for getting around, while the better off not only have bicycles, but may also possess motorcycles, and even four-wheeled transport across the income-wealth ranges. To the extent that the transport factor may not have been picked up in a more casual analysis, then, this exercise was worth doing. For example, finding ways to enable the poor to purchase bicycles could be identified as a valid poverty reduction objective. Figure 10.5 also emphasises that the poor are poor in all assets except household size.

Lessons for livelihoods analysis

This chapter has described an approach to the investigation of rural livelihoods that involves combining participatory techniques with a small-scale sample survey. It was argued that these methods should not be seen as mutually exclusive, but rather as playing different roles in achieving a clear picture for policy purposes of the liveli-hoods situation of the rural poor. In particular, it was suggested that focus group dis-cussions and other participatory methods might be well-suited to discovering the 'vulnerability context' of rural livelihoods, including issues of access, change, and trends; while sample survey data would be better suited to examining more con-cretely how the assets and activities of the poor differ from those of the better off.

The chapter has been concerned with elicitive rather than empowering attributes of field methods. While empowerment may be built into project or policy design, and constitute a core feature of project implementation, nevertheless there are occa-sions in the life history of rural poverty reduction projects when there is a need to elicit information in a timely and cost-effective fashion. This may occur as a precursor to project design, or as a part of monitoring project or policy effects and outcomes.

The approach produced mixed results with respect to its components and objec-tives. The focus group discussions were indeed found useful for describing the broad community context of rural livelihoods, and identifying key trends and emerging con-straints. It is probable that additional relevant information could have been obtained utilising a more complete range of participatory methods, especially with respect to finding out more about social institutions and organisations which were relatively ne-glected in this exercise. A participatory wealth ranking exercise was broadly successful at distinguishing the poor in the case-study villages from the better off. The lesson learnt is that a structured and selective combination of participatory techniques, that focuses consciously on the livelihood context and strategies of the rural poor, can go quite far in discovering policy relevant livelihood characteristics.

The small-scale sample survey was efficient in its execution and data entry, but more demanding than had been envisaged for data analysis. Moreover, it proved dif-ficult to pin down the activity strategies of different social groups utilising summary measures and indices, due to high variation within the sample as a whole, as well as in sub-samples, and to the failure of the measures adopted to portray strategies in a form that would be tractable for policy purposes. In this respect, the devising of liveli-hood typologies based on the majority contributor to total incomes was more suc-cessful than either income portfolios or diversity indices for the purpose of distinguishing critical aspects of livelihood strategies.

The sample survey was rather more successful at capturing the distinct asset capa-bilities of the poor compared to the other income-wealth groups identified in the wealth-ranking exercise. By asking questions about assets that are self-evidently im-portant for livelihoods in the social and economic setting under study, asset profiles between social groups can be devised quickly and easily, enabling the ready identifi-cation of the principal asset deficits of the poor. For this purpose, it is unnecessary to be artificially constrained by the five broad asset categories identified in the liveli-hood framework, although these remain relevant as a rough guide to achieving a balance in the items about which information is sought.

Depending on the subsequent intentions of the data collection exercise, the sam-ple survey could probably be reduced in scope quite considerably. As far as sample size is concerned (number of households interviewed), the case-study described here (90 households across three villages) is probably the minimum required if statistical inference about larger populations is being contemplated. However, smaller samples may be sufficient if the intention is simply to provide a cross-check of the findings of participatory methods, with the possibility of discovering factors overlooked by the latter. Moreover, if the researcher or policy maker is prepared to forgo quantitative verification of income portfolios, the survey could focus just on household asset profiles, substantially reducing the time and cost demands of all stages of the survey.

As far as the particular case-study presented here is concerned, the fieldwork did achieve some important livelihood insights. An area of rural Tanzania thought of as depending predominantly on coffee as the mainstay of livelihoods was found instead to depend mainly on milk production from stall-fed dairy cattle. The focus group discussions highlighted this, but the sample survey confirmed just how minor coffee had become in livelihoods, albeit the year in question was a poor one for coffee harvests in that region. Being poor in Hai district is often associated with the inability to participate in dairying as a livelihood activity. More widely, poor households in the case-study villages were distinguished from better-off households more sharply by their assets than by their activities. In particular, lack of education, dairy cattle, and transport strongly marked the differential asset status of poor households compared to better-off households.

— PART IV —
Looking Ahead

— CHAPTER 11 —

Livelihoods, Diversification, and Policies

This book sets out a livelihoods approach to rural poverty reduction, and locates this framework in a larger context of dimensions of the development process, such as poverty, gender and the environment that concern researchers, policy makers and development practitioners in rural development. The book is not a practical guide to implementing the livelihoods approach; however, many of the points it raises and the examples used to illustrate those points, provide insights into the key components that should feature in applications of the framework. A central theme running throughout the book is that of livelihood diversification; in other words, the observation that poor rural families tend to adopt survival strategies composed of a diverse portfolio of activities that cut across orthodox economic sectors and transcend the rural–urban divide.

The livelihoods approach takes the form of an 'assets-access-activities' framework that has its origins in diverse literatures about poverty, vulnerability, coping with crisis, and adaptation by rural individuals and households to the changing circumstances and shocks they confront. This has come to be called the sustainable livelihoods (SL) framework (D. Carney, 1998), and is viewed as equally applicable to urban as to rural survival strategies. Assets in this framework include human capital (the education, skills, health and number of household members); physical capital (e.g. farm equipment or a sewing machine); social capital (the social networks and associations to which people belong); financial capital and its substitutes (savings, credit, cattle and so on); and natural capital (the natural resource base).

In pursuing livelihood strategies, both assets and the uses to which they can be put are mediated by social factors (social relations, institutions, organisations), by exogenous trends (principally economic trends), and by shocks (personal misfortune, drought, disease, floods, pests). The framework provides a checklist by which constraints on livelihood success can be prioritised for action to remove them, and the links between them identified.

In line with this framework, a livelihood is defined in the book as 'the activities, the assets, and the access that together determine the living gained by the individual or household'. Rural livelihood diversification is then defined as 'the process by which households construct a diverse portfolio of activities and social support capabilities for survival and in order to improve their standard of living' (see also Ellis, 1998: 4).

The diversification theme

Key considerations

With respect to diversification as a livelihood strategy, the tendency for rural households to engage in multiple occupations is often remarked in the rural development literature, but few attempts have been made to link this behaviour in a systematic way to poverty reduction policies. The livelihoods framework provides just such an opportunity to explore more robustly the diversity of rural livelihoods. In the past it has often been assumed that farm output growth would create plentiful non-farm income earning opportunities in the rural economy via linkage effects. However, this assumption is no longer tenable. For many poor rural families, farming on its own is unable to provide a sufficient means of survival, and the yield gains of new technology display signs of levelling off, particularly in those regions where they were most dramatic in the past.

The causes of the adoption by rural families of diversified income portfolios are better understood than the policy implications. Considerations of risk spreading, consumption smoothing, labour allocation smoothing, credit market failures, and coping with shocks can contribute to the adoption, and adaptation over time, of diverse rural livelihoods. However, livelihood diversity results in complex interactions with poverty, income distribution, farm productivity, environmental conservation, gender relations and the macro economy that are not always straightforward, and are sometimes counter-intuitive in the relationships that are discovered.

One key finding about diversification can be summarised fairly succinctly. There is a critical difference between individual level diversity and household level diversity. The individual taking on multiple occupations can typically only do so in low skill, casual and part-time occupations that are also insecure and low paid. Individual livelihood diversification of this type therefore tends to be closely associated with poverty and necessity. Individuals belong, of course, to households. However, a household can have a diverse activity portfolio while individual household members are specialising in single occupations, providing more security and higher wages or good returns to substantive self-employment. Therefore what often distinguishes the diversification strategy of the poor household from that of the better off household is that the former is found to diversify individually in unfavourable labour markets, while the latter is found to diversify as a group while securing more favourable returns in specialised occupations.

This finding is related to the asset status of the poor (e.g. low human capital) and barriers to entry, or lack of access, resulting from low assets (need for skills, ability to navigate bureaucratic hurdles etc.). Applying the livelihood framework, it becomes evident that facilitating the poor to gain better access to opportunities, or to create their own opportunities, is likely to be substantially more cost effective for poverty reduction than attempting, artificially, to support particular sectors or sub-sectors of rural economic activity. This is an important conclusion of the book that relates more to the access constituent of the livelihoods framework than to any other, and to which this chapter returns in its concluding observations.

Extent. Case-studies from a variety of different locations suggest that rural households do indeed engage in multiple activities and rely on diversified income portfolios. A selection of such case-studies is summarised in the text boxes of preceding chapters. In sub-Saharan Africa, a range of 30 to 50 per cent reliance on non-farm income sources is common; however, this proportion tends to be considerably higher in southern Africa where it may attain 80–90 per cent. In South Asia it would appear that, on average, 60 per cent of rural household income is from non-farm sources; however, this proportion varies widely between, for example, landless households and those with access to land for farming. In sub-Saharan Africa reliance on agriculture tends to diminish continuously as income level rises, that is, the more diverse the income portfolio the better-off is the rural household. Elsewhere, a common pattern is for the very poor and the comparatively well off to have the most diverse livelihoods, while the middle ranges of income display less diversity.

Poverty and income distribution. It is widely agreed that a capability to diversify is beneficial for households at or below the poverty line. Having alternatives for income generation can make the difference between minimally viable livelihoods and destitution. However, the role of diversification in reducing the intensity of poverty at the lower end of the income distribution does not mean that it has an equalising effect on rural incomes overall. As already noted, better-off families are able to diversify in more favourable labour markets than poor rural families, and total income and the share of income from non-farm sources are often positively correlated. Different income sources may have strongly differing impacts on rural inequality. For example, unequal land ownership may mean that a policy focus on crop income favours the rich above the poor; however, greater access to non-farm self-employment would have the reverse effect.

Agriculture. The conventional wisdom for many years has been that rising output and incomes in agriculture itself are the catalyst for diverse non-farm activities arising in rural areas. However, in sub-Saharan Africa this has rarely been the case, since most household level diversification is not just non-farm but non-rural in character. Nor does it work in Asia once the pace of technological change in agriculture slows and crop yields level off. Evidence is mixed regarding the gains and losses to agriculture of household-level diversification strategies: negative effects are associated with the withdrawal of critical labour inputs from the family farm; while positive effects include the alleviation of credit constraints and a reduction in the risk of innovation. Where on-farm diversification occurs, it is associated with similar contributions to improved household income security as off-farm diversification.

Environment. As with agriculture, the effects of diversification on environmental resource management are context-specific and contingent on the processes unfolding in particular locations. The growth of non-farm income sources, especially if accessible in remote rural areas, might be expected to reduce the need for landless rural dwellers to carry out extractive practices in local environments for survival. On the other hand, for settled agriculturalists, non-farm earning opportunities can result in neglect of labour-intensive conservation practices if labour availability is reduced. Sustainable rural livelihoods need not equate with the sustainability of all the components of underlying ecological systems due to substitutions that occur between assets during processes of livelihood adaptation over time. There is an intrinsic difficulty in the transmission of the notion of sustainability across scales of its application, since higher order systems can make substitutions that mean that lower order components do not themselves have to be sustainable.

Gender. Gender is an integral and inseparable part of rural livelihoods. Men and women have different assets, access to resources, and opportunities. Women rarely own land, may have lower education due to discriminatory access as children, and their access to productive sources as well as decision-making tends to occur through the mediation of men. Women typically confront a narrower range of labour markets than men and unequal earnings in such labour markets as are open to them. These factors add up to diversification being more of an option for rural men than for rural women, as a general proposition. In this sense, diversification can improve household level livelihood security while at the same time trapping women in customary roles. From a policy viewpoint, approaches that view women as instrumental to other objectives such as poverty reduction, farm efficiency or better environmental management possess serious flaws because they fail to recognise or to address the social relations and institutions by which gender inequality is perpetuated over time.

Macro policies and reform. Macro policies determine the broad economic context within which livelihood decisions are made, while reform influences the social and political context, especially with respect to the way government agencies discharge their functions. Macro policies affect livelihoods via relative price and market liberalisation effects, with the latter being more significant for diversification due to the removal of controls on private initiative, and the reduction of the profile in the economy of state and parastatal agencies that formerly curtailed diversity and constrained opportunities and outcomes. The adoption of diverse cross-sectoral livelihood strategies by rural and urban households influences, in turn, the efficacy of macro policies in achieving income distribution objectives based on sectoral price changes. A problem in low-income countries is the absence of markets or their uneven functioning. Recognition of this leads to states and markets being seen as complements rather than substitutes, with the government helping to create markets where they are missing, and providing the regulatory framework without which markets cannot function well.

Positive and negative diversification effects

A diverse portfolio of activities contributes to the security of a rural livelihood because it improves its long-run resilience in the face of adverse trends or sudden shocks. In this respect, individual and family livelihoods display similarities to larger social and economic groupings up to the level of the economy at large. In general, increased diversity promotes greater flexibility because it allows more possibilities for substitution between opportunities that are in decline and those that are expanding. Some positive impacts of diversification on livelihood security and resilience are detailed in the following paragraphs.

Seasonality. Seasonality causes peaks and troughs in labour utilisation in farming, and creates food insecurity due to the mismatch between uneven farm income streams and continuous consumption requirements. These are often called the 'labour smoothing' and 'consumption smoothing' problems respectively. Diversification contributes to reducing these adverse effects, by utilising labour and generating alternative sources of income in off-peak periods in the farm cycle.

Risk reduction. Diversification reduces the risk of income failure by spreading risk across activities that confront different risk profiles. The more this comprises activities that display uncorrelated risks between them, the more successful it is at achieving this end. In other words, the factors (e.g. climate) that create risk for one income source should not be the same as those (e.g. urban job insecurity) that create risk for another.

Higher income. Diversification may simply achieve higher income than farming could alone. It can do this by making better use of available resources and skills (as in seasonality, see above), and by taking advantage of spatially dispersed income-earning opportunities.

Asset improvement. Cash resources obtained from diversification may be used to invest in, or improve the quality of, any or all of the five classes of assets distinguished in the livelihoods approach, for example, sending children to secondary school or buying equipment like a bicycle or sewing machine that can be used to enhance future income-generating opportunities.

Environmental benefits. Diversification can potentially yield environmental benefits in two main ways. One is by generating resources that are then invested in improving the quality of the natural resource base. The second is by providing options that make time spent in exploiting natural resources, for example, gathering activities in forests, less remunerative than time spent doing other things.

Disadvantages that have been noted about the adoption of diverse livelihood strategies by rural households are often the converse of its positive effects, and reflect the different circumstances that arise historically in different locations. Diversification may have adverse effects on rural income distribution, agricultural productivity, and gender relations. Some points made in the literature are as follows:

Income distribution. Diversification can be associated with widening disparities between the incomes of the rural rich and poor. As we have seen, this occurs because the diversification options of the better off are in more highly paid and secure labour markets than those that are open to the poor. For example, the rich may be able to secure permanent full-time jobs for family members in government or business; while the poor are only able to secure part-time and casual work at low wage rates. This in turn reflects the different asset positions of rural families, with those which possess high human capital being in a better position to take advantage of opportunities that arise than those not so well endowed. The same is true of all the different forms of wealth, including cattle held for wealth purposes.

Farm output. Some types of livelihood diversification may result in the stagnation or decline of output on the family farm. This typically occurs when there are buoyant distant labour markets for male labour, resulting in the exit from agriculture of the male, the young and the educated, resulting in depletion of the labour force required to undertake peak farm production demands such as land preparation and harvesting. This occurred, for example, in southern Africa in the 1970s and 1980s, where many rural households came to depend on remittances from migrants to urban areas in South Africa for their food security.

Adverse gender effects. Adverse effects on the gender balance of the household, and, specifically, on the role and status of women, are primarily associated with the type of diversification that is also held to have adverse effects on agriculture. Where it is male labour that is predominantly able to take advantage of diversification opportunities, then women may be even more relegated to the domestic sphere and to eking out a livelihood from subsistence food production. A high level of male migration is also associated with the prevalence of *de facto* female-headed households in rural areas. However, there are significant pitfalls, both empirically and conceptually, in inferring livelihood success or failure from the gender of the household head (see Box 7.1 above).

On balance the positive effects of diversification appear to outweigh its disadvantages. The positive effects tend to be beneficial impacts of wide applicability (e.g. risk reduction; mitigating seasonality), while the negative effects typically occur when labour markets happen to work in particular ways in particular places. A provisional conclusion is that removal of constraints to, and expansion of opportunities for, diversification are desirable policy objectives because they give individuals and households more options to improve livelihood security and to raise their own living standards (Ellis, 1998: p. 1).

This conclusion is open to some potential misinterpretations. One is that diversification is being prioritized above specialisation and division of labour. This is not the case. It has already been noted that a household may possess a diverse portfolio of income sources, while individual household members specialise in particular occupations. Nor does this conclusion advocate that all households should diversify; it merely states that the option to diversify is helpful to poverty reduction and livelihood security because it provides greater opportunities for those individuals or households the assets and access of which prevent the achievement of viable livelihoods from single occupations.

Criteria for poverty reduction policies

The livelihood framework emphasises a focus on people, their assets, activities and access, rather than on sectors and their performance which is the conventional point of entry to policy. The framework can be utilised to yield a number of generalised statements about the livelihoods of the rural poor that potentially permit the formulation of a set of 'livelihood criteria' to be taken into account in evaluating the merits of alternative project proposals, and for seeking to strengthen the poverty reduction content of policies and projects. A provisional set of such criteria are put forward here as follows:

Remoteness is typically associated with greater poverty and few livelihood options, and therefore it may be valid to target remote locations rather than those places already well integrated into diverse economic activities; however, remoteness can also mean fewer absolute numbers of poor people so this is admittedly not always an unambiguous criterion.

Assets, or the lack of them, are fundamental to livelihood strategies, and for this reason, policies and projects that target individuals or families that already possess assets are likely to improve the incomes of those who are already better off, rather than those of the poor; indeed farm policies may have this effect due to the not always correct suppositions that (1) the poor are mainly poor farmers, and (2) that there are multiplier effects of rising farm income beneficial to the assetless poor.

Substitution, between assets and between activities, is a key attribute of viable and resilient rural livelihoods: substitution between assets is facilitated by the possession of a diverse range of assets rather than just a few, and by working markets that enable one type of asset to be converted into another; substitution between activities makes livelihoods more resilient, and thus better able to adapt to unforeseen trends and hazards.

Options are important; being poor is often a case of being trapped with no options, therefore poverty reduction requires facilitating the widening of choices and options, by taking action to improve information, encourage mobility, and reduce regulatory restrictions on feasible courses of action.

These livelihood criteria are thus summarised under the four headings of *location*, *assets*, *substitution*, and *options*. To this should be added *knowledge* about the livelihood strategies of the constituency that a policy or project is designed to help. One of the key conclusions to emerge from livelihood research is that untested assumptions about the survival attributes of rural families cannot be made. For example, it cannot be assumed from appearances that a particular rural social group is mainly dependent on the production of a particular crop or farming system for survival; investigation is likely to show that livelihood strategies are a great deal more complicated.

This last point is addressed by the methods discussion and case-study of Chapters 9 and 10 of the book. While there is nothing especially innovative in the approach recommended in those chapters, emphasis is placed on combining methods in order to achieve cost-effective and timely information on the livelihood circumstances and survival options of the rural poor. This requires rapid rural appraisal techniques supplemented by in-depth studies of some households in order to confirm the findings of focus group discussions, and to obtain a more accurate picture of livelihood strategies at the household and individual level.

Looking ahead

The livelihoods framework does not claim to constitute an entirely new approach to the problem of addressing rural poverty in low-income countries. Important components of the approach have been around in rural poverty reduction policies for many years. With respect to the threefold characterisation of the approach as assets, access and activities, a lot is already known about assets and a fair amount is known about activities. The area in which rural development practice has in the past possibly been on the least firm ground is with respect to the institutional and organisational aspects of access.

There are many existing branches of policy that set out to tackle the lack of assets of the rural poor. Equity of access to, and innovative approaches to the delivery of, rural education and health are designed to increase the human capital of the rural poor. Lack of education in particular is recognised as curtailing the options open to the individual, both directly by excluding people from all but unskilled labour markets, and, indirectly, by limiting the range of livelihood options that people might consider as within their reach. Poor educational attainment has been identified in empirical studies as a critical constraint inhibiting livelihood diversification.

Likewise, the popular emphasis on microcredit provision through group lending schemes addresses the lack of financial capital available to the poor, and their consequent inability to acquire other assets that would permit them to engage in income-generating activities. There are many different models and experiments in microcredit provision from which to adapt and to choose appropriate elements for local solutions. Credit policy is not only, however, about microcredit schemes, many of which depend heavily for their sustainability on the continuous involvement of NGOs. It is recognised that there is also scope to facilitate the spread of rural financial institutions that are self-sustaining on the basis of savings and loans organised according to conventional banking criteria. This requires the appropriate regulatory and guarantee provisions that would enable the formation of such institutions and ensure confidence in them in the long term.

Another long-recognised policy priority is that of rural infrastructural provision, which addresses one aspect of the category of physical assets upon which rural livelihoods are constructed. Infrastructure plays a significant role in poverty reduction by contributing to the integration of national economies, improving the working of markets, speeding the flow of information, and increasing the mobility of people, resources and outputs. As with education, future infrastructural capacity will require innovative approaches to provision and maintenance. Reliance on central government and *ad hoc* project finance from donors cannot be depended upon to keep existing infrastructure in good repair or to make heavy investments in new infrastructure. Decentralisation may, arguably, help to bring the prioritisation and financing of rural infrastructure closer to rural communities themselves. Privatisation of suppliers like electricity and telephone companies may help to raise investment levels, and improve outreach to remote rural areas, although past experience is uneven in this regard.

These policy areas are indicative of long established understandings of the role of assets in improving the livelihood prospects of the rural poor. Conventional agricultural policies have also in the past addressed the asset dimension of rural livelihoods, especially with respect to soil conservation and irrigation provision in small-farm agriculture. Other rural policies have addressed the activities side of the livelihoods equation; for example, support to agricultural outputs, facilitation of rural small scale industries (often undertaken under the heading of rural non-farm employment or RNFE), and active encouragement of backward and forward linkages to agriculture (input delivery, machinery repair services, food processing, food trading, and so on). Also in the context of activities, rural safety-net policies based on providing minimum wages or food in return for work provide, in effect, a new activity option for those needing new income sources in order to survive.

Access raises quite different issues to assets and activities. While the latter reside safely in domains that are quite normally the subject of economic policy decisions, the former involves issues of local institutions, rural administration, authority, power, and governance that hitherto have not received a lot of attention in mainstream rural development policies. Even after two decades of market liberalisation, it is a mistake to assume that an environment that facilitates rather than inhibits the formation and operation of diverse small-scale enterprise is now in place in rural areas of low-income countries. On the contrary, established modes of looking at the world in local agencies of government are notoriously resistant to change, even when apparently superceded by regulatory streamlining introduced at the national level.

The local level policy context often remains basically inimical rather than facilitating or supportive to self-employment and start-up businesses. Local enterprises often arise 'outside' the regulations, that is, as an unrecognised and unsupported informal sector activity, and they sometimes depend on paying off local officials to secure their ability to operate in the future. Alternatively, they must typically undergo a sequence of complex registration and licensing requirements, themselves requiring side-payments to speed up official processes, in order to achieve proper legal status. There is often great reluctance to dismantle regulations, or speed up the processing of applications, precisely because these provide lucrative income supplementation possibilities for the low paid local officials who collect licence fees and issue permits.

It is in this sense that reform, in terms of efficiency, effectiveness, transparency and fairness of state operations, although proceeding at different speeds in different countries, is still in its early stages. One of the biggest challenges for the future must be to secure the switch from antipathy to supportiveness in the relations between public administration at local levels in rural areas and private, non-farm, productive activity. Indeed the difficulty here is more intractable than is suggested just by reference to local public administration. In many rural areas, the access of individuals and families to resources of different kinds is determined by traditional authorities more than by local government officials. It cannot be safely assumed that these traditional authorities are efficient, or effective, or fair in the way they discharge their duties, just because they have been around a very long time and are the accepted focal point of community decision-making.

The access dimension of the rural livelihoods framework contains a challenging set of concerns for rural poverty reduction in the future. It comprises institutions, organisations and social relations, requiring new methods for identifying 'poor friendly' from 'poor unfriendly' hierarchies of authority and control at local levels in rural areas, and new ways of carrying forward the governance debate, hitherto predominantly conducted at national levels, down to local levels in rural areas. It also contains the opportunity context of livelihoods, requiring new ways of exploring the links between macro level policies and micro level outcomes, so that the latter can be facilitated to take proper advantage of new possibilities opened up by macro level policy changes.

The rural livelihoods approach provides an organising framework for trying to improve the effectiveness of rural poverty reduction policies. The components of this framework are deliberately broad and lacking in matters of detail, since the key constraints and policy issues that arise will always be specific to local circumstances. The relationships within the framework are a process, unfolding over time, and the task of the development practitioner is to select those elements of the particular process that appear most promising for accelerated change in order to secure better outcomes for poor people. Sometimes those elements will turn out to involve quite orthodox policy proposals, even, for example, trials of new disease-resistant varieties of an established food or export crop. At other times, entirely new insights may occur into the constraints inhibiting the generation of viable livelihoods by poor people. It is suggested in the preceding paragraphs that local level governance may prove a particularly interesting area to explore for such new insights in the future.

It is appropriate to end this book with the same cautionary note struck right at the beginning, in the preface. At the time of writing, the livelihoods approach is being adopted by donor agencies and development practitioners as the new way forward for rural poverty reduction. In this wave of enthusiasm, there is a serious risk that the approach will become over-codified and obligatory, leading to the suffocation of the new insights that it once seemed able to provide. This happened in the past to farming systems research (FSR) and to participatory rural appraisal (PRA), both deadened by being made into compulsory toolkits, the application of which then results in the suspension of imagination and intelligent observation. You do not need a livelihoods analysis to install a water pipe to a village. Not all worthwhile ways of improving the lives of the rural poor will require a livelihoods analysis to achieve that end.

References

Abbot, J. and I. Guijt, 1997, 'Creativity and Compromise', *PLA Notes*, No. 28, London: International Institute for Environment and Development.

Adams, R. H., 1993, 'The Economic and Demographic Determinants of International Migration in Rural Egypt', *Journal of Development Studies*, Vol. 30, No. 1, pp. 146–167.

Adams, R. H., 1994, 'Non-Farm Income and Inequality in Rural Pakistan', *Journal of Development Studies*, Vol. 31, No. 1, pp. 110–133.

Adams, R. H. and J. J. He, 1995, *Sources of Income Inequality and Poverty in Rural Pakistan*, Research Report No. 102, Washington, D.C.: International Food Policy Research Institute.

Adams, W. M. and M. J. Mortimore, 1997, 'Agricultural Intensification and Flexibility in the Nigerian Sahel', *The Geographical Journal*, Vol. 163, No. 2, pp. 150–160.

Addison, T. and L. Demery, 1989, 'The Economics of Rural Poverty Alleviation', Ch.5 in S. Commander (ed), *Structural Adjustment and Agriculture: Theory and Practice in Africa and Latin America*, London: ODI, pp. 71–89.

Agarwal, B., 1986, 'Women, Poverty and Agricultural Growth in India', *Journal of Peasant Studies*, Vol. 13, No. 4, pp. 165–220.

Agarwal, B., 1990, 'Social Security and the Family: Coping with Seasonality and Calamity in Rural India', *Journal of Peasant Studies*, Vol. 17, No. 3, pp. 341–412.

Agarwal, B., 1994a, 'Gender and Command Over Property: A Critical Gap in Economic Analysis and Policy in South Asia', *World Development*, Vol. 22, No. 10, pp. 1455–1478.

Agarwal, B., 1994b, *A Field of One's Own: Gender and Land Rights in South Asia*, Cambridge: Cambridge University Press.

Ahmed, I. I. and M. Lipton, 1997, 'Impact of Structural Adjustment on Sustainable Rural Livelihoods: A Review of the Literature', *IDS Working Paper*, No. 62.

Alderman, H. and C. Paxson, 1992, 'Do the Poor Insure? A Synthesis of the Literature on Risk and Consumption in Developing Countries', *Policy Research Working Papers*, No. 1008, Washington, D.C.: World Bank.

Alderman, H. and D. E. Sahn, 1989, 'Understanding the Seasonality of Employment, Wage, and Income', Ch.6 in D. E. Sahn (ed), *Seasonal Variability in Third World Agriculture: The Consequences for Food Security*, Baltimore: John Hopkins University Press, pp. 81–106.

Alderman, H., P. Chiappori, L. Haddad, J. Hoddinott and R. Kanbur, 1995, 'Unitary Versus Collective Models of the Household: Is it Time to Shift the Burden of Proof?', *World Bank Research Observer*, Vol. 10, No. 1, pp. 1–19.

Altieri, M. A., 1995, *Agroecology: The Science of Sustainable Agriculture*, London: Intermediate Technology Publications, 2nd edn.

Andrae, G., 1992, 'Urban Workers as Farmers: Agro-links of Nigerian Textile Workers in the Crisis of the 1980s', in J. Baker and P. O. Pederson (eds), *The Rural-Urban Interface in Africa: Expansion and Adaption*, Uppsala: Scandinavian Institute for African Studies in cooperation with Centre for Development Research, Copenhagen.

Anker, R., 1993, 'Labour Market Policies, Vulnerable Groups and Poverty', paper presented at the International Institute for Labour Studies Symposium, *Poverty: New Approaches to Analysis and Policy*, Geneva, November.

Baber, R., 1996, 'Current Livelihoods in Semi-Arid Rural Areas of South Africa', Ch.11 in M. Lipton, F. Ellis and M. Lipton (eds), *Land, Labour and Livelihoods in Rural South Africa Vol. 2: Kwazulu-Natal and Northern Province*, Durban: Indicator Press, pp. 269–302.

Baber, R., 1998, *The Structure of Livelihoods in South Africa's Bantustans: Evidence from Two Settlements in Northern Province*, unpublished doctoral thesis, Magdalen College, Oxford.

Baden, S. and A. M. Goetz, 1998, 'Who Needs [Sex] When You Can Have [Gender]?: Conflicting Discourses on Gender at Beijing', Ch.1 in C. Jackson, and R. Pearson (eds), *Feminist Visions of Development: Gender Analysis and Policy*, London: Routledge, pp. 19–38.

Baden, S. and K. Milward, 1995, *Gender and Poverty*, BRIDGE—Briefings on Development and Gender, Report No. 30, Brighton: Institute of Development Studies.

Bagachwa, M. S. D., 1997, 'The Rural Informal Sector in Tanzania', in D. F. Bryceson and V. Jamal (eds), *Farewell to Farms: Deagrarianisation and Employment in Africa*, Leiden, Netherlands: African Studies Centre.

Bagachwa, M. S. D. and A. Naho, 1995, 'Estimating the Second Economy in Tanzania', *World Development*, Vol. 23, No. 8, pp. 1387–1399.

Bagachwa, M. S. D. and F. Stewart, 1992, 'Rural Industries and Rural Linkages in Sub-Saharan Africa: A Survey', Ch.5 in F. Stewart, S. Lall and S. Wangwe (eds), *Alternative Development Strategies for Sub-Saharan Africa*, Basingstoke: Macmillan, pp. 145–184.

Bardhan, P. K. (ed), 1989, *The Economic Theory of Agrarian Institutions*, Oxford: Clarendon Press.

Basu, K. (ed), 1994, *Agrarian Questions*, Delhi: Oxford University Press.

Baulch, B., 1996a, 'The New Poverty Agenda: A Disputed Consensus', *IDS Bulletin*, Vol. 27, No. 1, pp. 1–10.

Baulch, B., 1996b, 'Neglected Trade-Offs in Poverty Measurement', *IDS Bulletin*, Vol. 27, No. 1, pp. 36–42.

Bayliss-Smith, T., 1991, 'Food Security and Agricultural Sustainability in the New Guinea Highlands: Vulnerable People, Vulnerable Places', *IDS Bulletin*, Vol. 22, No. 3, pp. 5–11.

Bebbington, A., 1999, 'Capitals and Capabilities: A Framework for Analyzing Peasant Viability, Rural Livelihoods and Poverty', *World Development*, Vol. 27, No. 12, pp. 2021–44.

Beckerman, W., 1992, 'Economic Growth and the Environment: Whose Growth? Whose Environment?', *World Development*, Vol. 20, No. 4.

Bell, C., P. Hazell and R. Slade, 1982, *Project Evaluation in Regional Perspective*, Baltimore: Johns Hopkins.

Benjamin, C., 1994, 'The Growing Importance of Diversification Activities for French Farm Households', *Journal of Rural Studies*, Vol. 10, No. 4, pp. 331–342.

Bernstein, H., B. Crow and H. Johnson, 1992, *Rural Livelihoods: Crises and Responses*, Oxford: Oxford University Press.

Berry, R. A., and W. R. Cline, 1979, *Agrarian Structure and Productivity in Developing Countries*, Baltimore: Johns Hopkins.

Berry, S., 1986, 'Macro-Policy Implications of Research on Rural Households and Farming Systems' in Moock, J. L. (ed), *Understanding Africa's Rural Household and Farming Systems*, Boulder, Colorado: Westview Press.

Berry, S., 1989, 'Social Institutions and Access to Resources', *Africa*, Vol. 59, No. 1, pp. 41–55.

Berry, S., 1993, *No Condition is Permanent: The Social Dynamics of Agrarian Change in Sub-Saharan Africa*, Madison, Wisconsin: University of Wisconsin Press.

Berry, S., 1997, 'Tomatoes, Land and Hearsay: Property and History in Asante in the Time of Structural Adjustment', *World Development*, Vol. 25, No. 8, pp. 1225–1241.

Besley, T., 1995, 'Savings, Credit and Insurance', Ch.36 in J. Behrman and T. N. Srinivasan (eds), *Handbook of Development Economics*, Vol. IIIA, New York: Elsevier, pp. 2123–2205.

Bevan, D. L., A. Bigsten, P. Collier and J. W. Gunning, 1988, 'Incomes in the United Republic of Tanzania During the "Nyerere Experiment"', Ch.3 in W. van Ginnecken (ed), *Trends in Employment and Labour Incomes*, Geneva: ILO, pp. 61–83.

Bevan, D. L., P. Collier and J. W. Gunning, 1989, *Peasants and Governments*, Oxford: Clarendon Press.

Bevan, P. and S. F. Joireman, 1997, 'The Perils of Measuring Poverty: Identifying the "Poor" in Rural Ethiopia', *Oxford Development Studies*, Vol. 25, No. 3, pp. 315–343.

Bhaduri, A., 1986, 'Forced Commerce and Agrarian Growth', *World Development*, Vol. 14, No. 2.

Biggs, S. and G. Smith, 1998, 'Beyond Methodologies: Coalition-Building For Participatory Technology Development', *World Development*, Vol. 26, No. 2, pp. 239–48.

Bigsten, A., 1988, 'A Note on the Modelling of Circular Small Holder Migration', *Economics Letters*, Vol. 28, pp. 87–91.

Bigsten, A., 1996, 'The Circular Migration of Smallholders in Kenya', *Journal of African Economies*, Vol. 5, No. 1, pp. 1–20.

Bigsten, A. and S. Kayizzi-Mugerwa, 1995, 'Rural Sector Responses to Economic Crisis in Uganda', *Journal of International Development*, Vol. 7, No. 2, pp. 181–209.

Binswanger, H. P., 1983, 'Agricultural Growth and Rural Nonfarm Activities', *Finance & Development*, June, pp. 38 40.

Blackwood, D. L. and R. G. Lynch, 1994, 'The Measurement of Inequality and Poverty: A Policy Maker's Guide to the Literature', *World Development*, Vol. 22, No. 4, pp. 567–578.

Blaikie, P. M. and H. Brookfield (eds), 1987, *Land Degradation and Society*, London: Methuen.

Blaikie, P. M., T. Cannon, I. Davis and B. Wisner, 1994, *At Risk: Natural Hazards, People's Vulnerability and Disasters*, London and New York: Routledge.

Blarel, B., P. Hazell, F. Place and J. Quiggin, 1992, 'The Economics of Farm Fragmentation: Evidence from Ghana and Rwanda', *World Bank Economic Review*, Vol. 6, No. 2, pp. 233–254.

Booth, D. (ed), 1994, *Rethinking Social Development: Theory, Research and Practice*, Harlow: Longman.

Booth, D., F. Lugangira *et al.*, 1993, *Social, Cultural and Economic Change in Contemporary Tanzania: A People-Oriented Focus*, Stockholm: Swedish International Development Authority.

Boserup, E., 1965, *The Conditions of Agricultural Growth: The Economics of Agrarian Change Under Population Pressure*, Chicago: Aldine.

Boserup, E., 1970, *Woman's Role in Economic Development*, New York: Allen & Unwin.

Boserup, E., 1981, *Population and Technological Change: A Study of Long-Term Trends*, Chicago: University of Chicago Press.

Breman, J., 1996, *Footloose Labour: Working in India's Informal Economy*, Cambridge: Cambridge University Press.

Broad, R., 1994, 'The Poor and the Environment: Friends or Foes?', *World Development*, Vol. 22, No. 6, pp. 811–822.

Bruce, J., 1989, 'Homes Divided', *World Development*, Vol. 17, No. 7.

Bruce, J. and C. B. Lloyd, 1997, 'Finding the Ties that Bind: Beyond Headship and Household', Ch.13 in L. Haddad, J. Hoddinott and H. Alderman (eds), *Intrahousehold Resource Allocation in Developing Countries: Models, Methods, and Policy*, Baltimore: Johns Hopkins, pp. 213–228.

Brundtland, G. H., 1987, *Our Common Future*, Oxford: Oxford University Press.

Bryceson, D. F., 1996, 'Deagrarianization and Rural Employment in Sub-Saharan Africa: A Sectoral Perspective', *World Development*, Vol. 24, No. 1, pp. 97–111.

Bryceson, D. F., 1999a, 'African Rural Labour, Income Diversification and Livelihood Approaches: A Long-Term Development Perspective', *Review of African Political Economy*, No. 80, pp. 171–89.

Bryceson, D. F., 1999b, 'Sub-Saharan Africa Betwixt and Between: Rural Livelihood Practices and Policies', *De-Agrarianisation and Rural Employment Network*, Afrika-Studiecentrum, Leiden, Working Paper No. 43.

Bryceson, D. F. and V. Jamal (eds), 1997, *Farewell to Farms: De-agrarianisation and Employment in Africa,* Research Series No. 10, Leiden: African Studies Centre, pp. 3–20.

Bryceson, D. F., C. Kay and J. Mooij (eds), 2000, *Disappearing Peasantries? Rural Labour in Africa, Asia and Latin America*, London: Intermediate Technology Publications.

Buvinic, M. and G. R. Gupta, 1997, 'Female-Headed Households and Female-Maintained Families: Are They Worth Targeting to Reduce Poverty in Developing Countries?', *Economic Development and Cultural Change*, Vol. 45, No. 2, pp. 259–280.

Byres, T. J., 1996, *Capitalism from Above and Capitalism from Below*, London: Macmillan.

Cain, M. and G. McNicoll, 1988, 'Population Growth and Agrarian Outcomes', Ch.5 in R. E. Lee, W. B. Arthur, A. C. Kelly, G. Rodgers and T. N. Srinivasan (eds), *Population, Food and Rural Development*, Oxford: Clarendon Press, pp. 101–117.

Cain, M., S. R. Khanam and S. Nahar, 1979, 'Class, Patriarchy, and Women's Work in Bangladesh', *Population and Development Review*, Vol. 5, pp. 405–438.

Carney, D., 1998, 'Implementing the Sustainable Rural Livelihoods Approach', Ch.1 in D. Carney (ed), *Sustainable Rural Livelihoods: What Contribution Can We Make?*, London: Department for International Development.

Carney, J. A., 1988, 'Struggles Over Crop Rights and Labour Within Contract Farming Households in a Gambian Irrigated Rice Project', *Journal of Peasant Studies*, Vol. 15, No. 3.

Carswell, G., 1997, 'Agricultural Intensification and Rural Sustainable Livelihoods: A "Think Piece"', *IDS Working Paper*, No. 64.

Carter, M. R., 1997, 'Environment, Technology, and the Social Articulation of Risk in West African Agriculture', *Economic Development and Cultural Change*, Vol. 45, No. 3, pp. 557–591.

Cassen, R., 1994, 'Structural Adjustment in Sub-Saharan Africa', Ch.1 in W. van der Geest (ed), *Negotiating Structural Adjustment in Africa*, London: James Currey, pp. 7–13.

Chambers, R., 1981, 'Rapid Rural Appraisal: Rationale and Repertoire', *Public Administration and Development*, Vol. 1.

Chambers, R., 1982, 'Health, Agriculture, and Rural Poverty', *Journal of Development Studies*, Vol. 18, No. 2, pp. 217–237.

Chambers, R., 1983, *Rural Development: Putting the Last First*, London: Longman.

Chambers, R., 1989, 'Editorial Introduction: Vulnerability, Coping and Policy', *IDS Bulletin*, Vol. 20, No. 2, pp. 1–7.

Chambers, R., 1992, 'Rural Appraisal: Rapid, Relaxed and Participatory', *IDS Discussion Paper*, No. 311.

Chambers, R., 1994a, 'The Origins and Practice of Participatory Rural Appraisal', *World Development*, Vol. 22, No. 7, pp. 953–969.

Chambers, R., 1994b, 'Participatory Rural Appraisal (PRA): Analysis and Experience', *World Development*, Vol. 22, No. 9, pp. 1253–1268.

Chambers, R., 1994c, 'Participatory Rural Appraisal (PRA): Challenges, Potentials and Paradigm', *World Development*, Vol. 22, No. 10.

Chambers, R., 1997, *Whose Reality Counts?: Putting the First Last*, London: Intermediate Technology Publications.

Chambers, R. and J. Blackburn, 1996, 'The Power of Participation: PRA and Policy', *IDS Policy Brief*, Issue 7, August.

Chambers, R. and R. Conway, 1992, 'Sustainable Rural Livelihoods: Practical Concepts for the 21st Century', *IDS Discussion Paper*, No. 296.

Chambers, R., R. Longhurst, and A. Pacey (eds.), 1981, *Seasonal Dimensions to Rural Poverty*, London: Frances Pinter.

Chambers, R., A. Pacey and L. A. Thrupp (eds), 1989, *Farmer First—Farmer Innovation and Agricultural Research*, London: Intermediate Technology Publications.

Chandrasekhar, C. P., 1993, 'Agrarian Change and Occupational Diversification: Non-Agricultural Employment and Rural Development in West Bengal', *Journal of Peasant Studies*, Vol. 20, No. 2, pp. 205–270.

Chang, H. S., 1997, 'Coking Coal Procurement Policies of the Japanese Steel Mills: Changes and Implications', *Resources Policy*, Vol. 23, No. 3, pp. 125–135.

Chant, S., 1997, 'Women-Headed Households: Poorest of the Poor? Perspectives from Mexico, Costa Rica and the Philippines', *IDS Bulletin*, Vol. 28, No. 3, pp. 26–48.

Chuta, E. and S. V. Sethuraman (eds), 1984, *Rural Small-Scale Industries and Employment in Africa and Asia*, Geneva: ILO.

Coleman, J. S., 1990, *Foundations of Social Theory*, Cambridge, Mass.: Harvard University Press.

Collier, P. and D. Lal, 1986, *Labour and Poverty in Kenya, 1900–1980*, Oxford: Clarendon Press.

Collier, P., S. Radwan and S. Wangwe, 1986, *Labour and Poverty in Rural Tanzania*, Oxford: Clarendon Press.

Commander, S. (ed), 1989, *Structural Adjustment and Agriculture: Theory and Practice in Africa and Latin America*, London: ODI.

Conway, G. R., 1985, 'Agroecosystem Analysis', *Agricultural Administration*, No. 20, pp. 31–55.

Conway, G. R., 1987, 'The Properties of Agroecosystems', *Agricultural Systems*, Vol. 24, No. 2, pp. 95–117.

Conway, G. R. and E. Barbier, 1990, *After the Green Revolution: Sustainable Agriculture for Development*, London: Earthscan.

Cook, P. and C. Kirkpatrick (eds), 1995, *Privatisation Policy and Performance: International Perspectives*, London: Prentice Hall/Harvester Wheatsheaf.

Corbett, J., 1988, 'Famine and Household Coping Strategies', *World Development*, Vol. 16, No. 9, pp. 1099–1112.

Cornia, G. A. and G. K. Helleiner (eds), 1994, *From Adjustment to Development in Africa: Conflict, Controversy, Convergence, Consensus?*, London: Macmillan.

Cornia, G. A., R. Jolly and F. Stewart (eds), 1987, *Adjustment with a Human Face: Protecting the Vulnerable and Promoting Growth*, Oxford: Clarendon Press.

Crehan, K., 1992, 'Rural Households: Making a Living', Ch.5 in H. Bernstein, B. Crow and H. Johnson (eds), *Rural Livelihoods: Crises and Responses*, Oxford: Oxford University Press, pp. 87–112.

Dasgupta, P., 1993, *An Inquiry into Well-Being and Destitution*, Oxford: Clarendon Press.

Dasgupta, P. and K.-G. Maler, 1995, 'Poverty, Institutions, and the Environmental Resource-Base', Ch.39 in J. Behrman and T. N. Srinivasan (eds), *Handbook of Development Economics*, Vol. IIIA, Amsterdam: North Holland, pp. 2371–2463.

David, R. *et al.*, 1995, *Changing Places: Women, Resource Management and Migration in the Sahel*, London: SOS Sahel.

Davies, S., 1993, 'Are Coping Strategies a Cop Out?', *IDS Bulletin*, Vol. 24, No. 4, pp. 60–72.

Davies, S., 1996, *Adaptable Livelihoods: Coping with Food Insecurity in the Malian Sahel*, London: Macmillan Press.

Davies, S. and N. Hossain, 1997, *Livelihood Adaptation, Public Action and Civil Society: A Review of the Literature*, *IDS Working Paper*, No. 57, Brighton: Institute of Development Studies, July.

de Haan, A. (ed), 1997, 'Urban Poverty: A New Research Agenda', *IDS Bulletin*, Vol. 28, No. 2.

de Haan, A., 1999, 'Livelihoods and Poverty: The Role of Migration—A Critical Review of the Migration Literature', *Journal of Development Studies*, Vol. 36, No. 2, pp. 1–47.

de Janvry, A., 1994, 'Farm-Nonfarm Synergies in Africa: Discussion', *American Journal of Agricultural Economics*, Vol. 76, pp. 1183–1185.

Deaton, A., 1997, *The Analysis of Household Surveys: A Microeconometric Approach to Development Policy*, Baltimore: Johns Hopkins.

Deininger, K. and L. Squire, 1996, 'A New Data Set Measuring Income Inequality', *The World Bank Economic Review*, Vol. 10, No. 3, pp. 565–591.

Delgado, C., P. Hazell, J. Hopkins and V. Kelly, 1994, 'Promoting Intersectoral Growth Linkages in Rural Africa Through Agricultural Technology Policy Reform', *American Journal of Agricultural Economics*, Vol. 76, pp. 1166–1171.

Delgado, C., J. Hopkins, V. Kelly *et al.*, 1998, *Agricultural Growth Linkages in Sub-Saharan Africa*, IFPRI Research Report No. 107, Washington, D.C.: International Food Policy Research Institute.

Demery, L., 1994, 'Structural Adjustment: Its Origins, Rationale and Achievements', Ch.2 in G.A. Cornia and G.K. Helleiner (eds), *From Adjustment to Development in Africa: Conflict, Controversy, Convergence, Consensus?*, London: Macmillan, pp. 25–48.

Demsetz, C., 1967, 'Towards a Theory of Property Rights', *American Economic Review*, Vol. 57, No. 2, pp. 347–359.

Dennis, C., 1991, 'Constructing a "Career" Under Conditions of Economic Crisis and Structural Adjustment: The Survival Strategies of Nigerian Women', in H. Afshar (ed), *Women, Development and Survival in the Third World*, London: Longman, pp. 83–105.

Dercon, S., 1998, 'Wealth, Risk and Activity Choice: Cattle in Western Tanzania', *Journal of Development Economics*, Vol. 55, No. 1, pp. 1–42.

Dercon, S. and P. Krishnan, 1996, 'Income Portfolios in Rural Ethiopia and Tanzania: Choices and Constraints', *Journal of Development Studies*, Vol. 32, No. 6, pp. 850–875.

Devereux, S., 1993, 'Goats Before Ploughs: Dilemmas of Household Response Sequencing During Food Shortages', *IDS Bulletin*, Vol. 24, No. 4, pp. 52–59.

Dey Abbas, J., 1997, 'Gender Asymmetries in Intrahousehold Resource Allocation in Sub-Saharan Africa: Some Policy Implications for Land and Labor Productivity', Ch.15 in L. Haddad, J. Hoddinott and H. Alderman (eds), *Intrahousehold Resource Allocation in Developing Countries: Models, Methods, and Policy*, Baltimore: Johns Hopkins, pp. 249–262.

Drèze, J. and A. Sen, 1989, *Hunger and Public Action*, Oxford: Clarendon Press.

Duncan, A. and J. Howell (eds), 1992, *Structural Adjustment and the African Farmer*, London: James Currey.

Dunham, D., 1993, 'Crop Diversification and Export Growth: Dynamics of Change in the Sri Lankan Peasant Sector', *Development and Change*, Vol. 24, 1993, pp. 787–813.

Duraiappah, A. K., 1998, 'Poverty and Environmental Degradation: A Review and Analysis of the Nexus', *World Development*, Vol. 26, No. 12, pp. 2169–2179.

Dwyer, D. and J. Bruce (eds), 1988, *A Home Divided: Women and Income in the Third World*, Stanford, California: Stanford University Press.

Ellis, F., 1982, 'Agricultural Price Policy in Tanzania', *World Development*, Vol. 10, No. 4.

Ellis, F., 1993, *Peasant Economics: Farm Households and Agrarian Development*, Cambridge: Cambridge University Press, 2nd edn.

Ellis, F., 1998, 'Survey Article: Household Strategies and Rural Livelihood Diversification', *Journal of Development Studies*, Vol. 35, No. 1, pp. 1–38.

Ellis, F., 2000, 'The Determinants of Rural Livelihood Diversification in Developing Countries', *Journal of Agricultural Economics*, Vol. 51, No. 2.

Engberg-Pedersen, P., P. Gibbon and P. Raikes, 1996, *Limits of Adjustment in Africa*, Oxford: James Currey.

Evans, H. E. and P. Ngau, 1991, 'Rural–Urban Relations, Household Income Diversification and Agricultural Productivity' *Development and Change*, Vol. 22, pp. 519–545.

Evans, N. J. and B. W. Ilbery, 1993, 'The Pluriactivity, Part-time Farming, and Farm Diversification Debate', *Environment and Planning A*, Vol. 25, pp. 945–959.

Farrington, J., 1998, 'Organisational Roles in Farmer Participatory Research and Extension: Lessons From the Last Decade', *ODI Natural Resource Perspectives*, Vol. 27.

Fei, J. C. H. and G. Ranis, 1964, *Development of the Labor Surplus Economy, Theory and Policy*, Homewood, Illinois: Yale University Press.

Ferreira, L., 1994, *Poverty and Inequality during Structural Adjustment in Rural Tanzania*, Research Paper No. 8, Washington, D.C.: World Bank, Transition Economics Division.

Fisher, T., V. Mahajan and A. Singha, 1997, *The Forgotten Sector: Non-farm Employment and Enterprises in Rural India*, London: Intermediate Technology Publications.

Flint, M., 1991, 'Population, Environment and Development', in V. Johnson (ed), *Lifestyle Overload? Population and Environment in the Balance*, Report of the Actionaid Seminar, London, Commonwealth House, November.

Folbre, N., 1986, 'Hearts and Spades: Paradigms of Household Economics', *World Development*, Vol. 14, No. 2.

Gasper, D., 1993, 'Entitlement Analysis: Relating Concepts and Contexts', *Development and Change*, Vol. 24, pp. 679–718.

Ghana, 1993, Ghana Statistical Service, *The Estimation of Components of Household Incomes and Expenditures from the First Two Rounds of the Ghana Living Standards Surveys, 1987/88 and 1988/89*, Accra.

Ghosh, J. and K. Bharadwaj, 1992, 'Poverty and Employment in India', Ch.7 in H. Bernstein, B. Crow and H. Johnson (eds), *Rural Livelihoods: Crises and Responses*, Oxford University Press, pp. 139–164.

Gibbon, P., 1992, 'A Failed Agenda? African Agriculture under Structural Adjustment with Special Reference to Kenya and Ghana', *Journal of Peasant Studies*, Vol. 20, No. 1, pp. 50–96.

Gibbon, P., 1996, 'Structural Adjustment and Structural Change in Sub-Saharan Africa: Some Provisional Conclusions', *Development and Change*, Vol. 27, No. 4, pp. 751–84.

Glewwe, P. and J. van der Gaag, 1988, 'Confronting Poverty in Developing Countries: Definitions, Information and Policies', *Living Standards Measurement Study*, Working Paper, No. 48, Washington, D.C.: World Bank.

Glewwe, P. and J. van der Gaag, 1990, 'Identifying the Poor in Developing Countries: Do Different Definitions Matter', *World Development*, Vol. 18, No. 6, pp. 803–814.

Goetz, A. M. and R. Sen Gupta, 1996, 'Who Takes the Credit? Gender, Power and Control over Loan Use in Rural Credit Programs in Bangladesh', *World Development*, Vol. 24, No. 1, pp. 45–63.

Goldman, A., 1995, 'Threats to Sustainability in African Agriculture: Searching for Appropriate Paradigms', *Human Ecology*, Vol. 23, No. 3.

Gore, C., 1993, 'Entitlement Relations and "Unruly" Social Practices: A Comment on the Work of Amartya Sen', *Journal of Development Studies*, Vol. 29, No. 3, pp. 429–460.

Greeley, M., 1994, 'Measurement of Poverty and Poverty of Measurement', *IDS Bulletin*, Vol. 27, No. 1, pp. 50–58.

Green, C., S. Joekes and M. Leach, 1998, 'Questionable Links: Approaches to Gender in Environmental Research and Policy', Ch.12 in in C. Jackson and R. Pearson (eds), *Feminist Visions of Development: Gender Analysis and Policy*, London: Routledge, pp. 259–283.

Griffin, K., 1979, *The Political Economy of Agrarian Change: An Essay on the Green Revolution*, London: Macmillan, 2nd edn.

Grown, C. A. and J. Sebstad, 1989, 'Introduction: Toward a Wider Perspective on Women's Employment', *World Development*, Vol. 17, No. 7.

Gueye, B., 1995, 'Development of PRA in Francophone Africa: Lessons From the Sahel', *PLA Notes*, No. 24, London: International Institute for Environment and Development.

Guyer, J. I., 1980, 'Food, Cocoa, and the Division of Labour by Sex in Two West African Societies', *Comparative Studies in Society and History*, Vol. 22, pp. 355–373.

Guyer, J. I., 1984, 'Women in the Rural Economy: Contemporary Variations', Ch.2 in M. Hay, and S. Stichter (eds.), *African Women South of the Sahara*, London: Longman.

Guyer, J. I., 1997, 'Endowments and Assets: The Anthropology of Wealth and the Economics of Intrahousehold Allocation', Ch.7 in L. Haddad, J. Hoddinott and H. Alderman (eds), *Intrahousehold Resource Allocation in Developing Countries: Models, Methods, and Policy*, Baltimore: Johns Hopkins, pp. 112–125.

Guyer, J. I. and P. E. Peters, 1987, 'Conceptualising the Household: Issues of Theory and Policy in Africa', *Development and Change*, Vol. 18, No. 2.

Haddad, L., L. R. Brown, A. Richter and L. Smith, 1995, 'The Gender Dimensions of Economic Adjustment Policies: Potential Interactions and Evidence to Date', *World Development*, Vol. 23, No. 6, pp. 881–896.

Haddad, L., J. Hoddinott and H. Alderman (eds), 1997a, *Intrahousehold Resource Allocation in Developing Countries: Models, Methods, and Policy*, Baltimore: Johns Hopkins.

Haddad, L., J. Hoddinott and H. Alderman, 1997b, 'Introduction: The Scope of Intrahousehold Resource Allocation Issues', Ch.1 in L. Haddad, J. Hoddinott and H. Alderman (eds), *Intrahousehold Resource Allocation in Developing Countries: Models, Methods, and Policy*, Baltimore: Johns Hopkins, pp. 1–16.

Haggblade, S. and P. Hazell, 1989, 'Agricultural Technology and Farm-Nonfarm Growth Linkages', *Agricultural Economics*, Vol. 3, pp. 345–364.

Haggblade, S., P. Hazell and J. Brown, 1989, 'Farm-Nonfarm Linkages in Rural Sub-Saharan Africa', *World Development*, Vol. 17, No. 8, pp. 1173–1201.

Haggblade, S., J. Hammer and P. Hazell, 1991, 'Modeling Agricultural Growth Multipliers', *American Journal of Agricultural Economics*, May, pp. 361–374.

Hanger, E. J., 1973, *Social and Economic Aspects of the Contribution of Women to the Farm Household Economy: Two East African Case Studies*, Unpublished MSc. Thesis, University of East Africa, Mathenene, Uganda.

Hardin, G., 1968, 'The Tragedy of the Commons', *Science*, No. 162, pp. 1243–1248.

Harriss, B., 1987a, 'Regional Growth Linkages from Agriculture', *Journal of Development Studies*, Vol. 23, No. 2, pp. 275–289.

Harriss, B., 1987b, 'Regional Growth Linkages from Agriculture and Resource Flows in Non-Farm Economy', *Economic and Political Weekly*, Vol. XXII, No. 1 and No. 2.

Harriss, J. R. (ed.), 1982, *Rural Development: Theories of Peasant Economy and Agrarian Change*, London: Hutchinson.

Harriss, J. R. (ed), 1997, 'Policy Arena: "Missing Link" or Analytically Missing?: The Concept of Social Capital', *Journal of International Development*, Vol. 9, No. 7, pp. 919–971.

Harris, J. R. and M. P. Todaro, 1970, 'Migration, Unemployment and Development: A Two Sector Analysis', *American Economic Review*, Vol. 60, pp. 126–142.

Harriss-White, B., 1997, 'Gender Bias in Intrahousehold Nutrition in South India: Unpacking Households and the Policy Process', Ch.11 in L. Haddad, J. Hoddinott and H. Alderman (eds), *Intrahousehold Resource Allocation in Developing Countries: Models, Methods, and Policy*, Baltimore: Johns Hopkins, pp. 194–212.

Hart, G., 1989, 'The Growth Linkages Controversy: Some Lessons from the Muda Case', *Journal of Development Studies*, Vol. 25, No. 4, pp. 571–575.

Hart, G., 1992, 'Imagined Unities: Constructions of "The Household" in Economic Theory', Ch.6 in S. Ortiz and S. Lees, *Understanding Economic Process*, Monographs in Economic Anthropology, No. 10, Lanham, NY: University Press of America, pp. 111–129.

Hart, G., 1993, *Regional Growth Linkages in the Era of Liberalization: A Critique of the New Agrarian Optimism*, World Employment Programme Research Working Paper No. 37, Geneva: ILO.

Hart, G., 1994, 'The Dynamics of Diversification in an Asian Rice Region', Ch.2 in B. Koppel *et al.* (eds), *Development or Deterioration?: Work in Rural Asia*, Boulder, Colorado: Lynne Reinner, pp. 47–71.

Hart, G., 1995, 'Gender and Household Dynamics: Recent Theories and Their Implications', in M. G. Quibria (ed), *Critical Issues in Asian Development: Theories, Experiences and Policies*, Oxford and New York: Oxford University Press.

Hart, G., 1997, 'From "Rotten Wives" to "Good Mothers": Household Models and the Limits of Economism', *IDS Bulletin*, Vol. 28, No. 3, pp. 14–25.

Hayami, Y. and V. W. Ruttan, 1985, *Agricultural Development: an International Perspective*, Baltimore: Johns Hopkins, 2nd edn.

Hazell, P. and S. Haggblade, 1993, 'Farm-Nonfarm Growth Linkages and the Welfare of the Poor', Ch.8 in M. Lipton and J. van der Gaag (eds), 'Including the Poor', *Proceedings of a Symposium Organized by the World Bank and the International Food Policy Research Institute*, Washington, D.C.: World Bank, pp. 190–204.

Hazell, P. B. R. and B. Hojjati, 1995, 'Farm/Non-Farm Growth Linkages in Zambia', *Journal of African Economies*, Vol. 4, No. 3, pp. 406–435.

Hazell, P. B. R. and C. Ramasamy, 1991, *The Green Revolution Reconsidered: The Impact of High-Yielding Rice Varieties in South India*, Baltimore: Johns Hopkins.

Hazell, P. B. R. and A. Roell, 1983, *Rural Growth Linkages: Household Expenditure Patterns in Malaysia and Nigeria*, Washington, D.C.: International Food Policy Research Institute.

Hearn, D. H., K. T. McNamara and L. Gunter, 1996, 'Local Economic Structure and Off-Farm Labour Earnings of Farm Operators and Spouses', *Journal of Agricultural Economics*, Vol. 47, No. 1, pp. 28–36.

Helleiner, G. K., 1994, 'From Adjustment to Development in Sub-Saharan Africa: Consensus and Continuing Conflict', Ch.1 in G. A. Cornia and G. K. Helleiner (eds), *From Adjustment to Development in Africa: Conflict, Controversy, Convergence, Consensus?*, London: Macmillan, pp. 3–24.

Herbst, J., 1993, *The Politics of Reform in Ghana, 1982–1991*, Berkeley and Oxford: University of California Press.

Heyer, J., 1996, 'The Complexities of Rural Poverty in Sub-Saharan Africa', *Oxford Development Studies*, Vol. 24, No. 3, pp. 281–297.

Heyzer, N., 1995, 'Gender, Population and Environment in the Context of Deforestation: A Malaysian Case Study', *IDS Bulletin*, Vol. 26, No. 1, pp. 40–46.

Hoddinott, J., 1994, 'A Model of Migration and Remittances Applied to Western Kenya', *Oxford Economic Papers*, Vol. 46, pp. 459–476.

Hoddinott, J. and L. Haddad, 1995, 'Does Female Income Share Influence Household Expenditure Patterns? Evidence from Côte d'Ivoire', *Oxford Bulletin of Economics and Statistics*, Vol. 57, No. 1, pp. 77–96.

Hoff, K., A. Braverman and J. E. Stiglitz (eds), 1993, *The Economics of Rural Organization: Theory, Practice and Policy*, Oxford: Oxford University Press.

Holling, C. S., 1973, 'Resilience and Stability of Ecological Systems', *Annual Review of Ecology and Systematics*, Vol. 4, pp. 1–23.

Hopkins, J., C. Levin and L. Haddad, 1994, 'Women's Income and Household Expenditure Patterns: Gender or Flow? Evidence from Niger', *American Journal of Agricultural Economics*, Vol. 76, pp. 1219–1225.

Horton, S., R. Kanbur and D. Mazumdar (eds), 1994, *Labor Markets in an Era of Adjustment*, Washington, D.C.: World Bank.

Hunt, D., 1979, 'Chayanov's Model of Peasant Household Resource Allocation and its Relevance to Mbere Division, Eastern Kenya', *Journal of Development Studies*, Vol. 15, No. 1.

Husain, I. and R. Faruqee (eds), 1994, *Adjustment in Africa: Lessons from Country Case Studies*, Washington, D.C.: World Bank.

Hussein, K. and J. Nelson, 1998, 'Sustainable Livelihoods and Livelihood Diversification', *IDS Working Paper*, No. 69.

Hymer, S. and S. Resnick, 1969, 'A Model of an Agrarian Economy with Nonagricultural Activities', *American Economic Review*, Vol. 59, No. 4.

Jackson, C., 1993a, 'Doing What Comes Naturally? Women and Environment in Development', *World Development*, Vol. 21, No. 12, pp. 1947–1963.

Jackson, C., 1993b, 'Questioning Synergism: Win-Win with Women in Population and Environment Policies', *Journal of International Development*, Vol. 5, No. 6, pp. 651–668.

Jackson, C., 1997, 'Post Poverty, Gender and Development?', *IDS Bulletin*, Vol. 28, No. 3, pp. 145–155.

Jackson, C., 1998a, 'Rescuing Gender from the Poverty Trap', Ch.2 in C. Jackson and R. Pearson (eds), *Feminist Visions of Development: Gender Analysis and Policy*, London: Routledge, pp. 39–64.

Jackson, C., 1998b, 'Women and Poverty or Gender and Well-Being?', *Journal of International Affairs*, Vol. 52, No. 1, pp. 67–81.

Jaffee, S. and J. Morton (eds), 1995, *Marketing Africa's High-Value Foods: Comparative Experiences of an Emergent Private Sector*, Dubuque, Iowa: Kendall/Hunt for the World Bank.

Jamal, V., 1995, 'Adjustment Programmes and Adjustment: Confronting the New Parameters of African Economies', Ch.1 in V. Jamal (ed), *Structural Adjustment and Rural Labour Markets in Africa*, London: St Martin's Press, pp. 1–37.

Jamal, V. and J. Weeks, 1988, 'The Vanishing Rural-Urban Gap in Sub-Saharan Africa', *International Labour Review*, Vol. 127, No. 3, pp. 271–292.

Jamal, V. and J. Weeks, 1993, *Africa Misunderstood or Whatever Happened to the Rural-Urban Gap?*, London: Macmillan.

Jazairy, I., M. Alamgir and T. Panuccio, 1992, *The State of World Rural Poverty: An Inquiry into its Causes and Consequences*, London: Intermediate Technology Publications for the International Fund for Agricultural Development.

Jimenez, E., 1987, *Pricing Policy in the Social Sectors: Cost Recovery for Education and Health in Developing Countries*, Baltimore: Johns Hopkins.

Jimenez, E., 1990, 'Social Sector Pricing Policy Revisited: A Survey of Some Recent Controversies', *Proceedings of the World Bank Annual Conference on Development Economics 1989*, Washington, D.C.: World Bank, pp. 109–138.

Jodha, N. S., 1990, 'Rural Common Property Resources: Contributions and Crisis', *Economic and Political Weekly*, June 30.

Joekes, S., M. Leach and C. Green (eds), 1995, 'Gender Relations and Environmental Change', *IDS Bulletin*, Vol. 26, No. 1.

Johnson, H. and L. Mayoux, 1998, 'Investigation As Empowerment: Using Participatory Methods', Ch.7 in A. Thomas, J. Chataway, and M. Wuyts (eds.), *Finding Out Fast: Investigative Skills for Policy and Development*, London: Sage, pp. 147–171.

Johnson, S. and B. Rogaly, 1997, *Microfinance and Poverty Reduction*, Oxfam Development Guidelines, Oxford: Oxfam.

Johnston, B. F. and P. Kilby, 1975, *Agriculture and Structural Transformation*, New York: Oxford University Press.

Kabeer, N., 1991, 'Gender, Production and Well-Being: Rethinking the Household Economy', *IDS Discussion Paper*, No. DP 288, May.

Kabeer, N., 1996, 'Agency, Well-being and Inequality: Reflections on Gender Dimensions of Poverty', *IDS Bulletin*, Vol. 27, No. 1, pp. 11–22.

Kabeer, N. (ed), 1997a, 'Tactics and Trade-Offs: Revisiting the Links Between Gender and Poverty', *IDS Bulletin*, Vol. 28, No. 3.

Kabeer, N., 1997b, 'Editorial: Tactics and Trade-Offs, Revisiting the Links Between Gender and Poverty', *IDS Bulletin*, Vol. 28, No. 3, pp. 1–13.

Kabeer, N., 1998, 'Jumping to Conclusions', Ch.3 in Jackson, C. and R. Pearson (eds), *Feminist Visions of Development: Gender Analysis and Policy*, London: Routledge, pp. 91–107.

Katz, E. and O. Stark, 1986, 'Labor Migration and Risk Aversion in Less Developed Countries', *Journal of Labor Economics*, Vol. 4, pp. 134–149.

Kelly, C. and B. W. Ilbery, 1995, 'Defining and Examining Rural Diversification: A Framework for Analysis', *Tijdschrift voor Economische en Sociale Geografie*, Vol. 85, No. 2, pp. 177–185.

Kennedy, E. and P. Peters, 1992, 'Household Food Security and Child Nutrition: The Interaction of Income and Gender of Household Head', *World Development*, Vol. 20, No. 8.

Kenya, 1996, Ministry of Planning and National Development, *Welfare Monitoring Survey II: Basic Report*, Nairobi: Central Bureau of Statistics.

Killick, T., 1993, *The Adaptive Economy—Adjustment Policies in Small Low-Income Countries*, Washington, D.C.: World Bank.

Killick, T (ed), 1995, *The Flexible Economy: Causes and Consequences of the Adaptability of National Economies*, London: Routledge.

Krueger, A. O., 1992, *The Political Economy of Agricultural Pricing Policy: Vol. 5: A Synthesis of the Economics in Developing Countries: A World Bank Comparative Study*, Baltimore and London: John Hopkins University Press.

Lageman, B., 1989, 'Recent Migration Flows and the "Net Reallocation of Labour" between Rural and Urban Sectors in Nigeria', *African Development Patterns Yearbook*, pp. 525–45.

Larson, D. and Y. Mundlak, 1997, 'On the Intersectoral Migration of Agricultural Labour', *Economic Development and Cultural Change*, Vol. 45, No. 2, pp. 295–320.

Leach, M. and R. Mearns (eds), 1996, *The Lie of the Land: Challenging Received Wisdom on the African Environment*, London: Heinemann and James Currey.

Leach, M., S. Joekes and C. Green, 1995, 'Editorial: Gender Relations and Environmental Change', *IDS Bulletin*, Vol. 26, No. 1, pp. 1–8.

Leach, M., R. Mearns and I. Scoones (eds), 1997, 'Community-Based Sustainable Development: Consensus or Conflict', *IDS Bulletin*, Vol. 28, No. 4.

Leonard, H. J. (ed), 1989, *Environment and the Poor: Development Strategies for a Common Agenda*, New Brunswick, NJ: Transaction Books.

Leones, J. P. and S. Feldman, 1998, 'Nonfarm Activity and Rural Household Income: Evidence from Philippine Microdata', *Economic Development and Cultural Change*, Vol. 46, No. 4, pp. 789–806.

Leurs, R., 1996, 'Current Challenges Facing Participatory Rural Appraisal', *Public Administration And Development*, Vol. 16, No. 1, pp. 57–72.

Lewis, W. A., 1954, 'Economic Development with Unlimited Supplies of Labour', *Manchester School*, Vol. 22, No. 2, pp. 139–91.

Liedholm, C., M. McPherson and E. Chuta, 1994, 'Small Enterprise Employment Growth in Rural Africa', *American Journal of Agricultural Economics*, Vol. 76, pp. 1177–1182.

Lipton, M., 1977, *Why Poor People Stay Poor: Urban Bias in World Development*, London: Temple Smith.

Lipton, M., 1980, 'Migration from Rural Areas of Poor Countries: The Impact on Rural Productivity and Income Distribution', *World Development*, Vol. 8, pp. 1–24.

Lipton, M., 1991, 'A Note on Poverty and Sustainability', *IDS Bulletin*, Vol. 22, No. 4, pp. 12–16.

Lipton, M., 1996, 'Comment on "Research on Poverty and Development Twenty Years after Redistribution with Growth"', in M. Bruno and B. Pleskovic (eds), *Annual World Bank Conference on Development Economics 1995*, Washington, D.C.: World Bank, pp. 73–79.

Lipton, M. and R. Longhurst, 1989, *New Seeds and Poor People*, London: Unwin Hyman.

Lipton, M. and S. Maxwell, 1992, 'The New Poverty Agenda: An Overview', *IDS Discussion Paper*, No. 306, August.

Lipton, M. and J. van der Gaag (eds), 1993, *Including the Poor*, Proceedings of a Symposium Organized by the World Bank and the International Food Policy Research Institute, Washington, D.C.: World Bank.

Lipton, M. and M. Ravallion, 1995, 'Poverty and Policy', in J. Behrman and T. N. Srinivasan (eds), *Handbook of Development Economics*, Vol. IIIB, Amsterdam: Elsevier, pp. 2551–2657.

Livingstone, I., 1991, 'A Reassessment of Kenya's Rural and Urban Informal Sector', *World Development*, Vol. 19, No. 6.

Lloyd, C. B. and A. J. Gage-Brandon, 1993, 'Women's Role in Maintaining Households: Family Welfare and Sexual Inequality in Ghana', *Population Studies*, Vol. 41, pp. 115–131.

Lockwood, M., 1997, 'Reproduction and Poverty in Sub-Saharan Africa', *IDS Bulletin*, Vol. 28, No. 3 pp. 91–100.

Long, N. and A. Long (eds), 1992, *Battlefields of Knowledge: The Interlocking of Theory and Practice in Social Research and Development*, London: Routledge.

Longhurst, R., 1994, 'Conceptual Frameworks for Linking Relief and Development', *IDS Bulletin*, Vol. 25, No. 4, pp. 17–23.

Low, A. R. C., 1981, 'The Effect of Off-Farm Employment on Farm Incomes and Production: Taiwan Contrasted with Southern Africa', *Economic Development and Cultural Change*, Vol. 29, No. 4, pp. 741–747.

Low, A. R. C., 1986, *Agricultural Development in Southern Africa: Farm Household Theory and the Food Crisis*, London: James Currey.

Lucas, R. E. B. and O. Stark, 1985, 'Motivations to Remit: Evidence from Botswana', *Journal of Political Economy*, Vol. 93, No. 5, pp. 901–918.

Lynam, J. and R. Herdt, 1992, 'Sense and Sustainability: Sustainability as an Objective in International Agricultural Research', in J. Moock and R. Rhoades (eds), *Diversity, Farmer Knowledge and Sustainability*, Ithaca, NY and London: Cornell University Press.

McCracken, J. A., J. N. Pretty and G. R. Conway, 1988, *An Introduction to Rapid Rural Appraisal for Agricultural Development*, London: International Institute for Environment and Development.

Maliyamkono, T. L. and M. S. D. Bagachwa, 1993, *The Second Economy in Tanzania*, London: James Currey.

Matlon, P. J., 1979, *Income Distribution among Farmers in Northern Nigeria: Empirical Results and Policy Implications*, African Rural Economy Paper No. 18, East Lansing: Michigan State University, Department of Agricultural Economics.

Maxwell, S. and M. Smith, 1992, *Household Food Security: A Conceptual Overview*, Geneva: UNICEF.

May, J., 1996, 'Assets, Income and Livelihoods in Rural Kwazulu-Natal', Ch.1 in M. Lipton, F. Ellis and M. Lipton (eds), *Land, Labour and Livelihoods in Rural South Africa Volume 2: Kwazulu-Natal and Northern Province*, Durban: Indicator Press, pp. 1–30.

Meillassoux, C., 1981, *Maidens, Meal and Money: Capitalism and the Domestic Community*, Cambridge: Cambridge University Press.

Meindertsma, J. D., 1997, *Income Diversity and Farming Systems: Modelling of Farming Households in Lombok, Indonesia*, Amsterdam: Royal Tropical Institute.

Mellor, J. W., 1966, *The Economics of Agricultural Development*, New York: Cornell University Press.

Mellor, J. W., 1976, *The New Economics of Growth*, Ithaca, NY: Cornell University Press.

Mellor, J. W., 1983, 'Foreword', in P. B. R. Hazell and A. Roell, *Rural Growth Linkages: Household Expenditure Patterns in Malaysia and Nigeria*, Washington, D.C.: International Food Policy Research Institute.

Mellor, J. W., C. L. Delgado and M. J. Blackie (eds), 1988, *Accelerating Food Production in Sub-Saharan Africa*, Baltimore: Johns Hopkins.

Mencher, J. P., 1988, 'Women's Work and Poverty: Women's Contribution to Household Maintenance in South India', in D. Dwyer and J. Bruce (eds), *A Home Divided: Women and Income in the Third World*, Stanford, California: Stanford University Press, pp. 99–119.

Mies, M. and V. Shiva, 1993, *Ecofeminism*, London: Zed Books.

Mkandawire, T., 1994a, 'Adjustment, Political Conditionality and Democratisation in Africa', Ch.8 in G. A. Cornia and G. K. Helleiner (eds), *From Adjustment to Development in Africa: Conflict, Controversy, Convergence, Consensus?*, London: Macmillan, pp. 155–173.

Mkandawire, T., 1994b, 'The Political Economy of Privatisation in Africa', Ch.10 in G. A. Cornia and G. K. Helleiner (eds), *From Adjustment to Development in Africa: Conflict, Controversy, Convergence, Consensus?*, London: Macmillan, pp. 192–213.

Mohan, G. 1998, 'Beyond Participation: Strategies for Deeper Empowerment', Paper presented at the conference on *Participation: The New Tyranny?*, Institute for Development Policy and Management, University of Manchester, mimeo.

Morduch, J., 1995, 'Income Smoothing and Consumption Smoothing', *Journal of Economic Perspectives*, Vol. 9, No. 3, pp. 103–114.

Mortimore, M., 1998, *Roots in the African Dust: Sustaining the Drylands*, Cambridge: Cambridge University Press.

Mosley, P., J. Harrigan and J. Toye, 1991, *Aid and Power: The World Bank and Policy-Based Lending*, Vol. 1, London: Routledge.

Moser, C. O. N., 1996, *Confronting Crisis: A Comparative Study of Household Responses to Poverty and Vulnerability in Four Poor Urban Communities*, Washington, D.C.: World Bank.

Moser, C. O. N., 1998, 'The Asset Vulnerability Framework: Reassessing Urban Poverty Reduction Strategies', *World Development*, Vol. 26, No. 1, pp. 1–19.

Mosse, D., 1994, 'Authority, Gender And Knowledge—Theoretical Reflections on the Practice of Participatory Rural Appraisal', *Development and Change*, Vol. 25, No. 3, pp. 497–526.

Murray, C., 1981, *Families Divided*, Cambridge: Cambridge University Press.

Nafziger, E. W., 1997, *The Economics of Developing Countries*, London: Prentice-Hall, 3rd edn.

Narayan, D. and D. Nyamwaya, 1995, *A Participatory Poverty Assessment Study—Kenya*, Report Prepared for the World Bank, Nairobi: UNICEF-ODA-AMREF.

Narayan, D. and L. Pritchett, 1999, 'Cents and Sociability: Household Income and Social Capital in Rural Tanzania', *Economic Development and Cultural Change*, Vol. 47, No. 4, pp. 871–897.

Netting, R. M., 1993, *Smallholders, Householders: Farm Families and the Ecology of Intensive, Sustainable Agriculture*, Stanford, California: Stanford University Press.

Netting, R. M., P. Stone and G. D. Stone, 1989, 'Kofyar Cash-Cropping: Choice and Change in Indigenous Agricultural Development', *Human Ecology*, Vol. 17, No. 3, pp. 299–319.

North, D. C., 1990, *Institutions, Institutional Change and Economic Performance*, Cambridge: Cambridge University Press.

Ostrom, E., 1990, *Governing the Commons: The Evolution of Institutions for Collective Action*, Cambridge: Cambridge University Press.

Pasek, J., 1992, 'Obligations to Future Generations: A Philosophical Note', *World Development*, Vol. 20, No. 4.

Pearce, D., A. Markandya, and E. B. Barbier, 1989, *Blueprint for a Green Economy*, London: Earthscan.

Pearson, R., 1998, '"Nimble Fingers" Revisited: Reflections on Women and Third World Industrialisation in the Late Twentieth Century', Ch.8 in C. Jackson and R. Pearson (eds), *Feminist Visions of Development: Gender Analysis and Policy*, London: Routledge, pp. 171–188.

Pearson, S., W. Falcon, P. Heytens, E. Monke and R. Naylor, 1991, *Rice Policy in Indonesia*, Ithaca: Cornell University Press.

Pinstrup-Anderson, P. and R. Pandya-Lorch, 1994, *Alleviating Poverty, Intensifying Agriculture, and Effectively Managing Natural Resources*, Food, Agriculture and Environment, Discussion Paper 1, 2020 Vision, Washington, D.C.: International Food Policy Research Institute.

Place, F. and P. Hazell, 1993, 'Productivity Effects of Indigenous Land Tenure Systems in Sub-Saharan Africa', *American Journal of Agricultural Economics*, Vol. 75, pp. 10–19.

Platteau, J.-P., 1991, 'Traditional Systems of Social Security and Hunger Insurance: Past Achievements and Modern Challenges', in Ahmad *et al.*, *Social Security in Developing Countries*, Oxford: Clarendon Press, pp. 112–170.

Platteau, J.-P., 1994a, 'Beyond the Market Stage Where Real Societies Exist—Part I: The Role of Public and Private Order Institutions', *Journal of Development Studies*, Vol. 30, No. 3, pp. 533–577.

Platteau, J.-P., 1994b, 'Beyond the Market Stage Where Real Societies Exist—Part II: The Role of Moral Norms', *Journal of Development Studies*, Vol. 30, No. 4, pp. 753–817.

Platteau, J.-P., 1996, 'The Evolutionary Theory of Land Rights as Applied to Sub-Saharan Africa: A Critical Assessment', *Development and Change*, Vol. 27, pp. 29–86.

Please, S., 1994, 'From Structural Adjustment to Structural Transformation', Ch.2 in W. van der Geest (ed), *Negotiating Structural Adjustment in Africa*, London: James Currey, pp. 14–24.

Pottier, J., 1983, 'Defunct Labour Reserve?: Mambwe Villages in the Post-Migration Economy', *Africa*, Vol. 53, No. 2, pp. 1–22.

Pottier, J. and P. Orone, 1995, 'Consensus or Cover-Up? The Limitations of Group Meetings', *PLA Notes*, Vol. 24, London: International Institute for Environment and Development, pp. 38–42.

Preston, D. A., 1989, 'Too Busy to Farm: Under-utilization of Farm Land in Central Java', *Journal of Development Studies*, Vol. 26, No. 1.

Preston, D. A., 1994, 'Rapid Household Appraisal: A Method for Facilitating the Analysis of Household Livelihood Strategies', *Applied Geography*, Vol. 14, pp. 203–213.

Pretty, J. N., I. Guijt, J. Thompson and I. Scoones, 1995, *Participatory Learning and Action: A Trainer's Guide*, London: International Institute for Environment and Development.

Putnam, R. with R. Leonardi and R. Y. Nanetti, 1993, *Making Democracy Work: Civic Traditions in Modern Italy*, Princeton, NJ: Princeton University Press.

Ranis, G., 1990, 'Rural Linkages and Choice of Technology', in F. Stewart, H. Thomas and T. de Wilde (eds), *The Other Policy: The Influence of Policies on Technology Choice and Small Enterprise Development*, Washington: Intermediate Technology Publications.

Ranis, G. and F. Stewart, 1987, 'Rural Linkages in the Philippines and Taiwan', Ch.5 in F. Stewart (ed), *Macro-Policies for Appropriate Technology in Developing Countries*, Boulder, Colorado: Westview Press.

Ravallion, M., 1992, 'Poverty Comparisons: A Guide to Concepts and Methods', *Living Standards Measurement Study, Working Paper*, No. 88, Washington, D.C.: World Bank.

Reardon, T., 1997, 'Using Evidence of Household Income Diversification to Inform Study of the Rural Nonfarm Labor Market in Africa', *World Development*, Vol. 25, No. 5, pp. 735–747.

Reardon, T. and S. A. Vosti, 1995, 'Links Between Rural Poverty and the Environment in Developing Countries: Asset Categories and Investment Poverty', *World Development*, Vol. 23, No. 9, pp. 1495–1506.

Reardon, T., C. Delgado, and P. Matlon, 1992, 'Determinants and Effects of Income Diversification Amongst Farm Households in Burkina Faso', *Journal of Development Studies*, Vol. 28, No. 2.

Reardon, T., J. E. Taylor, K. Stamoulis, P. Lanjouw and A. Balisacan, 2000, 'Effects of Nonfarm Employment on Rural Income Inequality in Developing Countries: An Investment Perspective', *Journal of Agricultural Economics*, Vol. 51, No. 2.

Reed, D., 1996, *Structural Adjustment, the Environment and Sustainable Development*, London: Earthscan.

Rempel, H. and R. A. Lobdell, 1978, 'The Role of Urban-to-Rural Remittances in Rural Development', *Journal of Development Studies*, Vol. 14, No. 3, pp. 324–341.

Richards, P., 1985, *Indigenous Agricultural Revolution: Ecology and Food Production in West Africa*, London: Hutchinson.

Robson, C., 1993, *Real World Research*, Oxford: Blackwell.

Rogaly, B., 1997, 'Linking Home and Market: Towards a Gendered Analysis of Changing Labour Relations in Rural West Bengal', *IDS Bulletin*, Vol. 28, No. 3, pp. 63–72.

Rosenzweig, M. R., H. P. Binswanger and J. McIntire, 1988, 'From Land Abundance to Land Scarcity: The Effects of Population Growth on Production Relations in Agrarian Economies', Ch.4 in R. E. Lee, W. B. Arthur, A. C. Kelly, G. Rodgers and T. N. Srinivasan (eds), *Population, Food and Rural Development*, Oxford: Clarendon Press.

Sahn, D. E. (ed), 1989, *Seasonal Variability in Third World Agriculture: The Consequences for Food Security*, Baltimore: John Hopkins Press.

Sahn, D. E., 1994, 'The Impact of Macroeconomic Adjustment on Incomes, Health and Nutrition: Sub-Saharan Africa in the 1980s', Ch.13 in G. A. Cornia and G. K. Helleiner (eds), *From Adjustment to Development in Africa: Conflict, Controversy, Convergence, Consensus?*, London: Macmillan, pp. 273–297.

Sahn, D. E. and A. Sarris, 1991, 'Structural Adjustment and the Welfare of Rural Smallholders: A Comparative Analysis from Sub-Saharan Africa', *World Bank Economic Review*, Vol. 5, No. 2, pp. 259–289.

Sahn, D. E., P. Dorosh and S. Younger, 1996, 'Exchange Rate, Fiscal and Agricultural Policies in Africa: Does Adjustment Hurt the Poor?', *World Development*, Vol. 24, No. 4, pp. 719–747.

Saith, A., 1992, *The Rural Non-Farm Economy: Processes and Policies*, Geneva: ILO, World Employment Programme,.

Sanghera, B. S. and B. Harriss-White, 1995, *Themes in Rural Urbanisation*, DPP Working Paper No. 34, Milton Keynes, UK: The Open University, Faculty of Technology.

Sarris, A. H. and P. Tinios, 1995, 'Consumption and Poverty in Tanzania in 1976 and 1991: A Comparison Using Survey Data', *World Development*, Vol. 23, No. 8, pp. 1401–1419.

Sarris, A. H. and R. van den Brink, 1993, *Economic Policy and Household Welfare during Crisis and Adjustment in Tanzania*, New York: New York University Press.

Savadogo, K., T. Reardon and K. Pietola, 1994, 'Farm Productivity in Burkino Faso: Effects of Animal Traction and Nonfarm Income', *American Journal of Agricultural Economics*, Vol. 76, August, pp. 608–612.

Schultz, T. W., 1964, *Transforming Traditional Agriculture*, Yale University Press, 1964.

Scoones, I., 1998, 'Sustainable Rural Livelihoods: A Framework for Analysis', *IDS Working Paper*, No. 72.

Scoones, I. and J. Thompson (eds), 1994, *Beyond Farmer First*, London: Intermediate Technology Publications.

Scott, J. C., 1976, *The Moral Economy of the Peasant*, New Haven, Conn.: Yale University Press.

Sen, A. K., 1981, *Poverty and Famines: An Essay on Entitlements and Deprivation*, Oxford: Clarendon Press.

Sen, A. K, 1993, 'Capability and Well-Being', in A. K. Sen and M. C. Nussbaum, *The Quality of Life*, Oxford: Clarendon Press.

Sen, A. K., 1997, 'Editorial: Human Capital and Human Capability', *World Development*, Vol. 25, No. 12, pp. 1959–1961.

Shipton, P. and M. Goheen, 1992, 'Understanding African Landholding: Power, Wealth and Meaning', *Africa*, Vol. 62, No. 3, pp. 307–326.

Shiva, V., 1988, *Staying Alive: Women, Ecology and Development*, London: Zed Books.

Shucksmith, D. M., J. Bryden, P. Rosenthall, C. Short and D. M. Winter, 1989, 'Pluriactivity, Farm Structures and Rural Change', *Journal of Agricultural Economics*, Vol. 40, No. 3.

Shukla, V., 1992, 'Rural Non-Farm Employment in India: Issues and Policy', *Economic and Political Weekly*, July 11, pp. 1477–1488.

Simon, J. L., 1977, *The Economics of Population Growth*, Princeton, NJ: Princeton University Press.

Simon, J. L., 1981, *The Ultimate Resource*, Princeton, NJ: Princeton University Press.

Singh, I., 1990, *The Great Ascent: The Rural Poor in South Asia*, Baltimore: Johns Hopkins.

Singh, I., L. Squire and J. Strauss (eds.), 1986, *Agricultural Household Models*, Baltimore: Johns Hopkins.

Standing, G., 1989, 'Global Feminisation Through Flexible Labour', *World Development*, Vol. 17, No. 7.

Stark, O., 1980, 'On the Role of Urban-to-Rural Remittances in Rural Development', *Journal of Development Studies*, Vol. 16, pp. 369–374.

Stark, O., 1982, 'Research on Rural-to-Urban Migration in Less Developed Countries: The Confusion Frontier and Why We Should Pause to Rethink Afresh', *World Development*, Vol. 10, pp. 63–70.

Stark, O., 1991, *The Migration of Labor*, Cambridge, Mass.: Basil Blackwell.

Stark, O. and D. E. Bloom, 1985, 'The New Economics of Labour Migration', *American Economic Review*, Vol. 77, pp. 173–175.

Stark, O. and D. Levhari, 1982, 'On Migration and Risk in Less Developed Countries', *Economic Development and Cultural Change*, Vol. 31.

Stark, O. and R. E. B. Lucas, 1988, 'Migration, Remittances, and the Family', *Economic Development and Cultural Change*, Vol. 36, pp. 465–481.

Stewart, F., 1994a, 'Are Short-Term Policies Consistent with Long-Term Development Needs in Africa?', Ch.5 in G. A. Cornia and G. K. Helleiner (eds), *From Adjustment to Development in Africa: Conflict, Controversy, Convergence, Consensus?*, London: Macmillan, pp. 98–128.

Stewart, F., 1994b, 'Are Adjustment Policies in Africa Consistent with Long-Run Development Needs?', Ch.7 in W. van der Geest (ed), *Negotiating Structural Adjustment in Africa*, London: James Currey, pp. 99–114.

Stichter, S., 1982, *Migrant Labour and Capitalism in Kenya*, London: Longman.

Stiglitz, J. E., 1998, 'Keynote Address: An Agenda for Development in the Twenty-First Century', in B. Pleskovic and J. E. Stigliz (eds), *Annual World Bank Conference on Development Economics 1997*, Washington, D.C.: World Bank, pp. 17–31.

Streeten, P., 1989, 'A Survey of the Issues and Options', Ch.1 in S. Commander (ed), *Structural Adjustment and Agriculture: Theory and Practice in Africa and Latin America*, London: ODI, pp. 3–18.

Swift, J., 1989, 'Why Are Rural People Vulnerable to Famine?', *IDS Bulletin*, Vol. 20, No. 2, pp. 8–15.

Swift, J., 1998, *Factors Influencing the Dynamics of Livelihood Diversification and Rural Non-Farm Employment in Space and Time*, Rural Nonfarm Employment Project, Chatham, UK: Natural Resources Institute, mimeo report.

Tanzania, 1969, Ministry of Planning and Economic Affairs, *Household Budget Survey, 1969*, Dar es Salaam: Bureau of Statistics.

Tanzania, 1977, Ministry of Planning and Economic Affairs, *Household Budget Survey 1976/77*, Dar es Salaam: Bureau of Statistics.

Tanzania, 1994, National Planning Commission, *Agricultural Diversification and Intensification Study* Vol. 1: *Summary of Conclusions*, Oxford: Food Studies Group, December.

Tanzania, 1995, National Planning Commission, *Agricultural Diversification and Intensification Study* Vol. 2: *Analysis*, Oxford: Food Studies Group, November.

Tanzania, 1997, Bureau of Statistics, *National Accounts Revision—Tanzania: Report at the Completion of the First and Second Phases*, Dar es Salaam: Bureau of Statistics, mimeo.

Taslim, M. A., 1989, 'Supervision Problems and the Size-Productivity Relation in Bangladesh Agriculture', *Oxford Bulletin of Economics and Statistics*, Vol. 51, No. 1.

Taylor, E. and T. J. Wyatt, 1996, 'The Shadow Value of Migrant Remittances, Income and Inequality in a Household-Farm Economy', *Journal of Development Studies*, Vol. 32, No. 6, pp. 899–912.

Thomas, A., 1998, 'Challenging Cases', Ch.14 in A. Thomas, J. Chataway, and M. Wuyts (eds.), *Finding Out Fast: Investigative Skills for Policy and Development*, London: Sage, pp. 307–332.

Thomas, D., 1990, 'Intra-Household Resource Allocation: An Inferential Approach', *Journal of Human Resources*, Vol. XXV, No. 4, pp. 634–664.

Thorner, D., B. Kerblay, and R. E. F. Smith, 1966, *Chayanov on the Theory of Peasant Economy*, Homewood, Illinois: Richard D. Irwin.

Tiffen, M. and M. Mortimore, 1992, 'Environment, Population Growth and Productivity in Kenya: A Case Study of Machakos District', *Development Policy Review*, Vol. 10, pp. 359–387.

Tiffen, M., M. Mortimore and F. Gichuki, 1994, *More People, Less Erosion: Environmental Recovery in Kenya*, Chichester: John Wiley.

Tinker, I., 1990, *Persistent Inequalities: Women and World Development*, Oxford: Oxford University Press.

Tisdell, C., 1988, 'Sustainable Development: Differing Perspectives of Ecologists and Economists, and Relevance to LDCs', *World Development*, Vol. 16, No. 3.

Todaro, M. P., 1969, 'A Model of Labor Migration and Urban Unemployment in Less Developed Countries', *American Economic Review*, Vol. 59, No. 1, pp. 138–48.

Tomich, T. P., P. Kilby and B. F. Johnston, 1995, *Transforming Agrarian Economies: Opportunities Seized, Opportunities Missed*, Ithaca, NY: Cornell University Press.

Toulmin, 1992, *Cattle, Women, and Wells: Managing Household Survival in the Sahel*, Oxford: Clarendon Press.

Tripp, A., 1992, 'The Impact of Crisis and Economic Reform on Women in Urban Tanzania', in L. Beneria and S. Feldman (eds), *Unequal Burden: Economic Crises, Persistent Poverty, and Women's Work*, Boulder, Colorado: Westview Press.

Tschirley, D. L. and M. T. Weber, 1994, 'Food Security Strategies Under Extremely Adverse Conditions: The Determinants of Household Income and Consumption in Rural Mozambique', *World Development*, Vol. 22, No. 2, pp. 159–173.

UK Department for International Development, 1997, *Eliminating World Poverty: A Challenge for the 21st Century*, White Paper on International Development, London: The Stationery Office.

Unni, J., 1991, 'Regional Variations in Rural Non-Agricultural Employment: An Exploratory Analysis', *Economic and Political Weekly*, Vol. 26, No. 3, pp. 109–122.

Unni, J., 1996, 'Diversification of Economic Activities and Non-Agricultural Employment in Rural Gujarat', *Economic and Political Weekly*, Vol. 31, No. 33, pp. 2243–2251.

Vaa, M., S. E. Findley and A. Diallo, 1989, 'The Gift Economy: A Study of Women Migrants' Survival Strategies in a Low-Income Bamako Neighbourhood', *Labour, Capital and Society*, Vol. 22, No. 2, pp. 234–260.

Vaidyanathan, A., 1986, 'Labour Use in Rural India: A Study of Spatial and Temporal Variations', *Economic and Political Weekly*, Vol. XXI, No. 52, pp. A130–A146.

Valentine, T. R., 1993, 'Drought, Transfer Entitlements, and Income Distribution: The Botswana Experience', *World Development*, Vol. 21, No. 1, pp. 109–126.

van der Geest, W. (ed), 1994, *Negotiating Structural Adjustment in Africa*, London: James Currey.

von Braun, J. and R. Pandya-Lorch (eds), 1991, *Income Sources of Malnourished People in Rural Areas: Microlevel Information and Policy Implications*, Working Papers on Commercialization of Agriculture and Nutrition No. 5, Washington, D.C.: International Food Policy Research Institute.

Walker, T. S. and N. S. Jodha, 1986, 'How Small Farm Households Adapt to Risk', in P. Hazell, C. Pomareda and A. Valdes (eds), *Crop Insurance for Agricultural Development*, Baltimore: Johns Hopkins, pp. 17–34.

Walker, T. S. and J. G. Ryan, 1990, *Village and Household Economies in India's Semi-Arid Tropics*, Baltimore: Johns Hopkins.

Watts, M., 1983, *Silent Violence: Food, Famine and Peasantry in Northern Nigeria*, Berkeley: University of California Press.

Watts, M., 1988, 'Coping with the Market: Uncertainty and Food Security Among Hausa Peasants', Chapter 11 in I. de Garine and G. A. Harrison (eds), *Coping with Uncertainty in Food Supply*, Oxford: Clarendon Press, pp. 260–289.

Webb, P., 1991, 'When Projects Collapse: Irrigation Failure in the Gambia from a Household Perspective', *Journal of International Development*, Vol. 3, No. 4.

Webb, P., J. von Braun and Y. Yohannes, 1992, *Famine in Ethiopia: Policy Implications of Coping Failure at National and Household Levels*, Research Report No. 92, Washington, D.C.: International Food Policy Research Institute.

Whitehead, A., 1985, 'Effects of Technological Change on Rural Women: A Review of Analysis and Concepts', Ch.3 in I. Ahmed (ed.), *Technology and Rural Women*, London: Allen & Unwin, pp. 27–64.

Woodhouse, P., 1998, 'People As Informants', Ch. 6 in A. Thomas, J. Chataway, and M. Wuyts (eds.), *Finding Out Fast: Investigative Skills for Policy and Development*, London: Sage, pp. 127–14.

World Bank, 1975, *Rural Development: Sector Policy Paper*, Washington D.C.: World Bank.

World Bank, 1985, *Tanzania Country Economic Memorandum*, Report No. 5019-TA, Washington, D.C.: World Bank.

World Bank, 1988, *Rural Development: World Bank Experience 1965–86*, World Bank Operations Evaluation Study, Washington, D.C.: World Bank.

World Bank, 1989, *Women in Development: Issues for Economic and Sector Analysis*, WID Division Working Paper, No. 269, Washington, D.C.: World Bank.

World Bank, 1990a, *Making Adjustment Work for the Poor: A Framework for Policy Reform in Africa*, Washington, D.C.: World Bank.

World Bank, 1990b, *World Development Report 1990: Poverty*, New York: Oxford University Press for the World Bank.

World Bank, 1992, *World Development Report 1992: Development and the Environment*, New York: Oxford University Press.

World Bank, 1993a, *Tanzania—A Poverty Profile*, Report No. 12298–TA, Washington, D.C.: World Bank.

World Bank, 1993b, *Human Resources Development Survey, Tanzania: Individual Household Questionnaire*, Washington, D.C.: World Bank, mimeo document available on the World Bank website.

World Bank, 1994a, *Adjustment in Africa: Reforms, Results, and the Road Ahead*, Policy Research Report, Oxford: Oxford University Press.

World Bank, 1994b, *Tanzania Agriculture*, Washington, D.C.: World Bank.

World Bank, 1995a, *Ghana Poverty Past, Present and Future*, Report No. 14504-GH, Washington, D.C.: World Bank.

World Bank, 1995b, *Kenya Poverty Assessment*, Report No. 13152–KE, Washington, D.C.: World Bank.

World Bank, 1996, *Tanzania The Challenge of Reforms: Growth, Incomes and Welfare*, Vols. I-III, Report No. 14982-TA, Washington, D.C.: World Bank.

World Bank, 1997, *World Development Report 1997: The State in a Changing World*, Oxford: Oxford University Press.

Wyeth, J., 1989, 'Diversification: Eight Lessons from Honduran Experience in the Coffee Sector', *IDS Discussion Paper*, No. DP 259, April.

Zoomers, A. E. B. and J. Kleinpenning, 1996, 'Livelihood and Urban-Rural Relations in Central Paraguay', *Tijdschrift Voor Economische en Sociale Geografie*, Vol. 87, No. 2, pp. 161–174.

Index of Names

Index of Subjects

Note: Definitions of terms and key explanations of concepts are indicated in the index by page numbers in **bold** print. In addition, selected definitions are collected together under a 'definitions' entry in the index.